How to Get More Out of Sex

How to Get
More Out of Sex*

BY DAVID REUBEN, M.D.

*than you ever thought you could

DAVID McKAY COMPANY, INC. New York

To my wife, Barbara,
who teaches me anew each morning
the true meaning of love.

ACKNOWLEDGMENTS

I want to thank my good friend and agent (in that order) Don Congdon for being there whenever I needed him. My faithful friend, Max Geffen, constantly encouraged me by his enthusiasm and youthful vigor. The singular contributions of Kennett Rawson, Oscar Dystel, Marc Jaffe, and Alan Barnard must be noted with appreciation. Arnold Stiefel played a vital role. Anne Tiffany made things easier on many occasions. Beth Mortland typed the manuscript expertly.

My wife, Barbara, who makes everything possible, made this book possible too . . . with an assist from the munchkins.

CONTENTS

clitoral-vaginal bridging . . . octopus love . . . man's four
tasks . . . final gift

INTRODUCTION

Dr. Reuben, why did you write another book on sex?

Back in 1969, two weeks after *Everything you always wanted to know about sex* was published. A letter arrived in the morning mail:

"I only wish I had read *Everything* . . . twenty years ago —although that's beside the point. At least I am still a young man at forty and I can make up for lost time. But now that you've told me the essential facts of human sexuality, won't you please write another book—in the same style—that tells me how to make sex more interesting, more exciting, and most of all, more satisfying? What I really want to know is: 'How to get more out of sex!' "

I dropped the letter into my drawer and went on to see the first patient of the day. The next morning there were three letters and by the end of the week the mailman was complaining.

Did all the letters say the same thing?

No, but they said the same kind of thing:

"I'm twenty years old and my measurements are 35½–

23½–35. I've been married six months and I love to go to bed with my husband. But although I had endless orgasms with him *before* we got married, after the first month as a wife we try just as hard but the orgasms don't seem to happen. My mind is ready, my body is *more* than ready, but something just won't work. Can you tell me what to do next?"

Other letters went on to reveal every variety of sexual experience, to relate amazing sexual discoveries and inventions, and to present ingenious and novel solutions to eternal sexual dilemmas.

How many letters did you receive?

I still don't know the exact figure. As the months went by I found my office slowly turned into one gigantic mailroom with letters on desks, letters in cardboard cartons, and letters stacked in endless piles on the floor. Although I still haven't been able to make a final tally, I know that I have personally read at least twenty-five thousand individual letters in the past three years. Most of the mail came from the United States, but there were letters from England, France, Germany, Italy, Japan, Yugoslavia, Israel, Lebanon, China, and virtually every other country in the world.

What kind of people wrote to you?

Every kind. Senators, prostitutes, cowboys, dentists, college professors, policemen, housewives, nuns, rapists, little old ladies, twelve-year-old girls, criminals in prison, ministers of every denomination, blackmailers (and blackmailees), psychiatrists, motel managers, homosexuals, attorneys, and literally thousands and thousands of others.

Selections from their letters are included in this book—but in a special way. Every possible identifying detail has been altered or eliminated to absolutely protect the identity of each writer. To conserve space, only the most important part of each letter is presented. (However, the original of each of the letters is preserved on microfilm in a bank vault where it is held under conditions of absolute security. Only two individuals in the entire world know the location of the vault and only one of them has unlimited access to the letters.)

Where does the rest of the material in the book come from?

Basically, three sources.

First, it is selected from the total accumulated scientific knowledge of human sexuality from around the world. Even in these days of computers and microfiche, it is impossible for anyone to read everything written on sex. But I have drawn on the medical and psychiatric literature of the past five years for the factual details in each chapter.

Second, I have been fortunate to have had the cooperation of many hundreds of fellow physicians, ministers, nurses, psychologists, and others who shoulder the responsibility for human happiness and fulfillment. These co-healers have shared their own personal experiences and observations of human sexuality on an absolutely confidential basis.

Third, I have been a physician and psychiatrist for nearly seventeen years now, and I have had the privilege of examining and treating approximately ten thousand men, women, and children with sexual problems. I can honestly say that this is what taught me more than my eight years of medical study after college.

Dr. Reuben, specifically, what is your medical and psychiatric background?

Here's a letter from the American Medical Association that summarizes it concisely:

AMERICAN MEDICAL ASSOCIATION

535 NORTH DEARBORN STREET · CHICAGO, ILLINOIS 60610 · PHONE (312) 527-1500 · TWX 910-221-0300

**OFFICE OF THE
GENERAL COUNSEL**

BERNARD D. HIRSH
  General Counsel

BETTY JANE ANDERSON
  Assistant to the
  General Counsel

January 12, 1972

David R. Reuben, M.D.
LaPresa Medical Clinic, Inc.
8708 Jamacha Road
Spring Valley, California 92077

Dear Doctor Reuben:

The records of the American Medical Association contain the following information pertaining to the professional training and practice of David Robert Reuben, M.D.:

Doctor Reuben received a B.S. degree from the University of Illinois in 1953 and an M.D. from the University of Illinois Medical School in 1957. He served an internship at the Cook County Hospital in Chicago from June, 1957 until June, 1958 and completed one year of residency in psychiatry at the same hospital before being inducted into the Air Force in July, 1959.

Doctor Reuben served in the Air Force from July, 1959 until July, 1961 as a Captain being assigned for five months to Strategic Air Command Project 1502 at Harvard Medical School as a clinical research associate in psychiatry and as chief of psychiatry at the Walker Air Force Base Hospital at Roswell, New Mexico. The Walker Air Force Base Hospital was a fifty bed institution serving approximately 14,500 military personnel and their families. Specialists in internal medicine, obstetrics and gynecology and surgery were assigned to the Hospital also.

Doctor Reuben is licensed to practice medicine and surgery in Illinois (1958), California (1959) and Arizona (1969). His major professional activity is private practice in the specialty of psychiatry. The current Physicians' Records and all future editions of the American Medical Directory will so list Doctor Reuben's major professional activity. The 25th edition of the American Medical Directory gives Doctor Reuben's practice designation as general practice in psychiatry.

Sincerely,

Betty Jane Anderson

(Miss) Betty Jane Anderson

BJA:gs

Dr. Reuben, will your book really help a person to overcome his sexual problems?

Although, when it comes to human beings, there are no guarantees, many hundreds of my patients—and others—have solved their sexual difficulties by using the techniques and insights described in this book. That's how the ideas got there in the first place—after they were tested and proved in the living laboratory of the bedroom and the bridal suite. If every man who reads this book makes sure that his woman reads it with him (and vice-versa), they have every possible chance in the world of getting—and *giving*—all the sexual happiness and fulfillment that they ever wanted.

Why is sex so important?

Because sex is *life*. Remember that all of us are here today because two human beings cared enough about each other to merge their protoplasm in that clumsily precise, magnificently vulgar, breathtakingly beautiful maneuver called sexual intercourse. If sex is "right," then everything else in the world is right. If sex is "wrong," then nothing else can be right. With that in mind, I hope that the information and the personal experiences of thousands of people in this book will show each and every reader *How to Get More Out of Sex*—and *more out of life.*

Any readers who would like to write me personally are welcome to do so at the address below:

Dr. David R. Reuben
c/o Harold Matson Inc.
22 East 40th Street
New York, New York 10016

How to Get More Out of Sex

1

SEXUAL ORGANS

What are the sexual organs for?

A lot more than just for reproduction. They are a form of entertainment, a means of communication, a symbol of power, and a vehicle for expressing love, hate, and virtually every other human emotion. Even more important, along with the eyes, ears, nose, and mouth—because of their multi-channel nerve supply—the sexual organs are direct extensions of the human brain itself. (Maybe that's one reason why the penis and vagina often act as if they have a mind of their own.) In any event, more than they are ever willing to admit, men and women are ruled by those brilliantly designed, exquisitely enjoyable, slightly clumsy appendages known as the sexual organs. Yet even though the pleasures they transmit are free, abundant, untaxed, and constantly renewable, there are still complaints. Take men for example:

Are most men satisfied with their sexual organs?

Unfortunately not. When it comes to the primary male sexual attribute, owner satisfaction seems to be sadly lacking. If every penis were suddenly endowed with a written guarantee —"satisfaction or your money back"—probably 50 percent of the male population would line up for a refund or exchange. Regrettably, most of the dissatisfaction is based on misunderstanding. Listen to what an expert like Bonnie says:

"Doctor, in a way, I consider myself an expert on the penis. After all, that's how I earn my living. And by the way, I don't like the term 'call girl.' I think 'professional partner' sounds better, don't you? Anyhow, I average about fifty tricks a week, and that adds up to, say, about a thousand *different* penises a year, considering that I do a lot of repeat business. I'd say that at least half the johns complain about their organs. But they don't know a couple of things that every girl in the trade picks up right away. Like when it comes to a man's penis, what you see is *not* what you get. I've seen guys that were practically down to their knees *before* they got hard and by the time they were ready for action you wondered where it all went. And the other way around—some fellows look like they don't even have enough for themselves, but before you know it, you're looking down the barrel of a cannon.

"The other thing is, it's what's up front that counts—not for a guy as much as for a girl. I don't feel much with the johns because I can't afford to—they pay for *their* kicks, not mine. But when I do it for fun with my old man, most of my action happens right at the opening—say, the first couple of inches of the vagina. So as long as a guy can come up with two inches, he can give a woman all the action she can handle. Any man ought to be able to manage that."

2

What do men complain about the most as far as their sexual organs are concerned?

In a world where big is supposed to be good, and bigger is supposed to be better, most men, like the four quoted here, bemoan the length of their penises:

"Is there any way to lengthen my penis through masturbation, operation, or any other means?"

"Help! I am the victim of a short penis! Isn't there some hormone from some gland or other that can make my penis longer?"

"My penis is so very small that I am embarrassed to take it out long enough to have sexual intercourse with a girl. I am seventeen years old and still growing—do you think my penis will grow too?"

"If there was any way I could build up my penis I would be willing to pay ten thousand dollars an inch—all I want is two inches more."

Is there anything that can actually make the penis longer?

Of course there is—and doctors are helping patients to grow longer penises by the thousands. But virtually all the treatment is restricted to those who are really in need. For example, some young boys fail to develop full-size organs at the time of puberty. In certain of these cases regular injections of a substance called "chorionic gonadotropin" work wonders. Over the course of a year the penis may triple or quadruple in size. Even more dramatic results are being achieved in helping male infants born with tiny, tiny phalluses. If the mother rubs on a hormone cream daily—the hormone is simply testosterone, the male sex hormone—the penis may almost enlarge before her very eyes. So far neither of these techniques has been successfully applied to grown men—and maybe it's just as well.

Why is it just as well?

Because there's a better solution. An old vaudeville joke sums it up:

Two men were talking in the country club locker room after a round of golf. One remarked to the other:

"Say, how come you hardly ever take a shower after a game?" The other winced and blurted out:

"Uh, well, to tell the truth, it's really that I have this kind of small penis that I'm ashamed to show in the shower."

"Yeah? Well, tell me something—does it work all right?"

"Oh, sure. It works great!"

"Hmm. How'd you like to trade it for one that looks good in the shower?"

Male complaints about too-short phalluses are rarely seconded by women, who are, after all, the ultimate consumers:

"I'm sure my penis is much too short and I want to change before my wife discovers it. She seems to have orgasms all right now but maybe she can have better ones."

Another woman complains: "I've known a lot of men in my time. I used to be singer with a band—the only woman on tour with thirty-five men—and I never liked the ones with the biggest penises. It seems that the ones with average or even smaller organs were always the most considerate and really the most exciting—and the most appreciative. It's like they say: 'It's not how long you make it but how you make it long.' "

Of course, there are always those men who want to subtract from their penises rather than add to them.

4

Some men actually want to make their penises shorter?

Only slightly. The process is called circumcision. Although the operation has been around for about ten thousand years, only recently has it moved to the top of the surgical hit parade. And there are some good reasons for its popularity. Originally it was more of a social grace than a sexual custom —all male members of a tribe were remodeled in a group ceremony. (Jews and Moslems still use individual ritual circumcision.) But then it became apparent that doing away with that little cap of skin provided real protection from cancer of the penis. That brought more men to the surgeon's knife—and more little baby boys left part of themselves at the hospital when they went home.

As far as women were concerned circumcision was no big deal—although a few fastidious ladies preferred circumcised gentlemen because they felt it "looked neater." Then some medical researchers announced that women who had regular intercourse with uncircumcised men ran a higher risk of cancer of the cervix than those who selected slightly abridged partners.

How come?

It seems that smegma, a kind of cheesy discharge, accumulates under the foreskin (or prepuce) of the penis. During the turmoil of intercourse, as the prepuce is skinned back the smegma is smeared over the surface of the cervix. When the news came out that smegma might contain a substance that provokes cancer of the cervix, there was a run on circumcisions. As one husband described it:

"You know how I decided to get circumcised, Doctor? Well, one evening my wife read in the paper about circumcision and cancer of the uterus. The next night when we were in bed, she said: 'John, I gave up my hymen for you. Why don't you give up a little something for me?' I didn't pay much attention—I guess I just sort of laughed. The following night we were just getting ready to have intercourse when she stopped, very gently picked up my foreskin between her thumb and first finger, and whispered: 'Either *it* goes—or *I* go.' The next day *it* went."

The argument for circumcision was just about clinched when three more recent discoveries surfaced. First, military doctors discovered that circumcised men were less susceptible to VD. If two GIs had intercourse with the same girl, the uncircumcised one was more likely to become infected. (No one knows exactly why—maybe the foreskin simply gives the germs a place to hide.) Secondly, careful statistical analysis suggested that circumcised men were less vulnerable to cancer of the prostate—a disease with most unfortunate sexual consequences. The clincher came with the revelation that being circumcised was giving a little to get a lot. Men who have their penises remodeled that way may well be rewarded with longer-lasting erections.

How can circumcision prolong erection?

Like this:

The foreskin fits over the end of the penis like a glove on a finger—and like a glove it protects the head of the organ from rubbing against clothing and other objects. When the glove is removed by circumcision, the head of the penis is toughened—even calloused—which takes away its hair-trigger sensitivity and allows more prolonged friction with the super-smooth lining of the vagina.

Of course, that sort of thing tends to be a matter of personal taste, but there have been very few recently circumcised men who try it the new way and then ask for their foreskins back. (Although one inspired surgeon has come up with an operation that does graft a sort of foreskin back onto a circumcised penis. Understandably he is not overwhelmed with customers for that procedure.)

Do men have any other complaints about their penises?

Oh, yes. A lot of men are frustrated about a penis that won't get hard—and if it should get hard, won't stay hard. And many of them don't want to bother with understanding the emotional factors involved—they yearn for a little surgical magic to get them back in the saddle again:

"If they can transplant a kidney, a lung, and even a heart, why can't the doctors do an old man a favor and transplant a penis? I would even be willing to make a trade—say, a kidney for what I consider to be a more important organ."

Well, don't think that penis transplants haven't been considered. Probably the biggest obstacle to progress in that area is a significant lack of donors. Anyone who has a penis that works doesn't want to let it go. But the lights burn past midnight in the research laboratories and now what once was a dream has *almost* become a reality.

How has the penis transplant **almost** *become a reality?*

By means of a plastic implant that not only makes erection possible—but makes it permanent. The procedure is a simple one: at surgery the doctor clears a tunnel through the shaft of the penis and inserts a plastic rod. Presto! Unless complications develop, the patient is now endowed with an impressive, permanent, and *perpetual* erection of the penis. (This is probably the only situation where a permanent erection is possible posthumously.)

There are a few final problems to be worked out, however.

For one, standing around at a cocktail party or lying on the beach with a penis that stands at attention can be a bit of a problem. Riding in a crowded elevator can also bring objections from both male and female passengers. Although the operation is a relatively new one, improvements are already underway. One surgical team now inserts two rods instead of one and there may be a chance that man will catch up with the "lower animals."

Catch up with the "lower animals"?

That's right. Except for the primates (like the monkeys and apes), and marsupials, virtually every other mammalian male has a built-in insurance policy against loss of erection. It consists of the one bone that every man should have, and yet, up until now, no man was ever born with: the *penis bone*. The cat and dog, the mouse and rat, and, of course, the proverbial rabbit, all have a dependable bit of bone built into the shaft of the penis. Even the humble squirrel, with his tiny splinter of bone to splint his miniature phallus, never has to say he's sorry. Probably the champion in that department is the male whale, whose penis bone can be six feet long and five inches thick. Of course, there are those rare complaints from men whose penises are simply too hard.

Why should a man complain about a super-hard penis?

Judge for yourself:

"I'd been away at sea for about three weeks—it was only a week after my wife and I had been married. When I got back home I was ready to do it on the doorstep—and so was she. We managed to hold ourselves back until we got into the bedroom and, Doctor, I never saw a woman who was so turned on to sex. The more excited she got, the more excited

I got. Everytime I'd come she'd work on me until I got hard again—I was so crazy to be with her that it didn't take much. We did it at least five times before midnight, and the sixth time everything was fine except my penis didn't get soft afterward. We tried to have intercourse again but I couldn't come. Then she took it in her mouth but even that didn't help. Then she tried playing with it and it just got harder. Then *I* tried playing with it and it got worse. It was like a 'penis revolution'—and I started getting scared."

"What happened then?"

"I stopped fooling around and had my wife drive me to the emergency room at the hospital. That was also an experience. Doctor, have you ever lain naked on an examining table in a brightly lit emergency room, surrounded by student nurses, with your penis poking upward like the Statue of Liberty? It really gives you a different outlook on life."

"Then what happened?"

"Then I got lucky. One of the interns had just read about a new drug—it was originally used as an anesthetic for gorillas, as a matter of fact. He gave me a shot of it. I went out like a light, and when I woke up I was home in bed with a marshmallow where the telephone pole used to be. They say that whatever goes up must come down—but I had my doubts there for a while."

This patient was lucky. He only had a touch of what is poetically known as "priapism," or the sexual version of "You Asked for It." (In Greek mythology Priapus was the god of sensuality but even *he* didn't have an erection all the time.) The cause of extended erection is somewhat obscure but it can happen from intense physical and emotional stimulation. It is a real medical emergency because prolonged pressure on the structures of the penis can cause permanent damage—and ultimately loss of the ability to have any erection at all. There are other men too who have erections that are hot, hard, and useless.

What else causes useless erections?

A condition known as Peyronie's disease, or, more descriptively, the "Bent Nail" syndrome:

"Can you tell me if I am normal? Looking down on my erect penis, it deviates to the left about 45 degrees. This poses a problem in insertion since my wife's vagina does not have a corresponding angle. Could this be a result of masturbating with my left hand exclusively?"

And, "I wonder how rare Peyronie's disease really is. Perhaps it is simply obscured by the fact that few men bother to report it. I am in my early fifties and I have had it for about five years: my penis curves upward toward my abdomen making it almost impossible to penetrate my wife except by a complicated system of acrobatics. I consulted my family doctor who cheerfully informed me that my condition was not 'progressive.' By that I presume he meant it would not spread to the rest of my body. . . . Pardon the pun, but could you help me to straighten out?"

In some cases the deviation of the phallus can even affect a man's livelihood:

"I am sure that I suffer from Peyronie's disease because my penis angles upward and to the right when it is erect. Otherwise I am not an unattractive person. But there are other complications. I am just getting started in the business world and since I am only twenty years old I need extra money. I saw an ad the other day asking for men to appear in pornographic movies. The ad said: 'Good-looking males; 7, 8, or 9 inches long; well-developed; $5.00 per hour.' I'm not crazy about the idea but I need the money badly. But with my corkscrew penis, I don't have a chance. I need to be cured so I can get the job."

Is there help for a "bent-nail" penis?

Yes. As a result of relatively recent discoveries, there seems to be a good chance of helping many men "unbend the nail." First of all, it's important to remember that some victims have a spontaneous recovery regardless of treatment. Understandably, however, few of them (or their wives) want to wait around to see if "things straighten out." Best results so far come from oral medications like vitamin E or potassium para-aminobenzoate, taken under careful medical supervision, of course. Injection of cortisone directly into the penis has helped some men, and ultrasound treatment has also proved beneficial. Fortunately, only one of the surgical problems that affects the penis also involves its female cousin, the clitoris.

What kind of surgery links the clitoris and the penis?

Circumcision.

A circumcised woman tells about it:

"Ten years ago, when I was a young bride unable to have an orgasm, I went to a doctor who 'circumcised' me. He trimmed the hood off my clitoris and said that would make it more accessible for stimulation. Ten years later I still don't reach a climax during intercourse, although I can still manage to do so by masturbation or if my husband manipulates me. Do you think I might be able to have the foreskin put back onto my reluctant clitoris? Or could it be something else?"

It could be something else. Since orgasm for this woman arrives on schedule by masturbation, the problem apparently isn't related to the clitoris at all—removing the "hood" from the part of the brain that blocks orgasm during intercourse might be more rewarding.

Considering that cancer of the clitoris isn't much of a problem, and that VD of the clitoris is not exactly overwhelming, female circumcision doesn't seem to be an important operation these days—except, of course, if you are a Bedouin.

Do the Bedouins consider female çircumcision important?

A letter from Israel goes into detail:

"The tradition of circumcising the clitoris can be found among the Bedouin tribes in the west of the desert, near the Suez Canal. The reason has almost nothing to do with sex but, even so, is most extraordinary. The Bedouins are famous because of their hospitality. When a guest appears, they immediately slaughter a sheep to prepare a feast. In those tribes, however, the men travel all over the desert while the women stay home. Since a woman is not allowed to slaughter, according to the tribal tradition, there would be serious complications. They solve the problem by *circumcising* the woman. She then becomes a temporary "man" for the purpose of slaughtering sheep and helps maintain the Bedouin tradition of hospitality."

By comparison with the penis, the clitoris—and to a greater extent, the vagina—are neglected structures. It really shouldn't be that way.

Why is the clitoris neglected?

Consider it from this point of view:

"Doctor, I demand equal time for the female sexual organs! Ever since I was a little girl, I've been painfully aware that the penis gets all the attention, while the vagina and all the rest aren't even supposed to exist. Men's clothes are designed to emphasize the bulk of the penis; women's clothes —what with skirts, panty girdles, and even the new pantyhose—are designed to pretend that we're smooth as billiard balls down there. And another thing, we're supposed to smother ourselves in 'feminine hygiene' products like sprays and douches and suppositories. What's so unhygienic about a woman? And how about coming out with some 'masculine hygiene' products just to even the score?"

The lady makes a good point. At least in modern society, it's supposed to be a case of the clandestine clitoris, the lost labia, and the vanishing vagina. Everything from pornography to prostitution is designed to increase the eroticism of the male, while the official message to women is "Don't look, don't touch, don't feel." Just wait, as the Japanese say, and "Someday a man will come along and Unlock the Gate to your Golden Garden with his Magic Key." Until then, Keep Busy. Other societies don't necessarily feel that way.

How do other societies increase the sexual arousal of females?

They emphasize female sexuality right from the start so that when a woman begins to have sexual intercourse she is already primed to respond at an advanced level. Many primitive tribes begin training their girls as soon as their breasts begin to swell—when they are about ten years old. In the evenings the young pupils gather at the hut of one of the older women who begins their very practical sex education. Step by step she teaches them the structure and function of the female sexual organs. Then, gradually, she shows them the different techniques of masturbation. As time goes by, she illustrates how to stretch and massage the clitoris and labia minora to develop them to their maximum size. Later on she may even bring a few small ants to the session.

What do ants have to do with erotic excitement?

That's the advanced course. Several of the tiny insects are placed around the opening to the vagina and encouraged to sting. The swelling and itching that follow stimulate rubbing and masturbation and further increase the sensitivity and response of the area around the vagina. After a couple of years of this intense preparation the labia becomes permanently enlarged and extended. During intercourse they can grasp the shaft of the penis like a sort of sexual glove to steady it as it drives in and out of the vagina. The final result is that, as far as these tribal lovelies are concerned, orgasmic impairment is about as foreign as an uplift bra—and about as uncommon. The point of view of these so-called uncivilized peoples emerges as rational, sensible, and eminently practical. Our immensely complex and expensive educational system teaches our citizens to use their eyes, ears, fingers, brains, and nearly every other part of their bodies to make their lives more fulfilling. It also teaches them *not* to use their sexual organs—potentially the most fulfilling of all human attributes. Of course, to get the most from a vagina, a girl first of all has to have one.

Are there some girls who don't have vaginas?

Unfortunately, yes. Occasionally a woman may be born with no vagina at all. Until recently the basic treatment for absence of a vagina was to laboriously construct a new one by cutting a pouch, lining it with skin or silicone plastic, and letting it go at that. It required multiple expensive operations and was only marginally satisfactory. Then someone got a bright idea.

Many girls had nothing at all where the vagina should have been—just a smooth expanse of skin curving under the pubic bone. Instead of complicated surgery, the doctors placed a small plastic wand against the area where the vagina should have been and pushed—gently. If they could make a small dimple, they gave the wand to the patient and she went home and pushed gently—every day. Eventually the dimple got deeper and deeper until it was an actual vaginal space. Then it was time to give up the plastic wand and let the patient's husband push—using another type of wand—every day. As long as the woman is careful to have regular and frequent sexual intercourse, her do-it-yourself vagina should operate perfectly and permanently. As the sensational news stories about organ transplants appeared, the ultimate transplant became inevitable.

The ultimate transplant?

Right. The *vaginal* transplant. Recently an enterprising surgeon removed the vagina from a woman in her mid-forties and transplanted it into her daughter, who was born without a vagina. Apparently the new vagina "took" and is functioning well. The girl is said to be very happy, the girl's mother, who donated the transplanted organ, remarked that she "didn't need it anymore," and the girl's father is unavailable for comment. Of course, when a man wants a vagina, there's a simpler way to do it.

Why should a man want a vagina?

That's not an easy question to answer but there are some men who do. Certain Australian tribes have gone farther toward "Men's Liberation" than the most militant bra-burner ever dreamed of. Most adult males of the tribes have their penises slit along the underside in direct imitation of the female vagina. In case there is any question about what they are trying to accomplish, the tribal word for the operation is the same as their word for "vagina."

The exact purpose of the procedure is obscure but one theory suggests that this represents a way for the men to express their kinship and closeness to the women of the tribe. Just as Bedouin women become "honorary men," these tribesmen become "honorary women." While the explanation may be uncertain, there is one thing that we know for sure: that quaint little custom, called sub-incision, has no chance of catching on in our society.

Circumcision, si. Sub-incision, no.

However, there is one other sex operation as essential and as far-reaching as circumcision for men that is denied to millions of deserving women everywhere.

What sex operation is denied to millions of women?

A simple procedure called an "A-P Repair," that takes less than an hour and yet can make a woman of forty almost the same sexually as a girl of eighteen. Listen to man's point of view:

"I never believed in miracles, Doctor. All my life I told myself that a person just has to learn to accept things as they happen. Well, now I know that isn't true. My wife and I have been married twenty-five years and I was beginning to take sex for granted—just like most husbands, I guess. After three kids she was pretty well stretched out; I don't know if that had anything to do with it, but I just didn't get the same kind of erections anymore. You know, half-hearted and half-hard —and sometimes half-hardly. So Tina, my wife, must have sensed that something was wrong—I guess she wasn't feeling that much herself—and she started reading all those articles in the ladies' magazines. She heard about this operation that they do on women's sexual organs and went to her doctor and asked him. Boy, he didn't want to have anything to do with it! He said as long as she wasn't sick, he wasn't going to operate. What he didn't know was that she *was* sick—half the time she couldn't reach a climax anymore and she was getting a real complex about being so big down there.

"Would you believe that she had to go to six doctors before she found *one* that would do the job? But it was worth it. For the past six months it's been like our honeymoon—I mean, I'll be honest with you. I get an erection just thinking about it. She's so tight I have to use extra lubrication and she grabs on to my erection like a suction pump. Would you believe that at fifty-five I can go twice a night almost every night? When I paid the doctor I sent him a box of cigars along with the check. Believe me, he earned it."

What does the "A-P Repair" operation consist of?

Turning back the clock. The vagina itself is originally like a small rubber balloon—tubular in shape and small in diameter. When sexual intercourse begins, the penis dilates the vaginal tunnel and stretches it slightly, although it still retains the shape of a stretchable tube. Then, inevitably for most wives, along comes pregnancy. The hormonal changes make the vaginal structures much more stretchable, and when the baby's head finally squeezes through on its way to the outside world, the penis's little grotto of pleasure is instantly converted into Carlsbad Caverns. Where vagina and penis once met in fond embrace, they now wave to each other as they go flashing by. An operation, known technically as an "anterior-posterior repair," takes care of all that. Excess tissue is pulled together, muscles and supporting tissues are reinforced, bladder and urethra are restored to their correct positions, and man and woman can really get *close* again.

How do women feel about this kind of instant sexual rejuvenation?

Like this:

"Doctor, I'm obviously not as young as I used to be. Every morning when I get up I can identify a few more wrinkles on my one-day-older-face. Six months ago my husband sold some property and he knows how I feel so he gave me two thousand dollars to have plastic surgery. I went into the hospital and had the surgery. When he came to see me afterward, he was shocked. He said, 'What's going on here? Where are the bandages?'

"As modestly as I could I pointed in the direction of my lower anatomy and explained that I decided to have the plastic surgery done on my vagina instead. He never said another word until four weeks later—after he had a chance to tell the difference. Two days after that I found another check for two thousand on my breakfast plate. I said, 'What's this for?' He just smiled and said, 'That's for the face-lift. You want to get rid of the *rest* of the wrinkles, don't you?' "

The vagina also can be put to other uses.

What else can the vagina be used for?

As a means of administering medicine, for example. Although it isn't used much that way medically anymore, the lining of the vagina has the ability to absorb certain drugs in liquid form that are poured into it and transport them into the bloodstream. One of the most bizarre variations of that technique is known to drug users as "balling crank." It works like this:

Just before intercourse, a measured dose of "crank"—that is, an amphetamine (methamphetamine) in liquid form—is pumped into the vagina. This is followed by the insertion of an erect penis which mixes the solution well and distributes it throughout the vagina. A few moments later the "crank" works its way to the brain to produce that sudden "rush" that addicts love—and another doper starts a trip. You don't actually have to be crazy to use drugs this way—but it helps. That goes double for cocaine—especially on the penis.

How is cocaine used on the penis?

Hazardously. A white crystalline powder, cocaine has two characteristics. Taken internally, by sniffing for example, the effect is similar to that caused by amphetamines. The user becomes excited and overstimulated. But there is another, incredibly dangerous, way to take "coke":

Just before intercourse, the man drops a few crystals through the end of the penis down into the urethra. At the same time he rubs a little cocaine mixed with saliva over the surface of the penis.

Why would anyone want to do that to a penis?

To get a "popsicle." The other effect of cocaine is a local anesthetic, like dentists inject before they pull teeth. Applied to a hard erection from inside (and outside), cocaine deadens feeling and prolongs the hardness of the penis. It also produces a peculiar cold sensation to the user—that's why they call a coked-up phallus a "popsicle." Oh, yes, there's one little problem. Cocaine energetically constricts the blood vessels of the penis. There is a real and constantly increasing risk of gangrene of that vital organ. So the motto of "popsicle" fans might well be: "Enjoy it quick—before it melts."

Is there anything a man and woman can do to make their sexual organs work better?

Yes. They can make the final connection. What happens at the tip of the penis and the tip of the clitoris is simply the result of a long series of events that begin and end on the surface of the *brain.* Plugging the penis into the vagina *begins* sex, but the real copulation occurs when a couple of million nerve cells in the man's brain slide into a couple of million nerve cells in the woman's brain. The moment those two gigantic computers synchronize, they set off that sensational short circuit known as orgasm. And the surest way to make that happen is to hook up one mind to another in the closest and most intimate way of all. It's known as L-O-V-E.

2

ORGASMIC IMPAIRMENT
. . . THE FIRST STEP

What is a woman's greatest sexual challenge?

Orgasm. No matter how sophisticated, attractive, or desirable a woman may be, two or three times a week she faces a critical moment of truth: "Does she or doesn't she?" During those sensational eight seconds when her sexual partner is exploding deep within her pelvis she becomes either a participant or a spectator.

"I just finished reading the chapter of your book on orgasmic impairment and I've had the hardest cry I've had in years. You made me face squarely a problem I've been avoiding all my life. I just can't believe there can be more than one person in the world like me.

"I'm thirty-one years old, an excellent wife and homemaker, a gourmet cook, and I appreciate all the compliments I receive from men. If they only knew that all my sexiness is on the outside and that when it comes to sexual intercourse, I am zero. I've never had an orgasm in my life. Well, maybe one when I was eighteen.

"I was at a boy's house and he was petting my vagina while I was playing with his penis. Finally he started to come and at the same time I had this crashing feeling in between my legs. It was sort of a combination of wetting my panties and losing half my insides. I tried to get up from the couch and walk away but I was shaking so hard I couldn't even walk.

"I must have had sex a thousand times since then—I've even tried it with some of my husband's friends—but I've never had that feeling again. I remember hearing my mother say she never enjoyed 'it.' Maybe that's where I got the idea?

"I know there is more to sex than I've been able to get out of it. Is there any help for me?"

Most women who suffer from orgasmic impairment are tortured by the vague suspicion that every other woman in the world is scaling the heights of orgiastic ecstasy every fifteen minutes. For what it's worth, it's not true. Fully 50 percent of sexually mature females spend a good part of their time on the sidelines. Fortunately there is good news for them if they take a moment to think about it. The first encouragement comes from anatomy.

What does anatomy have to do with orgasm?

Just this. Every woman is programed to have an orgasm *virtually every time she has intercourse.* To make this possible her genitals consist basically of a combination of specialized tissues designed to receive from the outside (and transmit to the brain) the maximum in pleasurable sensations. If she can only make them work the way they were supposed to, she can enjoy more excitement and satisfaction in a single moment than she may have anticipated in a lifetime.

Take the clitoris, for example. This little stick of sexual

dynamite has ten times more sexual nerve endings packed into it than the largest penis. And it is linked by a massive cable of nerves directly to the most marvelous and powerful sexual organ ever designed—the human vagina. When the vagina comes in contact with the erect penis, it expands or contracts to hold the male organ in a perfect genital handshake. And once it grabs hold, it never relaxes its grip until it soaks up the last drop of sexual satisfaction.

As the penis moves in and out, the vagina constantly transmits its heat and throbbing, and its soft, caressing friction to the clitoris. The labia minora hitch a ride on the shaft of the penis and with each stroke pull the exquisitely sensitive tip of the clitoris down toward the penile piston. As intercourse proceeds, the vulva engorges with blood and reaches out even more for the probing penis. With approaching climax, the clitoris begins to throb and the orgasmic countdown begins. The moment of no return flashes past and the hips thrust the vulva convulsively toward the penis, the breath comes in grasps, the pupils dilate, and the woman is engulfed by her own monumental orgasm. Almost every woman has the physical endowments for orgasm, almost every woman has the desire for orgasm, and almost every woman knows the ins and outs of simple sexual intercourse. Having a climax *should* be easy.

If having a climax is so easy, why do so many women miss out?

Because it actually *isn't* so easy. Back in the days when people copulated in caves and dined on dinosaur steak, reaching orgasm *might* have been easy. But for modern women there are a different set of rules. From the moment she is old enough to understand—and sometimes before— the tiny baby girl is told that there is something bad about the territory below the pubis. When that little hand begins

to explore the infantile clitoris Mommy looms on the scene
like an avenging angel:

1. "Nice girls don't do that!"
2. "That's dirty!"
3. "You should be ashamed of yourself!"

Three lies all in a row.

1. Nice girls *do* do that.
2. Sexual exploration is *perfectly clean* (much cleaner
   than mud pies).
3. It is *not* something to be ashamed of.

Twenty years later that little girl—now a big girl—may
write this letter:

"I know you must have heard this story a million times
before so I guess once more won't hurt. Here goes.

"I am twenty-four and my husband and I have been married nearly four years. I have nothing against sex—at least
consciously—and I want more than anything else to enjoy
everything that sex has to offer. When my husband and I play
with each other we both get tremendously excited. But when
his penis actually goes into my vagina I turn off completely.
He calls it 'an attack of the sexual blahs.' Whatever it is it's
driving both of us crazy. I wish I could do it every night with
him—I want it so bad I can taste it. But as soon as he gets
inside me, everything stops.

"I've been racking my brain to figure out the reason and
all I can think of is the way my parents acted about sex. My
mother never told me about menstruation until *after* it
started. All she told me about boys was to make sure they
never 'took advantage.' And believe me, I worried for years
about what *that* was supposed to mean. If it weren't for my
wonderfully patient husband, who taught me everything, I
would still be a sexual idiot.

"But believe me, this orgasmic impairment is really beginning to get me down."

This young lady's sexual upbringing was especially unfor-

tunate and will cost her extra time and effort to overcome—
although her youth and her understanding husband give her
a good chance to succeed. Virtually every female, as she
grows from girl to woman, gets the message that she is
allowed to express her sexuality only at certain times, only
with certain people, and only in a certain way. Usually she
is told the time is after the wedding, the person is her husband, and the way is him on top and her on the bottom.

What's wrong with that kind of sex?

Well, first of all, that's not the way little girls are made. Every
woman in this world has more sexual potential packed into
her pelvis than a corral full of wild stallions. Females are
designed, equipped, and destined to have as many as forty
orgasms an hour, three times a night, seven nights a week,
fifty-two weeks a year. Fortunately for the men of America,
even though they have it, most ladies don't flaunt it. And
that's part of the problem.

Most of the women who settle for a sedate session of sexual
calisthenics three times a week after the late movie on TV are
like millionaires eating in a soup kitchen. They can trade
those mild tingles and an occasional orgasm that registers
zero on the applause meter for a totally different experience.
Sex can be the most mind-blowing, bone-rattling, supercolos-
sal experience any female ever had—and it can happen every
night of the year and get better as time goes on. Sandy
described it in person:

"Doctor, I'm thirty-five now and to tell the truth, five
years ago I was ready to give up on sex. I mean, I went
through the motions but I only did it to please my husband
—it was like handing him the tools while he was working at
one of his hobbies."

Sandy thought a moment, then went on:

"As a matter of fact, that's a pretty good description of my sex life. I lay there in bed and provided the tools while he amused himself. Boy, that wasn't too much fun!

"But after reading your book I began to understand that I was really equipped to get more out of sex than he was—if I was willing to work for it—and it really made a difference. Now the kind of orgasm I used to think was a big deal is what I have a couple of even before I really get down to business. By the time we're finished I'm a wreck. My hair's a mess, I'm dripping with sweat, and . . ." Sandy grinned, ". . . I love every minute of it."

Why can't every woman do that?

She *can* if she's willing to fight the same battle Sandy did. For her—and for most women—the first sexual experience is the beginning of an almost impossible conflict. After being told all her life that the road to hell begins at the entrance to the vagina, a girl suddenly discovers that the wildest experience of all time—orgasm—also begins there. It is simply a case of an irresistible force—a woman's sexual drive—running head on into an immovable object—the grotesque superstition that the normal use of the sexual organs is somehow wicked or sinful. The result is predictable: no orgasm. It takes more than the charming ritual of the marriage ceremony to turn a petrified pelvis into Passion's plaything. No matter how much they would like to enjoy sex—and reach an orgasm —millions of women go through life with what one young lady called "a mental tourniquet twisted around my vagina." Ironically, it usually isn't even her fault. Most women who suffer from orgasmic impairment are innocent victims—good little girls who believed what their mother told them.

Do mothers really have that much to do with orgasmic impairment?

Here's the way one mother looks at it:

"I am fed right up to here with all this emphasis on sex nowadays. It's absolutely sickening! After thirty-one years of marriage and four lovely children I certainly don't see anything so great about it.

"Thank goodness that I am too old now (fifty-two) and can go to bed and just sleep instead of having to wrestle for an hour with a lustful man. I just feel sorry for all the young girls who are led to believe they are in for a great experience. I have three daughters who are being told the truth about all this *crap.*"

Would anyone be surprised if a few years later one of the daughters who "was told the truth about all this *crap*" wrote a letter like this?

"Try dealing with people like me who just plain don't care about sex! I don't have any mental blocks regarding sex—I would love to enjoy it—but I don't!

"I'm not frigid and I love the company of men. I don't have any hang-ups and I don't consider sex unwholesome or dirty or anything like that. It's just that I *do not* and *can not* experience orgasm. And I don't believe that the brain controls the ability to reach orgasm.

"I wish I liked sex—I would love to like sex—I would love to *love* sex. But I can do without it. I don't like it."

No textbook description of the emotional turmoil that blocks orgasm expresses it more poignantly than that last line.

What can a woman do to help herself to enjoy sex more?

Plenty. She can begin by seeing human sexuality—her own and her partner's—as it really is. Sometimes it isn't easy:

"I guess I must be a freak. I suffer from aversion to intercourse. My parents always told me that people are to wash their hands after handling personal parts: penis, vagina, etc. Yet some think nothing of stroking, handling, and putting the same items in one's mouth.

"We are taught never to use other's drinking vessels, comb, or toothbrush. Yet when kissing, it's thought quite all right to moisten each other's lips with saliva. Ugh!

"I can't abide the feel of the hot, hard, throbbing, moist penis or the wrinkly, moist testicles. Yet, for all of that, I want love, need love, enjoy affection and soft, warm (not wet) kisses. What is the answer to my aversion to the items that handle our body wastes?"

Our body—and that includes our genitals—is our friend, not our enemy. There are fewer harmful bacteria in a vagina than on the drinking glasses in your favorite restaurant. If stroking, handling, and putting penis and vagina in one's mouth were the cause of disease, the side effects of just one big Saturday night could wipe out the entire population of our nation. People have been copulating—and putting things in their mouths—much longer than they have been washing their hands.

Even more conclusive, sex is so important to the mental and physical health of a normal woman that her *unconscious sexual needs* smash through her *conscious* inhibitions.

Many women who go without sex—willingly or unwillingly—have spontaneous and sensational orgasms while they are asleep. These are the equivalent of male "wet dreams." One woman says:

"I find little need for intercourse due to the automatic

safety valve that pops off quite often. I have orgasms in my sleep which occur usually without waking me and without my even dreaming of sex."

Another woman writes:

"I don't know why everyone makes such a fuss over sex. By concentrating very hard I have found that I can get along without sex completely. The thought never even enters my mind.

"Of course, I have some wild dreams from time to time. . . ."

Sure, it's possible to live (or, more accurately, *exist*) without sex just as it's almost possible to live on bread and water. But just as good food enriches the body, sharing sex and love enriches every part of a woman's being. The penis and vagina are not there for decoration—they are designed to express the deepest feeling that men and women can have for each other in the most satisfying way. (And it is no coincidence that the same expression of love creates new human beings.) The woman who says "yes" to sex and love says "yes" to life. But just wanting it to happen may not be enough; that's what Laura found out:

"I don't reach a climax even after hours of all kinds of stimulation from my partner. The thing that makes it even more frustrating is that sometimes I wake up during the night in the middle of a wild orgasm just from a sexy dream. Until I read your book I sort of accepted the situation, but then I went to see a psychiatrist about it. I couldn't believe it but he said, 'It isn't important to have an orgasm as long as you are happy otherwise.' But Doctor, without orgasms, how can you be 'happy otherwise'?"

Was the psychiatrist right?

Yes, if he meant, "It isn't important to *me* whether or not *you* have an orgasm." But he had better be the world's best salesman if he is going to convince the women of America that "Orgasms Don't Count." On the other hand, he wouldn't be the first to try. Dr. S. I. McMillen said in his book *None of These Diseases:*

> In fact some authorities state that less than half of married women have ever experienced sexual orgasm. However the emotions they derive from the sexual act are beautiful and completely gratifying without any need of physical climax. Their emotions are diffused throughout their bodies.

How wonderful. Will all the gentlemen who are willing to trade their ejaculation for "emotions diffusing through their bodies" please step forward. Don't all rush at once.

The late Dr. Emil Novak of Johns Hopkins Medical School wrote:

> There are those women who . . . have never throughout their married lives experienced any great degree of physical satisfaction from the sex act. Nor do they feel frustrated or cheated.

If a certain group of doctors treated broken legs with the same compassion and understanding they reserve for women with orgasmic impairment, fracture cases would get the same therapy as race horses who limp.

Then a psychiatrist can't help a woman overcome her problem?

Oh, he can, if the woman qualifies. First she has to find a sympathetic psychiatrist who understands her problem. Then *he* has to find time in his busy practice for her. Then *she* has to find $50 an hour (and up) for a few years. That's a lot of finding. On the other hand, almost every woman who really wants to has a good chance of overcoming her orgasmic impairment *on her own.* Her first challenge is the barrier of the "three Un's."

What are the "three Un's"?

Every woman with orgasmic impairment views sex as *Unthinkable, Unmentionable,* and *Untouchable.* Her first job is trying to help herself eliminate the "Un's." For Jennifer, the big part was *Unthinkable:*

"I really don't get much enjoyment out of sex because I just can't keep my mind on what I'm doing. I keep thinking about everything I have to do the next day and worrying if the baby will wake up and I won't hear him. *Then*—after it's all over—I could kick myself because I missed out on *another* orgasm.

"It's crazy. I even find myself straining my ears to listen for cars passing in the street and dogs barking across the way. I try so hard to keep my mind on what we're doing that maybe I think I try too hard. I even try playing loud music or putting cotton in my ears, but it just makes it worse.

"Am I overdoing it?"

Well, she might be overdoing it a little. Loud music and cotton in the ears is not the perfect setting for an evening of romance. But it's simply a case of the mind trying to make a compromise with the crazy idea that sex is "wrong." "I can do it if I don't think about it—and, incidentally, don't enjoy it."

Betty stumbles over the *Unmentionable* part:

"I am twenty-five years old and I just don't enjoy sex very much. Often when my husband touches me I just don't want him near me. Sometimes he asks me to kiss him below and I do sometimes, but it doesn't do a thing for *me.* Even when he touches me below and caresses it, I still don't get excited."

Gwen has taken the final step—*Untouchable*—almost:

"I had to write to someone about my problem—frigidity. I've been married six years and I'm afraid to go to bed at night because I know what my husband wants. I know that I should give myself to him freely but sometimes I can't. Once in a while when he touches me, I get sick and throw up. I really love my husband and I want him to be happy and love me."

What can these women do about their blocked orgasms?

They can *and must* fight back. These girls—and millions like them—are risking their happiness and their marriages because of childish concepts of sex implanted by *someone else*. They must first seize control of their own minds and then take over control of their own bodies. Making sex *Thinkable* is a good place to start. Thinking about the next day's grocery shopping is *not* purer or more noble than thinking about the man you love and what you are doing to him and what he is doing to you. There is precious little love to be found in the supermarket and hardly any chance at orgasm.

Making sex *Mentionable* also requires a conscious effort. Up 'til now there are no cases on record where referring to a vagina as a "vagina" brought a bolt of lightning searing through the bedroom window to eternally seal the lips of a brazen woman. Besides, there is nothing so exotic about most sexual terms. "Vagina" is Latin for "sheath," penis is Latin for "tail," vulva is the Latin word for "a cover" and clitoris is Greek for "closed-up" or "hidden."

When a woman has to refer to essential parts of her body as "privates," "down there," or "you-know-where," she is admitting that they don't really belong to her. Even as recently as the Middle Ages people openly accepted their genitals. In those days a man appearing in court swore to tell the truth or forfeit his testicles—that's why it's called "testifying." (Unfortunately there is no indication as to what organ female witnesses laid on the line.)

By contrast, in modern society, no one ever questions the "mystery of the vanishing vagina." As soon as a girl is old enough to tell the difference between little boys and little girls, her own genitals are supposed to instantly become intellectually invisible. It doesn't make sense. The sooner she can completely accept the way God made her, the sooner she can find sexual happiness.

What's her first step toward sexual happiness?

The woman who wants to overcome orgasmic impairment needs to make her own sexuality *Touchable*. All it takes is fifteen minutes of privacy, good light, a magnifying mirror, and a pamphlet on how to brush your teeth from her dentist.

First, she reads the pamphlet about teeth. Notice how it treats the subject simply and directly. Use of the toothbrush and massage of the gums are discussed in a matter-of-fact way. The reader is encouraged to boldly examine her own mouth and gums daily and play an active role in preserving the function of those tiny bony prominences we call teeth. Every woman takes that sort of thing for granted. With that in mind, there is no reason why she shouldn't devote a fraction of her time to understanding and preserving a far more vital part of her body. If she doesn't take care of her teeth, her dentist can always make up a set of artificial ones. No gynecologist, unfortunately, can offer an equivalent service.

The next step is to undress, lie on her back on a bed (or the floor), raise her knees, open her legs, and teach herself what someone else should have taught her years ago. If she carefully spreads the labia majora ("large lips"—no one has ever explained why "acceptable" sexual words are always in Latin and Greek) she will get a clear view of the clitoris, which hangs over the pubic bone much the same way as the tongue hangs over the lower lip if one tries to touch the tip of the tongue to the tip of the chin. Like the tongue, there is a substantial part of the clitoris which always remains inside the body but is still available to sexual stimulation in many ways.

An inch or so below the clitoris is the urethra, which is basically (though not exclusively) for urination. Attached to each side of the clitoris are the labia minora ("small lips"—Latin again). They look—and feel—like a rooster's comb and extend around to the base of the vagina.

What's the idea of taking inventory of her sexual organs?

To sacrifice—in the cause of sexual happiness—*visual virginity.* At least 80 percent of women have never taken a good scientific look at their own genitals because somebody once told them it was "wrong." Visual virginity is like vaginal virginity—once it's gone, a woman never has to think about it again. And more important, she's ready for the next step—learning how her sexual organs work.

How does she start learning?

By making them work. A bit of surgical jelly on the tip of an index finger is all it takes. By gently sliding the lubricated finger over the labia, clitoris, and entrance to the vagina, a woman can discover more about her individual sexuality than a dozen psychiatrists can teach her in a dozen years. She can immediately identify the most sensitive—*and responsive*—parts of her body. In the process she may make some interesting discoveries.

What kind of discoveries?

That's the fascinating part. It will be totally different for every woman. A right-handed woman, for example, may find that the right side of the clitoris is ten times more sensitive than the left side. Another woman may discover that the tip of the clitoris—where her partner has been concentrating most of his attention—is actually *too* sensitive. Slow, gentle massage of the clitoral shaft from base to tip may be much more exciting. Other women may realize that a series of very gentle taps with the fingertip brings on rapid and vigorous erection of the tiny organ. The possibilities are endless and can open up a completely new world of sexual satisfaction for almost every woman. Instead of waiting for an erotic Prince Charming to fit his "foot" into her "glass slipper" (Cinderella had it backwards), she can discover and develop her own unlimited sexual potential. When Prince Charming arrives (and it could well be her own husband) she will be ready to show *him* a thing or two.

Does understanding how her sexual organs function really help a woman to enjoy sex more?

Yes, it does. Claudia tells about her own experience:

"When you first told me about it, Doctor, it didn't sound right. After all, deliberately *touching* myself? But I figured I wasn't getting that much out of sex anyhow, so what harm could it do?"

She shrugged.

"Well, let me tell *you,* it was like Columbus discovering America. I always thought of the vagina as just being a kind of passive sort of organ—maybe stretching a little to take the penis or something. But it almost has a mind of its own. For example, that little space between the clitoris and—what do you call it—the urethra? Well, I didn't know there was any feeling there at all. I never imagined it could be so sensitive. I even followed your suggestion and pulled gently on the labia. Like you said, I did feel it directly in the clitoris. It's really amazing to find out that after twenty-three years I know so little about my own body!"

Is there anything else a woman should do while she's exploring?

There is one last bit of exploration that can make a big difference when she goes to apply her new knowledge to intercourse itself. If she places a lubricated finger directly into the vagina, takes a deep breath, and bears down, she will feel the muscular ring at the opening to the vagina relax around her finger. Then she should tighten her muscles as if she is trying to hold back her urine—*hard.* The vaginal muscles will contract snugly around her finger. As she learns to open and close the vaginal entrance during intercourse, she will be able to intensify her own sensations *and* make a big difference to her partner.

Once a woman has the courage to make friends again with her own body she is prepared to embark on the most thrilling and exciting journey of all. She can begin to explore the uncharted territory of her deepest unconscious sexual feelings. If she is persistent and determined, she will ultimately take as her reward the one thing that every woman deserves and all too few women ever achieve—orgasm on demand.

3

CONQUERING
ORGASMIC IMPAIRMENT

Is it true that orgasmic impairment is basically an emotional problem?

Yes, it is. And because of that, at the same time a woman is working on the physical part of orgasm, she should also try to set her emotional house in order. Ideally, a psychiatrist can make her job easier. But in time of disaster, everyone has to help herself. To the millions of women in America who don't have regular orgasms, orgasmic impairment is a personal disaster, and they all can't wait their turn at the psychiatrist.

There are at least a hundred specific reasons why the brain —at that critical instant before orgasm—disconnects itself from the sexual organs. However, there are basically *three* emotional conflicts that cause most orgasmic impairment. The first conflict is:

Guilt

"I think I need your help. I have read every book and article on sex I could find and I have had long talks with my gynecologist, but he is very puzzled. You see, my partner can bring me to a climax with his fingers, but I never reach an orgasm with his penis. I know what I'm looking for but I just can't come the right way.

"We have tried everything—every position we could think of. Sitting, standing, sitting, lying side by side, me on top, him coming into me from behind—nothing helps. Yet I come so alive with his finger and my climax is so strong.

"Maybe this has something to do with it. When I was fifteen a boy I had been dating tried to rape me. Well, actually he *did* rape me. We were at his house watching television in his father's den and making out. He had his hands inside my panties and I got so excited I unzipped his trousers and took out his penis. I didn't want to have intercourse then but he sort of forced me. His parents were asleep in the next room and I didn't want to cry out and awaken them. It was over in an instant and he got so upset he began to cry. I hated him for what he did and I never wanted to see him again.

"A month later I discovered I was pregnant. Two weeks after that my mother and father insisted we get married. Would it surprise you to know that I never had an orgasm with him? My mother insisted that I try to make a success of my marriage, but two years later we got a divorce.

"Although the whole experience was frustrating, there was one consolation: it made me grow up fast. The only part I really regret is that I still don't have a climax no matter how many men I try it with.

"The one thing I want most out of sex—an orgasm during intercourse—is denied me. If I only knew why maybe I could do something about it."

Guilt over "rape" holds back orgasm. Guilt over sex outside of marriage also takes its orgasmic toll:

"I have no qualms about 'anything goes' as long as it pleases both partners. I love to have a man excite me with his mouth and I can hardly wait to do the same to him, but that's the only way I can come. I really want to feel a man's penis inside me when I climax, but I just can't seem to 'trip the hammer.'

"Several of my most recent lovers—all *very* experienced men—said I was passionate and sensual, but because I am so excited by oral-genital play, they implied there was something wrong. Even with the constant excitement of new partners and many different techniques, I still can't come with the penis in me. Am I asking too much?"

No, you're not asking too much at all. But sometimes the human mind insists on enforcing the moral code of Mother and Grandmother over the objections of the sexual organs. The usual result is an emotional compromise, like the one you know so well: "You can have all the sex you want—any way you want—just don't expect to enjoy it!"

"I hope you can settle an argument between me and my husband. I insist that a woman can be satisfied with sex even if she doesn't reach a climax—ever.

"My husband is always complaining and asking me why I never come when he does. He's afraid he's not man enough to satisfy me, but he does. I can't help it just because I don't reach a climax.

"I think I know the reason—although I don't want want him to know. Before I met him I was a prostitute, and to me sex was nothing but a job. I figure I must still think of it as work, so I never have a climax."

Most prostitutes slip on a suit of sexual armor before they go to work every night. Their emotional remoteness from their customers makes their job a lot easier. But when they finally hang up their work clothes for the last time and get married (most prostitutes eventually marry) it isn't so easy to adjust. Just as the horse who draws the milk wagon is conditioned to stop at every house, the prostitute has been trained to rigorously suppress her sexual responses. Impersonating orgasm a dozen times a night (not including matinees) is one thing; accepting the sexual love of a husband can be much harder. As one of this girl's former co-workers said, "Doc, I *know* how to fake it. Now I want to learn to *make it!*"

But there's an even bigger rock in the road to orgasm on demand.

What's in the way of orgasm on demand?

Sexual Ignorance

Many women know more about operating their washing machine than their sexual apparatus. The reason is obvious —the washer comes with an instruction book. The sexual organs are just *there.* There is no owner's manual, no dealer, and no toll-free number to call for instant service. (If there were such a number, it would be overwhelmed with calls every night about eleven o'clock.)

Orgasm requires a vagina that gets enough stimulation and a brain that has enough information. Sometimes lack of information leads to ingenious solutions:

"What I call the clitoris is a little pea-shaped thing on the outside at the top between the lips of the vagina. The only way I have ever been able to reach a climax is for a man (or me) to massage this with his finger completely to the end of intercourse, with his penis going in and out of my vagina.

"I wonder if I could have plastic surgery to have this

clitoris moved so that it would be massaged by the penis naturally. Is this possible?"

Fortunately, a clitoris transplant is not necessary. During intercourse the average penis has plenty of opportunities to get the attention of the clitoris. It pulls on the labia as it slides in and out of the vagina, it massages the base of the clitoris through the top wall of the vagina and causes the vulva to squeeze the entire clitoris with each thrust. The biggest obstacle is to get the clitoris to *respond* to all this activity.

As every woman who has ever worn a bra knows, the human mind has the power to turn off sensations it doesn't care about. A few minutes after putting on a brassiere, many women forget they are even wearing one. The feeling of compression and binding around the breasts just doesn't register in the brain anymore. Unfortunately, a woman's mind can also shut off all but the most intense sensations from the clitoris. All too often her clitoris (and her brain) have decided to respond only to the very intense finger-clitoris sensations instead of the less direct penis-clitoris stimulation. The solution is *not* to change the location of the clitoris—it's fine where it is. It's simpler—and more effective —to improve the receptivity of the brain.

Another misunderstanding involves that same vital organ, the clitoris.

"I'm going to graduate from college soon and I want to get over this problem before I get married.

"I can reach an orgasm every time I masturbate—and that's at least four times a week. But what worries me is that I never have a climax if I (or one of my boy friends) just work on the vagina by itself.

"What can I do about my 'spoiled clitoris'? I know that vaginal and clitoral orgasms are the same, but as a lover I am zero since I can only have the clitoral ones. I hope you can help."

Not much help is needed. No woman will ever have any kind of orgasm except the clitoral kind. No trophy has ever been awarded for the amazing feat of reaching an orgasm without involving the clitoris. The reason is simple: the center of female orgasm *is* the clitoris. Whether it is stimulated directly or indirectly, the "little pea-shaped organ" is where the action is.

What's the third emotional obstacle that stands in the way of orgasm?

Revenge

Instead of cutting off their noses to spite their faces, too many women cut off their orgasms to spite their husbands. The results are about the same. An unhappy wife would be much smarter to strike back at her husband with conventional weapons rather than unleash the nuclear arsenal of sexual rejection. The fallout invariably poisons her own chances for sexual satisfaction. Ironically, most women who give up their orgasm to get even with their spouses don't really understand what's happening to them:

"About a year ago, my husband was working late at the office. I was feeling kind of lonely so I went next door (we live in an apartment house) to visit with my neighbor. She is twenty-four—two years younger than me—and married. No one answered when I knocked so I let myself in—I thought she might be in the back bedroom or something.

"She was in the bedroom—in bed—and my husband was there too. They were both naked and having intercourse. To make matters worse she was on *top*, something he would never let me do to him. I was too shocked to do anything so I just sneaked out and they don't even know I saw them.

"Since then I have never had an orgasm with my husband.

Whenever he touches me all I can see is them together with her big breasts bouncing. My husband always complains because I happen to be small in that way. . . ."

Sexual intercourse with a double-crossing husband is about as much fun as a heavy date with a baboon—and about as likely to result in orgasm. A few things have to be straightened out in the living room (and maybe even the lawyer's office) before there is going to be improvement in the bedroom. Every woman is entitled to a better deal than that.

Sometimes the shoe is on the other foot:

"I am in my thirties and married about ten years. When I first met my husband I thought I could love, trust, and respect him. Now I know I can trust him. He has always been hard to love. He yells, curses, and makes sarcastic remarks constantly. Everybody else laughs at his barbed wit but it isn't so funny in bed—I have never had a climax during intercourse.

"Last night I took a lover. He is a man I have known for many years; yet he loves his wife and will not leave her. I am sure he has given many women a night to remember. After a brief hour in his embrace I am learning to love from an expert, and maybe someday I can finally have an orgasm during intercourse. Am I doing anything wrong?"

The real question is, "Are you doing anything *right?*" Your new "lover," selected out of frustration, seems to specialize in dispensing lessons in love to lonely ladies while his own wife waits patiently at home. But the disappointing thing is he didn't seem to bring you any closer to orgasm than the man you are married to. Maybe the next lesson will be better—or worse.

Sooner or later every woman with O-I (orgasmic impairment) has to face a harsh fact of physiology: *The human penis is an organ of copulation, not a magic wand.* Orgasm depends less on the way the man's penis touches the woman's vagina and more on the way the man's spirit touches the woman's spirit. The key to orgasm is above the eyebrows—not below the pubis. Once a woman learns that, she can stop throwing the master switch in her brain to *Standby* for sex and *Off* for orgasm. Back in the first grade, everyone learned three rules that have a new meaning when it comes to sex.

What rules of sex are those?

STOP, LOOK, and *LISTEN.* It works this way:

STOP living in the past with your present partner. No matter what happened with your mother, your father, and all the nasty men (or women) in your life, it doesn't have to interfere with what happens in bed tonight. An innerspring mattress is no place to re-fight a duel that should have been settled with someone else twenty years ago. To put it another way, the ghosts of the past will be powerless to frighten away orgasm unless you give them your permission—and cooperation.

LOOK at sexuality honestly. Human beings were given sexual feelings by their Creator—sex is built into each and every one of us at birth. The full expression of sexual feelings is not optional—it is the right and destiny of every man and every woman. During the few short years we are here on earth together we might as well use it creatively—and *enjoy* it at the same time.

LISTEN to your deepest sexual feelings and respond to them. Women particularly are capable of an almost unlimited range of sexual responses with their partners. They have a right to expect more from sex than nine minutes every other night as measured by the clock radio on the bedside table and discreetly illuminated by the pink doggie lamp on the dresser.

Most women do the dishes every night after dinner. But if they "do" sexual intercourse the same way, it turns out to be just as thrilling—a little heat, a little splashing, a little

44

wetness, a little drying off, and back on the shelf until next time. The woman who really wants to can now begin to take positive action to achieve orgasm on demand. Instead of being a slave to the whims of her own unconscious mind and the frailities of her partner, she can finally bring her climaxes under her own *conscious control.* Instead of wondering what her sexual organs are going to do next, she can make them perform exactly the way she wants. The nagging doubt that creeps between the sheets at bedtime for so many women, "Will I or won't I?," can be replaced by the decision, "How many times do I want to?" For the woman who only has occasional orgasms, regular orgasm brings new sexual security. For the woman who has never had a climax, it can open a whole new world to her—in every way.

How does she begin to bring her orgasms under conscious control?

By having an orgasm—the best way she can, as soon as she can, and as often as she can. The concept is a basic one. Instead of a mystical, magical, mysterious event that comes on capriciously, she makes an orgasm a physical fact of life. At the same time, she is retraining her vagina and clitoris and all the nerves between her genitals and her brain to respond eagerly and enthusiastically to erotic excitement.

Then you're telling a woman to masturbate?

No. Masturbation is a bad idea. The word comes from the (as usual) Latin word "masturbari," which means "to pollute oneself." Certainly these days no one needs to pollute themselves any more than the environment is polluting them already. The point is that self-induced sensory stimulation of the sexual organs to the point of orgasm doesn't deserve to be called masturbation or self-pollution. It is a harmless form of recreation for millions of people, sexual release for millions of others, and for the woman with O-I it can be an essential part of her self-cure.

How is that part of her self-cure?

In this way. Every woman who can't reach an orgasm during intercourse wonders, "Could there be something *physically* wrong that prevents me from reaching an orgasm?" A self-induced orgasm answers that question in five minutes.

More important, a self-induced orgasm provides the emotional (and physical) foundation for having orgasms the "regular way." There is virtually no difference between that kind of climax and the kind that comes from copulation. Once a woman can do it on her own, she should be able to transfer the response to intercourse with her partner. Beth's experience is typical:

"You won't believe this but I was married for twenty-five years before I had my first orgasm! And the way I had it was by using a vibrator. That may not sound like very much to you but it was the turning point of my life because a few months later I progressed to having climaxes with my husband. I don't know whether it was a case of bad reflex pathways or fifty years of accumulated guilt but that's all in the past. I still haven't told my husband why there is such an improvement in our sexual relationship. He seems happy with it just the same."

What's the idea of a vibrator?

To batter down the barriers of guilt, shame, and prudery that prevent so many women from finding the sexual fulfillment that they deserve.

Remember those old movies where the heroine is mysteriously paralyzed and confined to a wheelchair? The doctors

46

are convinced she has no physical illness but are powerless to help her. One night the house catches on fire, and in spite of her emotions, her instincts for self-preservation overwhelm her self-induced paralysis and instantly make her walk again.

Ironically, many women with O-I have unconsciously (and unknowingly) imposed the same kind of paralysis on their sexual organs. An electric vibrator provides intense, almost unbearable sexual excitement that overwhelms the emotional obstacles to orgasm and makes the genitals (and brain) respond explosively.

It works like this:

Buried just under the skin of the clitoris, labia, and lower third of the vagina are millions of microscopic sensors, like tiny electric switches. During intercourse the penis pushes and pulls against these areas and snaps thousands and thousands of these tiny switches. As each switch closes it fires off a electric impulse to the brain. Basically, the more sensors the penis stimulates, the wilder the sexual sensations. That's where the vibrator excels. In a given moment it can trigger at least a million more sensors than the most educated penis —and that adds up to a virtually inevitable orgasm.

How does a woman go about using a vibrator?

Vibrators come in three models. The simplest and cheapest is shaped like a small plastic penis and runs on its own batteries. A woman lubricates the tip and places it *gently* against her clitoris. Some women prefer to insert the device carefully into the vagina and press it against the vaginal roof to stimulate the clitoris *indirectly*.

The second type of vibrator is the kind barbers use for scalp massage. It is simply a small electric motor that straps on the back of the hand and converts each finger into a miniature vibrator of its own. The possibilities are limited only by the imagination. Some women place the heel of the hand on the pubic bone, others insert an index finger into the vagina and rest the thumb lightly on the clitoris to double the effect. This kind of vibrator can also be used for treating some forms of impotence in men.

The third variety of vibrator is a small motor in a pistol-shaped plastic handle with soft plastic tips. The tips are lubricated and placed against the clitoris, labia, or opening to the vagina. The vibration usually brings on a prompt orgasm.

Where can a woman get a vibrator?

The local drugstore is the handiest place but sexual awareness has now touched Sears Roebuck and Montgomery Ward—their catalogues offer a nice selection of vibrators in several price ranges.

Does a woman have to use a vibrator?

Certainly not. As part of her orgasmic retraining program she can often produce an orgasm with her hand or fingers, although it usually takes longer and the climax is not as intense. The whole idea of self-produced orgasm is simply to pave the way for satisfying sexual intercourse. *No woman should ever want an electrical gadget or a lubricated finger to replace the warmth and tenderness of another human being.* On the other hand, few modern women are willing to settle for second-class sexuality simply because it would shock their grandmothers if they "touched themselves." If a determined program of sexual self-help can enable her to claim what is rightfully hers—full sexual satisfaction with her man —she doesn't have to apologize to anyone.

Often it works like this:

"A few months ago I started using a vibrator and very quickly found out what an orgasm really is—after eighteen years of marriage! But there is still one problem: I find that after using the vibrator I have such a strong craving for intercourse between sessions that I find myself literally itching for a penis. And even after coming three or four times with my husband I still find myself wanting more!"

A few lucky individuals will be able to make the jump from self-induced orgasms to penis-vagina climaxes directly. For them, that's the end of their retraining program. But most women need a transitional technique that is more emotional and personal than a vibrator yet more intense and at the same time less demanding than regular intercourse. Cunnilingus has helped millions of women bridge this gap:

"My husband and I have been married eight years and we can honestly say that our marriage is just as fresh as our honeymoon. We grow fonder of each other as friends and seem to learn something new and helpful about each other with each sexual experience. Quite simply, this is my problem: I am unable to reach a climax from the usual position of copulation. I experienced my first orgasm recently by cunnilingus and I'm not exaggerating when I say it was like being born all over again.

"I know that I'm getting closer to having orgasm the regular way—it's only a matter of time."

This wife is on the right track. If she has progressed so rapidly from no orgasm to tongue-clitoris orgasm, then penis-vagina orgasm should be just around the corner.

Is cunnilingus all right?

Well, for one thing, it has been approved by popular demand. Even though it is technically illegal in many states, the law is almost never enforced. If all the cunnilinctors (and cunnilinctees) were locked up, there would be about fifty million Americans behind bars. (It would also be a swinging prison system.)

Besides, to the woman who wants to overcome O-I, the advantages are obvious. It allows her to easily share her orgasm with her man, which is the whole idea in the first place. In addition, the tongue, mouth, and lips are ideal for providing all the various kinds of stimulation the female genitals are turned on to. Heat, pressure, gentle friction, and (with a little practice) vibration provide maximum sexual excitement and almost guarantee an orgasm every time. A fringe benefit is that most men find cunnilingus almost unbearably exciting and are more than willing to cooperate.

When a woman can reach regular climaxes by cunnilingus she is ready for the next step on the road to orgasm on demand—unless guilt blocks her progress.

Guilt about what?

About the kind of situation Karen describes in her letter:

"I'll try to be brief. I'm twenty-six years old and I've been married for two years. During that time I must have had at least five hundred orgasms, which is fine except none of them were during sexual intercourse. I respond quickly and feel very excited from preplay and fondling of the area around the vagina but I never reach a climax that way. Does that mean I'm frigid?

"When I bring on the orgasm myself it is tremendously exciting and I can have up to twenty of them at one 'session.' All I have to do is rub the labia and the particularly sensitive piece of skin right at the head of where the 'slit' begins. The funny thing is that when my husband does the same thing to me, nothing happens and it seems just like he is masturbating me."

Karen isn't the only one with that dilemma. For many women, do-it-yourself orgasms come swiftly, but when a man caresses their clitorises, their brains turn off. After a lifetime of being told it's "nasty" to let anyone touch their "privates," they come to the reasonable—but incorrect—conclusion that a woman who feels anything is "nasty" too. Conclusive proof that the brain and not the genitals has the final say is summarized in Karen's experience. The same organ, the clitoris, stroked by the same structure, the finger, says YES or NO depending on whose hand that finger happens to be attached to.

Yes, but what can Karen do about it?

Well, she can try to understand why her brain won't listen to her sexual organs. In a way it's like the pregnant but unmarried young lady who was being examined by her doctor:

DOCTOR *(noticing her enlarged abdomen):* "Is it Miss or Mrs.?"

YOUNG LADY: "Let's think of it this way—from the waist up, it's Miss; from the waist down, it's Mrs."

Women like Karen are 91 percent adult. But the 9 percent of their bodies that consist of labia, clitoris, and vagina never had a chance to grow up. They accept masturbation as a physical necessity, although they still feel loads of guilt about it. But the genitals (and the brain that is connected to them) absolutely reject something so daring as letting a man "play with you" or "go all the way." Things will start to get better as soon as the twenty-six-year-old woman makes her twenty-six-year-old sexual organs act their age. If she succeeds in giving up the "little-girl vagina," a whole new world of orgasm unfolds. Sometimes it helps if she puts it in these terms:

"I am no longer a little girl subject to the sexual taboos enforced by my parents. I am a sexually mature woman and

I have the *absolute right* to experience orgasm with my partner—without interference from anyone."

One final word about masturbation. Karen says, "When my husband does the same thing to me . . . it seems just like he is masturbating me." Sexual brainwashing strikes again! If it's "masturbation" when she stimulates her own sexual organs, and "masturbation" again when her husband excites her, then isn't it "masturbation with a penis" when she has sexual intercourse? By that medieval reasoning, *all* sex is "masturbation."

That doesn't leave a girl much to look forward to, does it?

The truth is that a man who excites a woman sexually—and even brings her to orgasm—by titillating her clitoris can actually help her to make the transition to full penis-vagina orgasm. This technique, if intelligently employed, takes the form of *clitoral-vaginal bridging.*

What's **clitoral-vaginal bridging?**

Clitoral-vaginal bridging (or C-V-B, for short) is often the final step before orgasm on demand. It brings the vagina and clitoris into full-fledged partnership and impels them to work together to make a climax during intercourse inevitable. Here is an example of what it can do:

"I guess I was typical of so many American women. I was married five years, mothered three babies, felt guilty about masturbation, and never had an orgasm except by 'sixtynine.' I finally decided it was time to do something about it. I read your books and started myself on a program of research—with my husband's eager cooperation. In six months of experimentation I learned more than in four years at college. Here's some of the things I found out:

1. I need *constant* stimulation from the first kiss to just before orgasm if I am going to reach a climax.

2. It *is* true that the clitoris is the only way to reach an orgasm—*but* working on the vagina at the same time certainly helps a lot.

3. A husband has to do his part—just lying on top and going in and out doesn't make it easy for his wife.

4. I also discovered something else in the process—sex isn't all romance, it can be a lot of fun too!

"Hope this helps other women like it helped me."
C-V-B can be simple and effective therapy.

How does a woman go about it?

She simply arranges for her man to effectively caress her clitoris with a finger at the same time he is massaging her vagina with his penis. Each type of stimulation reinforces the other to the point where orgasm becomes almost irresistible. The combined stimulation, penis in vagina, fingers on clitoris, is repeated over and over with each act of intercourse. Gradually the intense excitement from clitoral caresses merges with the diffuse rhythmic sensations of the penis as it glides in and out of the vagina. Many women find the combined sensations so unbearably exciting that they are reluctant to give up the clitoral stroking and settle for penis penetration alone. As one patient described after trying it for the first time:

"Doctor, it's like being made love to by an octopus! You said C-V-B stands for 'clitoral-vaginal-bridging.' From the way it felt last night, a better description is 'clitoral-vaginal-*blitzkrieg!*' "

In orgasm, as in life, position is everything. C-V-B often works best if the woman mounts her man and sits firmly astride his penis. This literally puts *her* in the driver's seat and lets her steer his penis into her most responsive sexual area. It also allows her partner to reach the clitoris easily with his fingers and helps everybody to see what they are doing. A few nights devoted to conscientious practice will pay immense dividends. Sometimes direct friction between the clitoris and the man's pubic bone are enough to solve the problem of O-I once and for all. A little American ingenuity may also come to the rescue:

"Before my husband and I were married I had no trouble reaching a climax every time we had intercourse. *After* marriage I was lucky to have an orgasm every third time. I was very concerned, so I started thinking. Then it dawned on me. When we were engaged we usually made love in the back seat of his car—like so many other couples. He would sit on the seat and I would sit on his lap facing him. So I tried it the same way at home in bed.

"It was an exciting discovery and it helped a lot. However, one day in this position he had already reached his climax and I was still not satisfied. Maybe I am oversexed because one or two orgasms are not enough for me. I experimented a little and managed another orgasm. This is how I did it.

"I let him play with my breasts first and then I rock back and forth with his limp penis against my clitoris. After a few moments, I stop and rest and he plays with my breasts again. When I start in again I am even more stimulated. I keep this up, rocking and stopping, until the final climax comes. And when it does it is of such magnitude that it dwarfs all others. I think this information might be of interest to other women because I feel they should get as much satisfaction as possible from sex—I do!"

*Doesn't the man have some responsibility for
helping a woman to overcome her O-I?*

There's no question about it. Copulation is the most complicated activity a woman ever engages in—most women realize that. Some men don't.

A husband and wife were being interviewed together about their mutual problems:

> HUSBAND *(pompously):* You can't teach *me* anything about sex, Doctor. *I* just do what comes naturally.
>
> WIFE *(with raised eyebrows):* How do you know you're doing it right?

What may be a colossal finish for the gentleman can still leave the lady at the starting gate:

"Every time we have intercourse my husband snatches his penis out of me just at the moment of ejaculation. That may feel all right for *him* but, let me tell you, it comes at just the wrong time for me. I don't want to get pregnant every time we have sex but I want more out of it than a wet tummy."

It takes some men a long time to face the fact that sex is a team project:

"My wife and I have been married since May 29, 1942. She has yet to enjoy a sexual intercourse. I guess she does it occasionally for my benefit. We wish to receive your advice concerning this."

This fellow obviously has the right idea, but thirty years is a long time for him—and his wife—to suffer. In a sense, when it comes to sex, man is the manufacturer and woman is the consumer. His job is to

1. manufacture a rigid and erect penis
2. deliver it to the customer—in good condition
3. help her to install the product
4. remain on the premises long enough to be sure it provides her with satisfactory service

That's all a man has to do?

Not quite. If these four requirements were sufficient, then a good hard rubber dildo would be the ideal sexual partner. It isn't. In addition to performing mechanically, a man must also bring a woman love and kindness and understanding. He must be dedicated to using sex as a means of expressing the otherwise inexpressible devotion that only a man and a woman in love can share. He must also be willing to fight shoulder-to-shoulder with her in her battle for orgasmic fulfillment.

Is it really worthwhile to go to all that trouble just to reach an orgasm during intercourse?

That's the decision every woman has to make for herself. One woman who said "yes" expressed it this way:

"Doctor, before I achieved it I used to think that her orgasm was the most beautiful gift a woman could give to the man she loved. Then, when it finally happened, I discovered something else—it's also the greatest gift a man can give to a woman. Those are the two things that made it really worthwhile."

4

ABORTION
AND BIRTH CONTROL

What's the most effective method of birth control?

Abortion. Ironically, it satisfies nearly all the requirements of a perfect means of contraception. It doesn't interfere with foreplay, requires no technical skill on the part of the couple, is 100 percent effective in preventing birth (at least *live* birth), and does not stain the clothing. It is also cheap—if the actual cost is spread out over the total number of copulations, it can run as low as fifteen cents per act of intercourse. It also has a high degree of safety.

But is abortion really safe?

Not only safe but *legal.* Recommended by your local social worker, endorsed by Family Planning, and stamped with the seal of approval of none other than the U.S. Supreme Court. Things have really changed:

"Doctor, I've had two abortions in my life. The first one was six years ago, when I was eighteen. It cost $500, was done in Tijuana in a motel room, and I almost died. The latest one was done last month. My minister helped me arrange it, the U.S. Government paid for it—my husband's in the service—my doctor did it in his office, and afterward when I couldn't get my car started one of his patients, who's a police sergeant, drove me home. Boy, was I amazed!"

These days abortion has nearly become the gynecological equivalent of having your tonsils taken out. Of course, it wasn't always that easy. In the old days, back in 1969, most legal abortions involved raking around inside the uterus with a looped instrument called a "curette" to drag out the embryo. After the sixteenth to twentieth week of pregnancy it was too late for that, so the uterus had to be opened up at surgery and the baby taken out. It was primitive at best.

Then American doctors started using a new machine—the suction-abortion device—invented some years before by Polish and Israeli scientists. That started the Abortion Revolution.

How did one machine start an Abortion Revolution?

Well, if you think of the embryo in the pregnant uterus as being like a mouse in a breadbox, the idea comes into focus. The old way was like using a broomstick to force out the mouse. It did the job but it tore up the bread. The new abortion machine works on the principle of the vacuum cleaner: just hook it up, turn it on, and it sucks out the mouse —or the embryo. Basically it is nothing more than a small electric suction pump hooked up to a length of plastic tubing. The tube is carefully inserted into the uterus, the pump builds up a powerful suction, and another pregnant woman becomes unpregnant. No muss, no fuss, no bother.

Nowadays the vast majority of abortions are the "vacuum cleaner" type—walk-in-walk-out. (Lest any amateurs be tempted, that vacuum cleaner you have in the closet will end up turning your whole body inside out and stuffing it into one of those little paper dust bags. Save money some other way.) Of course, there are some women who don't qualify for a vacuum abortion.

Who doesn't qualify for an abortion?

The women who wait too long. After about the sixteenth week or so, the baby can't be whooshed out by suction—the head is just too big. But Modern Science only sees that as a challenge. These "late abortions" are usually handled in the hospital. A nurse who assists describes it:

"Well, after the mother—I mean, patient—is prepared and on the operating table, the doctor comes in. He inserts a large-bore hypodermic needle right through her enlarged abdomen into the uterus. Then he slides a narrow plastic tube through the needle and sucks out about a cupful of the amniotic fluid that surrounds the baby. After that he pumps in a strong solution of table salt—and that's it."

"What do you mean, 'that's it'?"

"You know, the rest is routine. The baby usually dies in a few minutes and it's born dead within twenty-four hours. We usually have the mothers—I keep forgetting, the patients—drop them in a bed pan. I guess that's the worst part."

"The worst part?"

"Yes. The doctor rarely sees the baby, the patient doesn't want to see it, and I'm the one who has to get rid of them day after day. I can pretty much handle that. It's only the ones who are born alive that bother me."

Some aborted babies are born **alive?**

Oh, yes. In New York State alone, one of the pioneer states in legal abortion, more than thirty late abortions have produced living babies. Most of those died subsequently, although at least two infants marked for destruction have survived and will probably grow up into more or less normal children—in spite of their hazardous debut.

Isn't there a better way to do it?

That, of course, is the problem—and a thoughtful reader summarizes it very well:

"I notice, Doctor, that all the news stories about the advantages of abortion emphasize the safety of the procedure as far as the mother is concerned. I do not think, nevertheless, that abortion is too safe for the baby."

Not only does abortion have to be *unsafe* for the baby, it has to be *lethal* for him. That's what it's all about. The word abortion itself comes from the Latin term *aboriri,* which means "to disappear," and the only way to really "disappear the baby" is to snuff it out. If nobody interferes, that little embryo or fetus—or as some delicate souls like to call it, "the product of conception"—is going to turn into a full-fledged human being. Pretending that the tiny organism in the uterus isn't alive because it doesn't have a social security number or can't watch television doesn't fool anyone. The truth is, there is a trace of killing in every abortion—as well as a violation of the Hippocratic Oath. (To get around that, a lot of medical schools just don't bother giving the oath anymore.) Ending a human life—even if it's only a potential human life—is a sobering undertaking.

But then should abortion be made illegal again?

Hardly. That's like the story of the man who was being interviewed on his ninety-second birthday. He was complaining to the reporter about losing his hearing, about his failing vision, and about his arthritis. The reporter said: "It really must be a nuisance to be so old!" "I used to think so," said the old fellow with a smile, "until I considered the alternative."

That's about the way it is with abortion. Inflicting an unwanted child on an unwed mother blights the lives of two human beings at once. Adding another unwelcome baby to a long string of ten other malnourished and miserable kids multiplies unhappiness for thirteen people.

In most cases abortion is simply a form of retroactive birth control—second-thought contraception for children who never should have been conceived (as far as their parents were concerned) in the first place. These days our society feels that only wanted children should be born, so anybody can have an abortion anytime so long as it's done in the doctor's office—or, in later stages, in the hospital. But even that may be in the process of changing.

How is abortion changing?

The great American obsession with do-it-yourself is about to spread to the field of abortion.

Linda is twenty-two, blonde, beautiful, and an airline stewardess:

"Doctor, we both know the kind of reputation that stewardesses have and we both know it isn't true. We're just like any other bunch of healthy, red-blooded American girls—which means we don't sit around crocheting between flights. I mean, we're not supposed to be the Vestal Virgins, are we? Anyhow, I personally don't believe in sleeping around. I happen to be living with my fiancé—he's going to law school and we'll probably get married when he passes the Bar. But I don't want to get pregnant. Right?"

Linda paused, smiled, then answered her own question:

"Right! Well, I took the pill and it made me gain weight. The company says that's a no-no—no chubby charmers for *our* tired businessmen. I don't care to mess with diaphragms and foams and all that. I want sex to be fun—not work. And I don't like the way those condoms feel—it's like making love to a plastic baggie. I was in trouble—until this came along—"

Linda opened her purse and dumped some plastic tubing and a large plastic syringe on the desk top.

"With these little goodies, like they say on TV, 'Relief is only moments away!' "

In a sense, she was right.

What did she mean by "Relief is only moments away!"?

Linda was referring to the ultimate weapon in the field of abortion. More and more unmarried girls (and some married ladies) are turning to the trail-blazing technique of "menstrual extraction." Immediately after the first missed period, they insert a length of soft plastic tubing into the vagina, through the cervix, and into the uterus. They attach the other end to a large disposable plastic syringe and carefully apply suction. If they happen to be pregnant, they draw out the embryo at the very earliest moments of its existence.

They sidestep the biggest burden of guilt because they deliberately avoid knowing whether or not they were actually pregnant. And they save even the cost of a simple vacuum abortion. But there are a few little details that Linda didn't mention.

What details are those?

Pushing a foreign body up into the uterus is no job for an amateur. Even though a plastic tube isn't a knitting needle or a coat hanger, menstrual extraction is still vaguely reminiscent of the old "backyard scrape" in the days of illegal abortions. There is a constant danger of infection and related problems. The same woman who calls a plumber to fix her kitchen sink should at least put an equivalent value on her own body. But fortunately for the do-it-yourselfers, there might soon be another way to go about it.

What's the other do-it-yourself way?

Prostoglandins. Prostoglandins (or PGs) are a recently discovered type of hormone produced by each cell of the body individually. (In contrast to the usual hormones which require special gland factories like the thyroid or adrenal gland to produce them.) Although still in the experimental stage, prostoglandins have been used by intravenous injection to produce thousands of relatively safe abortions without surgery.

The next wrinkle is to develop PG vaginal suppositories so a woman can simply slip one into place after missing a period —and that will be that. The ways things are going, it should be perfected in short order. There is no area of medicine where research activity is so intense as the territory between the knees and the navel. Take the field of contraception, for example.

What's going on there?

A better question might be, "What's going *in* there?" The hottest item in the contraceptive catalogue these days is the intrauterine device, or IUD. Originally developed as a means of family planning for camels (Remember, pregnant camels wouldn't leave the caravans?), the IUD is now taking the center of the stage in human birth control. Since the early days of the first crude plastic loops and bow ties, a whole new generation of plastic doodads and gimcracks has evolved. Perhaps not by coincidence most of them look like refugees from the costume jewelry counter at the dime store.

There's one that looks like a little miniature accordion, another in the form of a shield, and a third of white plastic wrapped in copper wire. To make it more confusing some of the snappier IUDs have actually been made into costume jewelry so a pretty young lady may have the same coils dangling from her ear lobes as she has floating in her uterus.

How effective are the IUDs as contraceptives?

Better than they are as costume accessories. The rate of protection is right up there in the same league as the pill, the best foam, and conscientious use of the diaphragm. Besides, the IUD is convenient, greaseless, and always there when you need it. But the problems are the predictable ones, considering that it *is* a foreign body. It can cause pain, irritation, bleeding, and on rare occasions it penetrates through the wall of the uterus to cause real trouble. The copper-wrapped IUD is easily the most effective of all, but unfortunately copper is a poison and the long-range effects of inner exposure are still unknown. That pretty much applies to IUDs in general—no one has used them long enough to know if they cause cancer —like earlier IUDs did shortly after the turn of the century. Time will tell. In the meantime, two other developments have occurred. First the U.S. Government has recalled the entire production (over 200,000) of one brand of stainless steel IUDs as hazardous to health. Second, the American Medical Association has begun a nationwide survey of physicians to find out what's really going on with these widely used gadgets. On the other hand, a woman can always rely on Silly Putty for protection.

Silly Putty is a contraceptive?

In a way. Doctors are in the final stages of testing a little doughnut of similar material that sits high in the vagina next to the cervix. This silicone ring is impregnated with a female sex hormone, progesterone, that is slowly absorbed through the walls of the vagina and gets into the bloodstream. It works pretty well as a contraceptive, but a woman has to take it out for seven days each month if she wants to have a normal period. That's probably all right as long as she doesn't let the kids get hold of it and bounce it around the family room.

To avoid that problem there is also a tiny piece of the same silicone that can be injected under the skin or even placed directly into the uterus where it hopefully drifts around keeping sperm from accomplishing anything for at least a year. (Both these ideas have yet to be approved by the Food and Drug Administration, although it may be only a matter of time.)

Is there anything new that a woman can use right now?

The latest arrow in the birth control quiver is a drug that's been around for about forty years and is well-known to veterinarians. They've been using it for a long time to keep cats and dogs from having kittens and puppies. Finally it's worked its way up the evolutionary scale to the point where it is now available for canceling people. It is a synthetic hormone called "diethylstilbesterol," or DES, for short.

DES is the famous "morning-after" pill that gives a girl three full days after each unprotected act of sexual intercourse to decide whether or not she wants to become a mother. If she decides to drop her baby's option, she simply takes fifty milligrams a day for five days in a row. (DES isn't 100 percent effective but it comes pretty close.)

This method has become very popular recently with college girls, what with co-ed dorms and all that. Finally the Food and Drug Administration has given in and approved DES for use as a human second-thought contraceptive with the insistence that it be used "For Emergency Only," an ambiguous restriction if there ever was one.

As one girl from Vassar said,

"Does that mean I have to keep those pills in a bright red box on the wall of my bedroom next to the fire extinguisher?"

DES does have a couple of drawbacks, however. If by chance it doesn't abort the impending pregnancy, there is a small chance that trouble is on the way. Some girl babies born to mothers who have taken the drug during pregnancy tend to develop cancer of the vagina at about the age of twenty. No one knows why, but it can happen. And like other oral contraceptives, there is a real hazard of death or illness from sudden blood clots.

These days whenever the question of safety comes up someone always mentions the traditional birth control pill.

Are birth control pills really safe?

Well, they're safe for the doctor who prescribes them, they are safe for the man who copulates with the woman, but maybe they aren't so safe for the female who takes them.

At least the people who make them don't seem to think they're so safe. Listen to what the manufacturers say in their private ads, aimed at doctors:

"The physician should be alert to the earliest manifestations of thrombolic disorders (blood clots). Should any of these occur or be suspected, the drug should be discontinued immediately."

That's *easy* to understand. Then the ad lapses into scientific gobbledy-gook:

"Retrospective studies of morbidity and mortality in Great Britain and studies of morbidity in the United States have shown a statistically significant association between thrombophlebitis, pulmonary embolism, and cerebral thrombosis and embolism and the use of oral contraceptives."

That's to make sure no female patient comes across the inside information by accident in the waiting room. A literal translation goes like this:

"Scientific studies of illness and death rates in Great Britain and illness rates in the United States have shown that birth control pills cause blood clots of the legs, blood clots of the lungs, and blood clots of the brain in some women."

The ad goes on to state—in technical jargon—that women *taking* the pill have anywhere from a 440 to a 700 percent greater chance of having these serious blood clots than women who *don't* take the pill.

Then things really get scary:

"Discontinue medication pending examination if there is a sudden, partial or complete *loss of vision,* or if there is a sudden onset of proptosis, diplopia, or migraine."

Translation: "If the woman suddenly goes blind, don't give her any more birth control pills. And if her eyes bulge out or she sees double or has migraine headaches, stop the pill."

Does that mean a woman shouldn't take birth control pills?

What that really means is that taking birth control pills is an individual decision between the woman and her doctor. About two million women have already decided *against* taking the pill and another two million have indicated (in surveys) that they're thinking about switching to other means of contraception.

Doctors have their own problems when it comes to the pill. Two of America's leading drug companies together controlled 20 percent of the very profitable oral contraceptive market. Doctors felt confident when they prescribed the products of such prestigious manufacturers. Suddenly and without warning the two companies stopped selling oral contraceptives in the U.S. It seems that laboratory animals got breast tumors from the little pills.

To make matters worse, women who were crippled allegedly as a result of taking birth control pills started suing —and winning. As woman after woman was awarded staggering settlements—a quarter of a million dollars and more —things began to get sticky. Some of the malpractice insurance companies insisted that their M.D. policyholders get a signed agreement from each woman taking the pill agreeing not to hold the doctor responsible for illness or death from the pill. That did absolutely nothing to inspire confidence in the drugs.

As a postscript, most doctors have long ago stopped letting

their wives take birth control pills. Maybe they know something the drug companies don't feature in their ads?

Some defenders of birth control pills continue to insist that taking the pill is safer than pregnancy. Well, so is having the vagina sewn shut—or having the penis cut off. But no one stands in line to have it done. Besides, that sort of logic compares apples and oranges. Pregnancy is a normal physiological experience that is unavoidable if one wants to perpetuate the human race. Birth control pills are only one way —and a relatively dangerous way—of slowing down the reproductive process. For the human race as a whole there are many alternatives to birth control pills—there are no substitutes for pregnancy.

What about the other methods of birth control?

Many of them are effective and no one has ever gotten a blood clot on the brain from using a condom, or gone blind from vaginal foam, or lost a leg from a diaphragm or an IUD. All these methods are, according to pill manufacturers themselves, from 440 to 700 percent safer than birth control pills.

For those who want to compare actual statistics, the safety of the various methods work out something like this: birth control pills—about 99 percent; condoms—about 98 percent; IUD—about 97 percent; foam—about 98 percent; diaphragm—about 97 percent.

But no matter how reassuring these figures may look, they are absolutely unrealistic. The true dependability—over a person's sexual lifetime—is at least 10 percent *less.*

Why does contraception lose so much of its effectiveness?

Because nobody takes precautions *every* time he has sexual

intercourse. From time to time everyone succumbs to the temptation to put aside all the paraphernalia of plastic and rubber and slippery jelly and engage in good old-fashioned free-style frolicking. That may raise havoc with contraception statistics, but it sure is a lot of fun.

Unfortunately, a lot of husbands then have to sweat out the next few weeks until their wives' periods start. However, according to the surgeons of the world, husbands need sweat no more.

How come?

Because there are thousands of masked and gowned surgeons who stand ready—scalpels gleaming—to provide fast, fast, fast relief from the miseries and anxieties of unwanted fatherhood. The package that relief comes wrapped in is called: VASECTOMY. What circumcision did for the penis, vasectomy is supposed to do for the rest of the male reproductive system.

Last year as many as one million American males were reproductively reprocessed, according to the Association for Voluntary Sterilization, which has emerged as sort of a trade association for those who are vasectomized. The operation itself is relatively simple:

The patient lies on his back on the operating table, naked from the waist down. His genitals are covered with a sterile sheet which allows only his testicles to protrude. After injecting a local anesthetic into the skin of the scrotum, the doctor snaps a steel clamp around the vas deferens, that small tube about the diameter of a pencil lead that carries sperm from the testicles to the penis. He then makes his incision, ties off and cuts the tubing, and sews up the wound. After repeating the procedure on the other side, another proud vasectomee is returned to the sexual scene.

Why should men be proud of this operation?

It's hard to say. Although few men brag about gall bladder surgery, and hardly anyone takes pride in having his appendix out, vasectomized fellows tend to be a different breed. Many of them even wear the equivalent of a campaign ribbon —a little gold-plated male symbol with a chunk nipped out of the left lower corner. (To be perfectly accurate, that chunk should be taken out of *both* corners.)

But vasectomy wasn't always that popular. As recently as fifteen years ago the procedure was virtually confined to lunatics in mental hospitals—to prevent them from fathering millions of other little lunatics. A few senior citizens also lost their tiny sperm ducts during surgery for prostate problems. Suddenly the nineteen sixties became the decade of the vasectomy. The *Journal of the American Medical Association* announced that vasectomy ". . . seems to offer the ideal contraceptive for a husband when his family has become as large as he and his wife can afford."

Free or almost free clinics sprouted overnight. Baseball players—who presumably had acquired expertise in medicine somewhere between second and third base—bragged about their own vasectomies and touted them to sports fans throughout the country. Some enterprising gents found that the dollar invested in a vasectomy lapel pin was the ticket of admission to previously unapproachable young ladies. Some of the girls found out later that the surgery had been done to the pin and not necessarily to the gentleman—but the morning-after pill was there when they needed it. Then suddenly the honeymoon was over.

What finished the honeymoon?

The medical profession. They took a closer look at the operation. What they found wasn't exciting. First of all, most of the men who had the operation gave it great reviews—for public consumption. You know, sex was much better and everything like that. But when satisfied users were given intense psychological testing their real feelings came out. In one survey, 40 percent of those who were sterilized showed increased psychological disturbance after the operation and 20 percent finally admitted that they noted a decline in sexual performance.

Second, and more ominous, there were isolated reports of men who developed multiple sclerosis, rheumatoid arthritis, and blood clots a year or so after the operation. Nothing definite, but not an exciting prospect.

Then, the final blow. Men had always been assured that they could have the tiny ducts hooked up again with a fair chance of success if they changed their minds. But there's good news and bad news. About 75 percent of those who undergo the surgery can be plugged in again—that's the good news. But only 25 percent—at the most—will father children again—that's the bad news.

Why do so many "hook-ups" fail?

No one knows for sure, but this is the current theory: After the operation, the testicles are isolated from the rest of the body as far as sperm are concerned. The spermatazoa are still produced but they have nowhere to go. That means they are absorbed by the body and produce antibodies against themselves. In a sense, a man becomes allergic to his own sperm. When he is re-operated and the sperm start flowing again, those antibodies start zapping any live sperm that come through. (Some people think that's the same reason, among others, that prostitutes don't get pregnant all the time—sensitization to sperm.) As if that isn't bad enough, the ace-in-the-hole seems to be falling through.

What's the ace-in-the-hole?

The frozen-sperm bank. Fresh from the science-fiction films, it originally seemed like a good idea. All a man had to do was send off a generous supply of sperm to be permanently frozen in a sperm bank before he had his ducts cut—and that was that. If he and his wife changed their minds later on—or if he changed wives—all he had to do was get a doctor to defrost some sperm and artificially inseminate his partner. Veterinarians had been doing it for years with prize cows and prize bulls.

There was only one little flaw: men are not bulls, women are not cows, and babies are not calves. After a year or two in the freezer, human sperm has sentimental value and not much else. Within five years, it becomes the world's most expensive douche—and easily the world's coldest.

Four years after endorsing vasectomy, the AMA announced in their *Journal* that they weren't quite so sure. The editorial was entitled: "Vasectomy—A Note of Concern." It said, in part: "No surgical operation which results in severe impairment or loss of a major body function should be undertaken casually." And further on: "The medical profession should not condone vasectomy 'on demand' any more than it would tolerate any other biological mutilation 'on demand.' The procedure is not innocuous. The most optimistic surveys indicate a potential 3 percent psychosexual casualty rate, and others report a much higher incidence of psychological complications." The editorial then proposes a number of guidelines for physicians and patients, including the following: "In view of the probable irrevocability of the surgery and the potential of serious postoperative psychosexual problems, vasectomy should never be considered casually by either the patient or the physician."

But isn't it possible that the men who had sexual problems before vasectomy are the only ones who have trouble afterward?

That's what some people say:

"As a wife I can find no evidence that vasectomy is risky for a man. Men who have problems after vasectomy had them before the surgery, and there is no scientific evidence that vasectomy caused it."

And, of course, there is no scientific evidence that vasectomy didn't cause it:

"My husband told me that he would have a vasectomy and he did. Now he is impotent and we are both quite concerned —to put it mildly. How do we handle this? Believe me, this is the kind of trouble neither of us needs."

And:

"I used to have trouble reaching an orgasm but my husband worked hard on me and I usually climaxed finally. But then I talked him into having a vasectomy and now he has as much control as the Easter Bunny. I wish the doctor could put him back the way he was before."

And:

"Doctor, while I'm on the subject, one of my husband's friends is afraid that after having that bit of surgery done, nothing will spurt out of his Glorious Penis—something like the dry heaves, I guess. I'd like to tell him the real story, but no one can tell him anything."

What's the "real story"?

Simply this: Vasectomy only does away with about 5 percent of the fluid ejaculated. The other 95 percent comes from the prostate and other associated structures. So there's no problem with the penile equivalent of the "dry heaves." That still leaves a big cloud over the whole procedure of vasectomy.

74

Does that mean vasectomy is no good?

Not necessarily. But it does mean that quite a few questions have to be cleared up before it can be recommended without reservation. Reversibility is one nagging problem. The Japanese, however, are hard at work on a tiny faucet that can be inserted in the sperm duct. Then when a man wants to have children, he just has the valve turned. Then it boils down to: "Where do you get a plumber in the middle of the night?"

Another current hazard is that even after a vasectomy, there are still millions and millions of sperm backed up in that maze of tubing between the testicles and the penis. By estimate it takes at least fifteen ejaculations to flush out all those tiny wigglers. Some men who are in a hurry try to clear the passageway all in one night. It's much better to let nature take its course and use contraceptives the first *sixteen* times. By contrast the equivalent of a vasectomy for women has many fewer difficulties.

Which operation is that?

The old standby—tubal ligation. Instead of keeping the sperm from getting out of the testicles, the goal of tubal ligation is to keep the egg from getting out of the ovary. If the fallopian tubes are tied off and cut, hopefully the tiny egg will never keep its appointment with all those eager little sperm. But until recently, tying off the fallopian tubes was an expensive and reasonably hazardous procedure. It cost up to $500 and required five days in the hospital. For most women it was a procedure of desperation after the fourth or fifth child. But the magic of glass fibers has changed all that.

Glass fibers?

Right. When thin strands of glass are placed alongside each other, they transmit light like crazy. That allows doctors to use a flexible length of tubing with a bulb inside, called a "fiberoptics scope," to look right inside the body. So using a tiny electrode on a long handle plus a fiberoptics scope a surgeon can now cut the fallopian tubes without significantly cutting open the patient. The procedure takes about fifteen minutes, costs about $125 and lets the patient go home the same day.

How does fiberoptics sterilization work?

Like a charm. Under anesthesia the doctor makes two tiny incisions—one at the lower rim of the belly button, the other just below the pubic hair line. He puts the scope in one opening and the electrode in the other. He cooks and seals the tubes electrically and after a few moments takes out the instruments. The incisions are so small and inconspicuous that the operation has become famous as "band-aid sterilization"—two band-aids could almost cover the incisions. By now there are many variations, including crushing the tubes, tying them off with tiny instruments, and even snapping them shut with plastic clips in the hope of restoring fertility by slipping the clips off at some future date. But the attack on the fallopian tubes has just begun.

What else is happening in space age sterilization?

One of the greatest contradictions in all of modern medicine is happening. For years physicians struggled to save women from the ravages of gonorrhea—specifically from the complication that causes permanent sterility. As the infection progresses, it often seals off the fallopian tubes with scar tissue and makes pregnancy impossible—once and for all. (That's why the old-time prostitutes used to call gonorrhea "Cupid's Catarrh"—it solved a lot of problems for them.) Nowadays, on the same morning a doctor may desperately try to keep one woman's fallopian tubes open while he tries with equal determination to seal another woman's tubes shut without surgery—because she *doesn't* want to become pregnant.

How can a woman's tubes be sealed without surgery?

In a way that will startle and amaze millions of ex-GIs who remember that daily atabrine tablet they were forced to swallow to protect them against malaria. Reluctant soldiers offered many suggestions about alternate ways of disposing of these bitter little pills, but none of them imagined that the drug would one day be pumped into the vagina, through the cervix, past the uterus, and into the fallopian tubes. Ironically, it seals off the tubes as effectively as a galloping case of gonorrhea. Currently it is an exotic technique, still in the experimental stage. It shares, unfortunately, the same problems as most of the current "new" methods of contraception.

What problems are those?

It's a last-ditch attempt to prevent pregnancy. Instead of fending off the enemy—sperm—at the outer walls of the castle—before they are launched by the millions into the vagina, modern contraception welcomes them right into the Queen's Private Chambers—even as far as the uterus—and then tries to sneak up behind and zonk them when they aren't looking. It would be so much easier to simply stop them before they get started.

How do you stop sperm before they get started?

Some people think a male contraceptive pill is the answer. Killing or maiming the sperm before they go forth into action would prevent conception. That's easy enough to do—there are a dozen chemicals that accomplish the goal. But if a man wants to have children again, he has to make his sperm strong and vigorous—and nobody has come up with a dependable way to reverse the effects of male contraceptives. Besides, the same drug that poisons the sperm has a tendency to poison the gentleman who makes the sperm—and that's not exactly the idea. There's another big reason that scientific research into male contraceptives has lagged far behind female birth control methods.

What's that big reason?

Men don't get pregnant. If only one man were to come home from a business trip with the same problems that a seventeen-year-old unmarried girl faces after she's missed her second period, research into male contraceptive would take a great leap forward.

As it is, many experts think that the whole thrust of research into human contraception has gone in the wrong direction.

Why is contraceptive research going in the wrong direction?

Ever since the development of the "pill" the emphasis has been on exotic "Buck Rogers" techniques that seriously intrude on the delicate and poorly understood mechanisms of

78

the human body. Popping pills that distort the workings of every cell of the body, poking plastic pinwheels deep inside the uterus, tying off vital pipelines indiscriminately, all have the faint aroma of a gorilla playing the violin. Human sexuality is so subtle, so complex, and so incompletely understood that massive tinkering can only produce unpleasant surprises —sometimes twenty years later. Separating copulation from conception is the basic idea—maybe it requires basic solutions. For example, the condom has not really been improved since its invention in 1400. How about a spray-on-peel-off silicone plastic version that is unbreakable and provides excellent sensation? (As a built-in bonus, it would also protect against VD at the same time.) How about using the same substance to seal off the cervix before intercourse? How about a dozen other simple, cheap, safe concepts? How about taking the same type of genius that put our team on the moon to a far more important project? After all, if he's lucky, a man only visits the moon once in a lifetime. On the other hand, if he's really lucky, he copulates every night. It's worth thinking about.

5

ORAL SEX

Is oral sex normal?

That's really part of a larger question: "Is *sex* normal?" Once human beings accept the idea that the enthusiastic, spontaneous use of their sexual endowments is normal, natural, and desirable, life will become easier and more fulfilling for everyone. A great part of the anxiety over oral sex springs from failure to recognize that the human mouth is an important sexual organ.

Is the mouth really a sexual organ?

Yes, it is. That's one of the reasons most women paint their mouths with that red dye called "lipstick"—so no one will ever forget what it's there for. But not only is the mouth a sexual organ, it's probably one of the busiest sexual organs of them all. Every aspect of human sexuality, from the first tentative "hello" to the last passionate "good-night" begins and ends with the mouth. By contrast, the genitals themselves are bit-players who only get onstage for the final scene of the last act. It all starts with an innocent kiss:

"I'm fourteen and just starting to date so this question may sound dumb. Why is it when a boy kisses me I get sort of excited all over? I mean, he's not touching me anywhere else —I don't let him do that until later. But just feeling his lips against my lips makes me feel all sexy—is that okay?"

Congratulations on your curiosity. Most fourteen-year-olds are too busy enjoying the new physical sensations they are feeling to take the time to understand them. But it's worth the effort to try. The lip-to-lip kiss, probably the most socially acceptable intimate gesture in our society (next to the handshake), is actually a sexual time bomb. Under the right circumstances it causes instant erection of the penis, prompt response from the clitoris and vagina, and sets all the circuits buzzing in anticipation of sexual intercourse. Most of the aphrodisiac effect of the lip kiss springs from an accident of anatomy called the "muco-cutaneous junction." Stated simply, most parts of the body where the skin meets a mucous membrane are susceptible to intense sexual stimulation. That includes the entrance to the vagina, the tiny opening at the tip of the penis, and certainly the mouth. (There are also a few other specially designed areas of the body with hot lines to the sexual centers of the brain—they include the nipples, the clitoris, the labia minora, and most of the surface of the penis.) Muco-cutaneous junctions are greedy and they never seem to be satisfied. The more stimulation they get, the more they want—as a result the French get credit for something they never invented.

What didn't the French invent?

The "French" kiss. As the sexual excitement from kissing spreads beyond the lips to the tongue and inner surfaces of the mouth, a miniature version of sexual intercourse takes place. The tongue becomes compressed into a cylinder much like the penis, and the mouth of the recipient closes around it like the vagina. The combination of heat, well-lubricated friction, and ever-spreading stimulation often leads to the next stage of oral sex—and a more controversial one.

Why controversial?

Because of the social disapproval of "the kiss that slips below the lips." If the sexual reflexes are working normally, the inevitable happens:

"I've only been married about six months and something strange goes on before my husband has sex with me. He likes to kiss my breasts, lick my nipples, and then suck on them. I admit it feels good, especially after a while when my nipples get hard and stick out, but do all men do this?"

Only about 98 percent of them. The overwhelming attraction of mouth-breast sex is one of the great riddles of human sexuality. Why contact between the male mouth and the female breast should bring on such intense sexual stimulation has baffled generations of researchers. Even the meager scientific evidence available is more frustrating than revealing:

1. Mouth and breast are both dual-purpose structures; they provide sexual stimulation *and* nutrition.
2. Both breast and penis—as well as clitoris—have erectile tissue.
3. There is a direct nervous and hormone (neurohormonal) connection between the female breast and the uterus. For example, the sucking action of a nursing

82

infant triggers immediate responses in the mother's uterus. Nursing mothers often experience the same feeling of satisfaction that comes from sexual intercourse.

4. Orgasm in the female is almost invariably linked to involuntary erection of the nipples.

There is even some convincing nonscientific evidence of the mouth-breast link. During the past few years breast feeding and sex have met over the lunch table. All over the country, in topless restaurants, bare-breasted waitresses serve well-developed mammary glands with the blue-plate special. (Careless girls sometimes serve their charms *in* the blue-plate special.)

While solving the riddle of the breast's role in sex may not exactly earn some eager researcher the Nobel prize, it will clear up one of the more obscure areas of human sexuality. But that's an easy job compared to the next one.

Why is the next one so hard?

Because it means explaining the tremendous attraction—and occasional repulsion—of mouth-vagina and mouth-penis sex. When a man's tongue and lips begin to compete with his penis for the attention of the vagina and when a woman's mouth takes over the penis, the participants start feeling good and bad at the same time. In accordance with Aunt Nellie's Law of Sex, "It's all right to do anything as long as you don't enjoy it," mouth-vagina and mouth-penis sex bring on all kinds of anxieties, as these queries demonstrate:

"I would like to have your opinion about oral sex. Is it practiced in the U.S. or mostly in foreign countries?"

And

"After practicing such things as fellatio and cunnilingus could one ever enjoy normal sex again?"

And

83 ORAL SEX

"I don't know if all girls have this problem or just me. But like I really love to have my boy friend put his mouth to my vagina while I love his penis. The only trouble is I feel guilty afterward and I kind of think he does too. What's the answer?"

The answer is to understand what brings on the guilt about oral sex. Part of it starts in the nursery where Mother, with good intentions and bad information, gets the message to Baby that the sexual organs are "dirty." Well, no one wants to put something dirty in his mouth, does he? The follow-up comes later on when teacher and nearly everyone gets into the act. The human mouth is represented as the unsullied last outpost of clean living, to be protected at all costs from the forces of dirt that threaten it. That's one of the big reasons for compulsively brushing your teeth, rinsing your mouth with funny-tasting chemicals, spraying your palate with cloying aerosols, and constantly sucking on phenol-flavored candy. Imagine bringing that gleaming mouth in contact with someone else's sexual organs!

But reality doesn't necessarily correspond to the mouthwash commercials. The truth is that nearly every form of virulent bacteria thrives in the oral cavity of a normal individual. The intruders range from the germs that cause pneumonia and diphtheria to those that transmit gonorrhea—and worse.

By contrast, the worst germs found in a healthy vagina are the meek *Lactobacillus acidophilus*—found in every pint of health-giving yogurt. In effect, there is far more danger involved in a casual peck on the lips than in either fellatio or cunnilingus. But that never stopped anyone from snatching a kiss.

What is fellatio?

Fellatio is a sexual technique in which a woman uses her mouth, tongue, lips, and (very, very gently) her teeth to stimulate her partner's penis. The word *fellatio* comes from the Latin word *fellare,* which means "to suck," but as any man will verify, sucking is *not* the idea. The principle of fellatio is to apply to the penis the same kind of heat, pressure, lubrication, and friction provided by the vagina. A woman who is dedicated and skillful can make fellatio a truly exhilarating experience.

How does she make fellatio exhilarating?

Like this:

"As a woman, I think it's about time someone spoke up in defense of fellatio. I have done it for dozens of men over the past twenty years and all of them have been extravagant in their praise. I think sex the regular way is better but still, the mouth is the only part of a woman that has a tongue.

"I think every wife should know about the three most sensitive parts of a man's penis. They are the rim that runs around the head, the tiny opening right at the end, and that little flat spot just under the head of the penis. If they will concentrate most of their attention at those three areas, they will be amazed at the compliments they will get. Too many wives look down on oral sex—as if it were beneath them. Please remind them that men will do almost anything to have this kind of satisfaction, and if the wife won't do it, take it from me, there is always somebody else who will."

Is that true?

It seems to be. The following letter is typical:

"After thirty years of marriage I found that my husband

was occasionally seeing another woman who lived on our street. He admitted that it was just because she would suck on his penis whenever he asked her. I had always considered this act to be degrading and had refused to participate in it. However, since my marriage was in danger, I have tried to comply and now I find I actually enjoy it." The point is not necessarily that the wife denied herself the pleasures of fellatio for thirty years but that her husband was so eager for it that he was willing to endanger their marriage.

Does fellatio mean that much to men?

According to their wives and girl friends, it seems to be one of the biggest things on their minds:

"My husband is always trying to get me to take his penis into my mouth. He tells me it is normal and almost everyone does it. To prove his point, he even took me to see a movie where a woman did it to a man's penis right on the screen. Both of them seemed to enjoy it, and to tell the truth just watching it made me a little excited sexually. I think I might like it, but do you think it is all right for us to do it regularly?"

Is fellatio really a pleasure for a woman?

Many women say it is. Some of them hold back at first because of misconceptions about fellatio. They may worry about "choking" on the penis or fear that there is something "perverted" about orality. However, after one or two experiences with an understanding and appreciative partner, they usually become ardent advocates of this form of oral sex. And they make an interesting discovery in the process.

What do they discover?

That the partner who takes the initiative in fellatio (or cunnilingus, for that matter) gets as much gratification—or more—as the one whose genitals are being stimulated by the mouth. There is something about feeling the erect, throbbing penis pulsating against the lips that can be exquisitely exciting to a woman. And in the same way, most men are driven to the limits of delight by the sensation of the clitoris straining eagerly to meet their tongues. That is part of the reason why the one who performs oral sex often reaches near-orgasm without any other sexual stimulation whatsoever. Another confirmation of the pleasure that oral sex brings the practitioner is that it is the "doer" rather than the "done-to" who usually brings up the idea of oral sex in the first place.

Do men really like fellatio so much?

Apparently they do.

In fact, the male desire for oral gratification has supported two major industries in the United States.

Which industries are those?

The massage parlor is one. The "personal" column of most major papers carries ads like these:

EXCITING HOT FOAM TREATMENTS—LEONA'S MAGIC MASSAGE TAKES ALL THE DISCOMFORT OUT OF STIFF MUSCLES. FEELING UP-TIGHT? LET LEONA HELP DISCHARGE YOUR TENSIONS. 24 HOURS. HOUSE CALLS TOO. 459–1212.

The "magic massage" usually emanates from the lips of Leona—dressed in a micro-miniskirt and a see-through blouse. The "discomfort" that she "takes-out" probably comes from all that blood building up in the penis. And it's a safe bet that the "stiff muscles" are mainly concentrated in the pubic area. During the ten-minute session (costing fifteen dollars) more sperm than "tensions" are discharged.

Why don't the police do something about places like that?

They try, but it isn't easy. They are dealing with clever criminals and the job requires dedicated men. One police report reads:

"I entered the suspect premises and was directed to a small room. The subject was a female about twenty-two years old clad only in bikini panties. She directed me to remove my clothing and assume a supine position on the small padded table in the center of the room. I paid her fifteen dollars in marked bills, in advance, and lay down on the said table. She proceeded to rub warm perfumed oil (a sample has been sent to the crime lab) onto my private parts producing an immediate erection. She then applied her mouth to my erection and orally copulated me until the act was concluded. While she was wiping her mouth, I quickly arose, secured my badge from my trouser pocket, identified myself, and placed her under arrest, charging her with 21:49, lewd and lascivious conduct. As I was reading the suspect her rights, she spat the contents of her mouth all over my shirt. She was further charged with 21:19, assaulting an officer."

As a result of this dramatic encounter, an all male jury acquitted the accused. A policeman's lot is not an easy one.

What's the second industry?

The reluctance of some wives to perform fellatio provides most prostitutes with a profitable sub-specialty. Betty, who has had a lot of experience in that line, tells about it:

"Well, Doctor, thanks to all those goody-goody wives, I've spent the last two years living from hand-to-mouth, if you know what I mean. And it's been a good living. I can 'trick' four johns in the time I used to waste on one, I don't have to take my panties off, and I can work thirty days a month instead of the usual twenty-five. Besides, I'm getting a reputation as a specialist and I'm building up a referral business. Some nights I even got a waiting list. Like tonight, I got two guys on 'standby.' All I can say to all those wonderful ladies out there is, 'Keep those lips together, honey. You're making a better life for one little girl!' "

But isn't fellatio against the law?

In most states the moment the penis crosses the lower lip, man and woman become desperados, often liable for twenty years in the penitentiary if apprehended. (By comparison, manslaughter usually brings one-to-fourteen.) Fortunately, laws against oral sex are fairly difficult to enforce in the privacy of one's bedroom and convictions are very, very rare.

Why do men like fellatio?

For several reasons. First of all, it feels so good. Most fellatrices (female practitioners of the art) take pride in their work. They can judge the man's reactions, both from the expression on his face and the more automatic responses of the penis itself. They quickly map out the most sensitive areas of their partner's anatomy and concentrate on them. In the situations where fellatio proceeds to orgasm some women even claim to anticipate the moment of ejaculation by detecting a short puff of air a moment or two before.

The second reason is more profound. Between two people in love, fellatio is one of the most intimate and expressive forms of sexuality that exists. It brings the conscious and civilized part of a woman's being—her lips and mouth—into direct and passionate contact with the primitive fountain-head of male sexuality, the penis. The intimate kiss between the lips that say the love words and the organ that actually performs the act of love can be one of the deepest expressions of affection between man and woman.

Why do women enjoy fellatio?

For many similar reasons. Every woman wants to bring the man she loves the ultimate in happiness. By fellatio she is dramatically demonstrating her love and acceptance of the most masculine part of his physical being. As she takes his penis into her mouth she bestows on him the ultimate kiss at the same time she is making the most exciting part of his body part of her own body.

But there are some other uses of fellatio too, including sexual self-defense:

"In your book you mentioned oral sex and I thought you might be interested in my own experiences. I went to a small college in the South and it was an impossible situation for a girl to be in. On one hand, you were supposed to be a virgin until the stroke of midnight on your honeymoon. On the other hand, if you wanted to have any kind of social life you had to participate in some kind of sex. Here is the solution I worked out and I know a lot of other girls who did the same thing.

"I managed to be very popular—I was the homecoming queen as well as the senior class president—and for what it was worth I managed to keep everything I was born with until my wedding night. That was almost six years ago, and I don't know if girls worry about things like that anymore, but when I got married I wanted to be a virgin—at least from the neck down.

"The way I did it was simple. I never refused sex to any of my dates—after I got to know them, of course. But I always insisted on oral sex. I never had any complaints, and the fascinating thing about it was that all those boys would rather go out with me than the girls who gave it to them the regular way. Aren't men funny?"

Yes, men are funny. But then so are women. Like when it comes to birth control:

"I think I found a way to keep from getting pregnant that even beats the birth control pills. When I first got married, I used the diaphragm. A year later we had little Karen. Then I switched to the 'pill' and I guess I must have skipped it a couple of times because then we had little Jimmie. Now I'm back to the diaphragm—except around the time of ovulation. Then instead of regular sex my husband and I have sex the oral way. So far it's worked fine and since I'm the one that has the babies, I take it seriously. My husband likes to make jokes about it. He says, "The stork brings the babies and the swallows keep them away." I tell him he's vulgar but he just laughs."

Is it all right for a woman to swallow semen?

A lot of them seem to worry about it:

"In performing fellatio, what's a woman to do with the semen if the man reaches an orgasm? To put it bluntly, does she swallow or spit?"

It's up to her. Semen is not a mystical, magical potion that corrodes the insides of every woman that comes in contact with it. As a matter of fact, it is just another body fluid derived from the same basic source as saliva, sweat, and tears. Swallowing it or spitting it out are just about the same —with two exceptions.

What are those?

The first is a matter of etiquette. If a young lady concludes what might otherwise be a stellar performance by staggering to the bathroom with bulging cheeks, hawking and gagging, she probably isn't cut out for that sort of thing anyway.

The other exception has deeper implications. Although it is high in protein and relatively low in carbohydrates, a man's ejaculate may add as much as one hundred calories to a woman's daily diet. Maybe that provides a way out for the more reluctant fellatrices:

"It isn't that I don't love you, Harry, but you really wouldn't want me to get fat, would you?"

According to women who know, the taste of human semen varies from man to man. Because of their diet, the semen of Greeks and Italians has a garlicky flavor, that of vegetarians has a bland taste, and Latin lovers tend toward the spicy side. So far the mouthwash people have not come up with a semen-flavorer but it is probably only a matter of time. "For the man who doesn't want to offend . . ."

But isn't fellatio a homosexual sort of thing?

Yes, when done by one man to another. When a woman does it to a man, by definition, it's heterosexual. And so is kissing on the mouth and holding hands. Just because homosexuals do these things too doesn't mean that heterosexuals have to give them up. Fellatio between men and women is usually the preliminary to penis-vagina sex—and so far no one has been able to tag *that* as homosexual.

Aren't most religions against oral sex?

Yes—if it is used as a substitute for copulation. Understandably if members of any group substituted oral sex for the regular kind, membership (and church attendance) would soon shrink to zero. Even official Catholic marriage manuals approve of mouth-penis and mouth-vagina activities provided they do not result in ejaculation. And that goes for cunnilingus too.

What is cunnilingus?

Cunnilingus is one of the most fascinating sexual experiences available to human beings. The term, as usual, comes from Latin. "Cunnus" means *the female genitals* and "lingus" means *tongue*. Put them together and the result is cunnilingus, which is the whole idea in the first place. Most women enjoy this form of oral sex almost as much as regular intercourse. As far as men are concerned, usually their desire to be fellated is exceeded only by their wish to cunni-ling.

What makes cunnilingus so special?

First of all, it brings the two most sensitive and sensual structures of the human body into tantalizing contact with each other. No other organs even approach the millions upon millions of tiny nerve endings packed into every inch of the tongue and clitoris. These two organs are alike in many ways. They are both exquisitely sensitive to pressure, touch, heat, and motion. Both have a massive blood supply. And both are directly connected to the sexual areas of the brain. When they are brought together under ideal conditions of warmth, moisture, and supercharged sexual excitement, the results can be almost unbearably delightful. And they usually are. Cunnilingus provides a man with by far the most effective means available for bringing a woman to orgasm—and that can be important to both of them.

Why can cunnilingus be important to both of them?

Take this woman's experience, for example. Her letter comes on crisply engraved pale blue stationery; the envelope is postmarked "Boston."

"I've never written to anyone like this before, but after reading what you have written about cunnilingus I thought it might be appropriate to share my feelings with other women and perhaps their husbands as well. My ancestors came over on the *Mayflower*—that's where I got my name. But for all I can tell, they must have left their sexual inclinations back in England. As far as I can determine, no one on either side of the family has had an orgasm since 1620—or slightly before. And I was no exception. After seven years of marriage I was getting desperate—so desperate that I finally let my husband try oral sex on me. I must have been out of my mind at the time because I had always considered it perverted—at least that's the way my mother always referred to it whenever any reference to it came up.

"This may sound overdramatic but it was the turning point of my married life. I had my first three orgasms ever that night and neither of us got to sleep until almost four o'clock in the morning. What a difference it has made in our lives! I hope other women can find the same satisfaction I did."

For the 50 percent of women who suffer from some degree of orgasmic impairment, cunnilingus can make the difference between happiness and disappointment. Even more vital, for many it can be the emotional bridge that leads them to eventual penis-vagina orgasms. Cunnilingus, properly performed, can transform a woman's sexual experiences from a

94

sedate ritual after the late news into a series of nightly orgasms so exhilarating that each morning she looks back fondly on yesterday's and eagerly forward to tonight's.

What is the "proper" way to perform cunnilingus?

Tenderly. Although the clitoris and labia are unbelievably sensitive, they are also extremely delicate. Gentleness and restraint can make all the difference. A gentle nudge with the lips against the clitoris will usually be rewarded by a gentle nudge in return. Clitoral erection is so prompt and dependable that any penis would be jealous. Almost simultaneously the labia become engorged and pout invitingly forward.

Then, gentle exploration with the tongue will quickly reveal the most responsive areas. The shaft of the erect clitoris, the tiny dimple under its head, the inner surface of the erect labia minora, all respond to the probing tongue. Vibration, slow caressing, *gentle* suction, and anything else that seems appropriate will propel the proceedings toward the ultimate goal. Most girls will eagerly do their part by maneuvering their pelvises into just the right position as things move along. Of course, that isn't enough for some men. They pride themselves on their "technique."

What's special about their cunnilingus "technique"?

Well, they apply the basic principles of competition bowling or championship golf to the far more abstract art of making love. They see cunnilingus as a challenging athletic event rather than a particularly expressive form of making love.

Some men who think this way may roll the clitoris between their lips while sliding an index finger in and out of the vagina and caressing their partner's breasts with the other hand. Others track the tongue around the vagina while caressing the clitoris with one hand and the inner thighs with the other. More often than not this frantic sort of activity is aimed at turning on a prostitute—most of whom are not turn-on-able. In fact, the girls have a good-natured nickname for customers like this. They call them "one-man bands."

Aren't there some special techniques a woman can use to make cunnilingus more effective?

There are dozens of techniques she can use—but it is doubtful that any of them make cunnilingus more effective. Once the two sexual organs—mouth and vagina—are in contact, things pretty much take care of themselves. Actually there is no position, however contorted, that can improve on that relationship.

For those who welcome a challenge, however, there are always grimy little books that give detailed instructions. For example, there is a position where the woman stands on her head while the man seats himself in a chair. Aside from giving the lady a migraine headache and making the gentleman more round-shouldered than he is already, there seems to be no advantage to undertaking this feat of skill. And the same is true for most of the other elaborate positions of oral sex.

In a real sense, the most effective thing a woman can do to increase her partner's pleasure as well as her own during cunnilingus is to provide him with ample words of affection and encouragement.

But doesn't cunnilingus tend to take the place of regular intercourse?

Not for most people. Mouth-clitoris stimulation usually brings on such an overwhelming urge in a woman for penis penetration that she literally drags her partner onto and into her as she hurtles toward her final orgasm. The man can help by using his tongue as an orgasm-detector. Slow pulsations of the turgid clitoris usually mean a powerful climax is moments away. Once a rhythmic throbbing takes over, the man might as well forge ahead because there is no time to turn back.

Like any other profoundly satisfying sexual experience cunnilingus often arouses deep emotional and affectionate reactions in women:

"I have always had a keen curiosity about the workings of the human mind. Over the past twenty years, as a professor of psychology, I have had ample opportunity to observe and record human behavior. I think you might be interested in some observations I have made on one effect oral sex has on my wife and myself.

"About two years after our marriage I made the following discovery. One evening, just before bedtime, we had a rather heated argument. Both of us were angry and we went to bed furious at one another. Neither of us could sleep, and about ten minutes later I was overwhelmed with the desire to perform cunnilingus on my wife. I made the appropriate advances and I was amazed to see that she was more passionate than I. Within three or four minutes I brought her to orgasm and both of our tensions were swept away in her climax. On more than a hundred occasions since then I have used this method of erasing those feelings of mutual antagonism that inevitably crop up between husband and wife. I hope these observations are useful in some way to your patients."

Besides the sexual gratifications there also may be physical rewards to mouth-vagina sex.

What are those?

Hazel tells about it. She is forty-one, looks thirty-five, and has a busy career as a fashion designer for a small clothing manufacturer:

"It's not as if I take inventory down there every morning, Doctor, but with these vaginal foam contraceptives you tend to pay more attention, if you know what I mean. Well! About three months ago I found out I was getting smaller! I mean, my clitoris seemed to be shrinking, those little lips were getting all wrinkled, and even the entrance to the vagina seemed smaller. I mean, as we girls say, 'tight is all right'—but not *too* tight. Then I started going with a new man who liked oral sex—I mean, he liked to do it to me. Anyway it seems that everything is getting better—like I'm getting younger—all over. Do you think what we're doing might have something to do with it?"

There is no doubt that the vigorous massaging action of cunnilingus improves the blood flow to the clitoris, labia, and surrounding tissues. It also tones up the genital skin and prevents the atrophy of disuse. There is the added bonus of maintaining a high level of sexual performance by constantly reinforcing the basic sexual reflexes. In short, it is the ideal form of self-improvement—no dieting, no expensive equipment to buy, no classes to attend, and a very low percentage of dropouts. To those who pursue it too vigorously there may be one minor drawback.

What's the drawback to cunnilingus?

The vulvar equivalent of dishpan hands. On the other hand, a bit of baby oil after each session of calisthenics usually solves the problem. There is also a chance that cunnilingus can be therapeutic for men.

Cunnilingus can be therapeutic for men?

It all started with mice. Male mice have an aphrodisiac substance in their urine which excites a female mousling to the peaks of passion if she passes a place where Mr. Mouse has urinated. As if that weren't enough, the average mouse Casanova exhales this same chemical in every breath. As a result, there is no doubt that if he kisses her once, he won't have to kiss her again. These powerful sexual chemicals are called *pheromones*—substances that both males and females can inhale without knowing it and which irresistibly influence their sexual feelings.

Things really got interesting when the researchers worked their way up to monkeys. When male monkeys catch a whiff of the vaginal secretion of the female they go wild. Instant erection, furious masturbation, and frenzied attempts at intercourse occur immediately. To prove that this type of pheromone acts through the nasal passages, the researchers plugged certain males' nostrils with cotton. These males turned off completely.

And pheromones mean business. The four male monkeys featured in the experiment made a few half-hearted attempts at intercourse *before* being exposed to the vaginal scent. Right after the first sniff, they plunged into a simian orgy of *over two hundred attempts* at copulation.

Do human females secrete the same substance?

They might. For one thing, they have all the necessary equipment. There are small glands in the labia which can produce pheromones. There are also special tufts of hair designed to waft the aroma into the night air. Even the clitoris and its foreskin constantly produce a substance that may have a powerful aphrodisiac effects on any male that is exposed to them.

But that's just a theory, isn't it?

Not quite. There are examples of male sexual behavior that indicate cunnilingus may in fact have aphrodisiac qualities. Almost every man who has the opportunity finds cunnilingus tremendously exciting—over and over again. Many cunnilinctors have spontaneous erections and even ejaculations *without any other sexual stimulation other than mouth-vagina /clitoris.* Some men are so excited by cunnilingus—or the pheromones that it exposes them to—that they are willing to pay for the privilege of cunnilinging prostitutes. (Ironically, this is one of the few situations where the girls get the money and occasionally the orgasm too.)

Aren't there some men who don't like cunnilingus?

Certainly. But probably they consist mainly of those who haven't gotten around to trying it. They—and the women who are turned against it—are victims of a relentless crusade in the name of "feminine hygiene." It all started back in the days when menstruation was considered "unclean"—it isn't —and women, by extension, were considered "dirty"—they aren't. It wasn't long before moral experts were complaining that "mankind is brought into the world between urine and excrement." (How did they do *their* research?) Aside from the fact that urination, defecation, and reproduction are basic indispensable bodily functions, the vagina is the only orifice designed to deliver newborns. (The nostrils, for example, are totally unsuitable.)

The fact is that the female sexual organs smell better than "gourmet" cheese, are cleaner than the mouth that is applied to them, and fifty years of cunnilingus is more healthful than five minutes of cigarette smoking—as well as infinitely more enjoyable. (Also cheaper, more acceptable to others in the room, and doesn't mar furniture or burn holes in clothing.) But the final obstacle to the popular enjoyment of cunnilingus is the notion that the human vagina and accessories must be douched with antiseptic, flooded with perfume, doused with dusting powder, and finally blasted with vaginal spray deodorant from a little aerosol can before it is "socially (sexually) acceptable." Realistically, being served up like an embalmer's masterpiece does little to enhance the loveliest and most alluring part of the female body. And any and all aphrodisiac pheromones are swept away in the process of fumigation.

But aren't perfumes sexually stimulating?

To whom? The active ingredient of most expensive perfumes is a substance that causes prompt erection and insertion by male wildcats, deer, muskrats, and other four-footed friends. Musk, the basis for "tropical-type" perfumes, comes from a gland at the end of a deer's penis. It is an effective pheromone aphrodisiac for Bambi. Civet, another perfume base, will precipitate rape by the hyena-like animal from whose genital glands it is derived. The woman who wants to attract male muskrats does well to anoint her pubis with thirty-dollar-an-ounce perfume. The one who seeks sexual happiness with men might want to do it another way.

How should she do it?

One way is by being natural. To be *really* clean, all her genitals need is a little soap and water. Even the menstrual fluid itself is *odorless.* (Any odor that arises comes later on as the fluid seeps through the napkin, decomposes, and comes in contact with the outside air. Using a tampon instead, along with soap and water as indicated, will help solve that problem.) Being "natural" about themselves has a lot to offer women. It makes their lives easier, saves them hundreds of dollars and hundreds of hours in a year, and has the bonus of making them—in the long run—more sexually attractive to men. Those tragic little melodramas on television that show a man fleeing the embrace of a sexy chick because she doesn't use somebody's sanitizing spray just don't ring true. To a real man, a woman who smells like a woman is a thousand times more attractive than one who smells like an explosion at the dime-store perfume counter.

Doesn't the same thing apply to men?

It sure does. Men are also equipped with all the devices to produce their own aphrodisiac-type pheromones. It may well be that the man who performs cunnilingus on a woman simultaneously releases his own pheromones to excite the female. Thus cunnilinctors quickly learn by experience that a woman primed with this invisible aroma is a thousand times more exciting when it's *her* turn to work on him. Fortunately there is a way that any man can test this concept.

How can he test the aphrodisiac effect of pheromones?

The first thing in the morning, before taking a shower, he draws a clean cotton handkerchief across the underside of his scrotum. After dressing, he places the pheromone-saturated hanky in the breast pocket of his jacket and sallies forth to meet (or conquer) the world. It is too early in the experiment to tabulate the outcome, but some of the preliminary results are sensational. A few of the pioneers in pheromone therapy have had to shut off the flow—in self-defense.

What about performing cunnilingus and fellatio at the same time?

Cunnilatio does have some advantages. It is a dependable means of birth control, at the beginning it is new and exciting, and it probably releases more pheromones than any other sexual technique known. That makes it a powerfully stimulating prelude to actual intercourse. On the minus side, it requires a lot of room (making it unsuitable for small foreign cars, telephone booths, and similar informal settings), demands some athletic ability from the performers, and tends to be distracting. About 50 percent of ex-cunnilatio addicts complained that they were so involved with what was being done to them that they couldn't concentrate on what they were doing. The other 50 percent complained that they were so absorbed in what they were doing that they couldn't concentrate on what was being done to them. Cunnilatio has its attractions but it has never been as popular as its antecedents, cunnilingus and fellatio. That applies even more emphatically to supermarket sex.

What's supermarket sex?

A collision between the grocery store and the genitals. In those cutesy sex manuals some coy little lady is always simpering about stuffing the vagina with marshmallows or dipping the penis in melted chocolate. A few of the more wild-eyed thrill-seekers anoint their reproductive organs with orange juice, ice cream, champagne, honey, and whipped cream. There are even those who suggest (presumably with straight faces) that a woman suck on peppermint candy before performing fellatio—to add just that hint of mint? Other suggestions for exotic mouth-penis involvement include a pre-fellatio rinse with vodka, rum, or brandy. For the girl who seeks revenge there is always the chance to fill her mouth with ice cubes before the big moment.

In actual practice about all these exciting variations accomplish is an astronomical escalation of the laundry bills.

But what should parents tell their children about oral sex?

The easiest thing—in the long run—is to tell them the truth. This is how one mother did it:

"Last night my daughter Robin was helping me do the dishes. She's seventeen and just about to graduate high school. Suddenly she turned to me and said: 'Mother, if a man and a woman really love each other, do you think it's right for them to have oral sex relations?'

"I'm ashamed to admit I almost died! The picture that went through my mind! My little baby being taken advantage of by some pervert! The fear and disgust were almost too much for me to handle. The best I could do was to bite my lip and say, 'If it's all the same to you, let's wait until your father gets home so we can all sit down together.' Fortunately, that gave me an opportunity to do some of the hardest thinking I ever did in my life. Then I knew what I had to do.

"About an hour later the three of us sat down, and this is what my husband—a very understanding man—told her:

" 'Yes, it is all right for a man and a woman who really love each other to have oral sex.

" 'Oral sex—fellatio and cunnilingus—is a normal part of mature love-making, with the emphasis on *love*.

" 'Sometimes childish people try to cheapen every part of love by giving it nasty names and making us feel guilty about it—that applies especially to oral love.

" 'Because oral sex is so intimate and so personal and so full of the deepest emotional feelings, many people want to reserve it for those who are most important to them.'

104

"It would have been so much easier for us to try to just gloss it over, but during the hour I waited for my husband to come home I kept reminding myself how much easier my life would have been if my mother had just told me those same four sentences twenty-four years ago. I love Robin and I want her to have the same happiness my husband and I have had together. Did I say the right things?"

Yes, you said the right things. You said *exactly* the right things.

6

MASTURBATION, FETISHES, AND PERVERSIONS

Is masturbation harmful?

Some experts used to think so. In *The American Family Physician,* an influential reference work published about the time of the Civil War, it got this kind of review:

"Masturbation is the production of the venereal orgasm by artificial means. It is a vice by no means uncommon among the youth of both sexes and is frequently continued even into the riper years. It usually retards growth, impairs the mental faculties, and brings on debasement of the human soul and a mind filled with obscenities and beastliness. Cowardice is a striking peculiarity—a masturbator cannot look a person full in the face."

Is it really true that masturbators can't look a person in the face?

No, it isn't true.

The truth is that nearly every human being from the African pygmy grandmother to the twenty-year-old blonde movie starlet, from the Japanese teen-ager to the fifty-year-old British businessman, from the professor of mathematics to the bum on Skid Row, masturbates, has masturbated, or is going to masturbate. No matter what anyone says against it—or for it—self-produced orgasms are the missing piece in the sexual jig-saw puzzle. It is the first sexual adventure of adolescence, the better-than-nothing sexual release of the adult years, and the final sexual consolation of old age. Beyond that, "therapeuatic masturbation," or "orgasm-to-order," plays a vital role in overcoming both male impotence and female orgasmic impairment. Like practicing tennis strokes against a backboard, in its ideal form, sexual solitaire is simply playing a one-handed game to learn how to play better with a partner.

Isn't masturbation habit-forming?

It sure is. Like eating, sex, and being alive, masturbation tends to grow on you. Even the somber old *American Family Physician* grudgingly admits: "The more the vice is indulged in, the greater will be the desire to continue it."

With that kind of recommendation, masturbation can't be all bad.

Why do people masturbate?

Well, for one reason, it's handy. In a way, masturbation is the original do-it-yourself project. Anybody can do it, it doesn't require any skill or equipment—and it's free. There is no risk of VD, pregnancy, or jealous husbands. On the debit side, however, there is also no chance of the emotional fulfillment that comes from a warm and loving experience of sexual intercourse. But at certain stages of a person's life, sexual self-sufficiency plays a very important role:

"Doctor, I'm sixteen now and I'm sure most of the other girls in my class would tell you about the same thing if you asked them. For the past two years I've been masturbating at least three times a week—sometimes, if I feel like it, I do it every day. The most satisfying way for me is to gently manipulate my clitoris with the heel of my hand. I usually do it when I take a bath, but on weekends I like to have a couple of orgasms in bed before I get up in the morning. I enjoy it the most when I've been out on a date the night before and I can imagine that it's my boy friend who's playing with me. I've thought a lot about it and I don't feel guilty at all. I look at it this way: When I get married I'll already know what an orgasm is, I'll know exactly what I'm looking for, and I'll know how much I really enjoy it. That's more than a lot of married women can say."

Unfortunately, not every masturbating adolescent is as free of guilt:

"As an eighteen-year-old who used to masturbate each and every day, I would like to know if four years of doing it will affect intercourse with my wife three or four years from now. I have just about completely stopped last month and I don't think I will ever masturbate again. Please tell me what to do since I am just starting college and I am away from my girl friend for the first time. We are very close and I miss her very much."

Most teen-agers will gleefully discard masturbation just as soon as they begin regular intercourse: "Wow! After playing with myself for the last four years—I'm seventeen—I found a girl who loves sex as much as I do! I just threw away all my nudie centerfolds that I used to masturbate over. Compared to intercourse, masturbation was just spinning my wheels!"

But why do adults masturbate?

For a lot of different reasons. At this precise moment there are as many as one hundred-thousand adult Americans in the midst of an act of masturbation. Many of them are women—single, widowed, or divorced—who choose it as the lesser of two evils:

"As a single twenty-six-year-old girl, I cannot accept the state of celibacy that society has forced on my body. I find masturbation necessary at the time of the month just before my period when I get absolutely frantic for sex. However, I am always very careful to do it by putting one finger in my vagina and my thumb gently on my clitoris. I do it that way for two reasons: First, it makes my climax about twice as powerful, and second, I think it is close to what my husband will do to me when I get married. I have thought about getting an artificial penis to make it even closer to actual intercourse but I think I'd rather hold out for the real thing."

Do many women use artificial penises?

Not as many as most men think. Although porno movies feature sensational scenes of frenzied cuties impaling themselves on yard-long pink plastic phalluses while they stare wide-eyed into the camera, the taste of most women is somewhat less flamboyant. Some ladies are even puzzled about where to start:

"How about including a how-to-do-it section on masturbation for females? The taboo against autoerotics is even stronger for women than men, and combined with the obvious where-is-it problems—(How in the dickens do you find that little clitoris?)—it leaves many women unequipped to enjoy the *fruits* of their anatomy. (Sorry about that.)"

The lady has a point. The taboo against a woman touching herself plus the two-layered arrangement of the female genitals (labia majora plus labia minora) make the clitoris as hard to find for some women as a parking space in Times Square. Those women who do masturbate often use this technique:

Lying on their backs and spreading their legs apart, they gently caress the area from the pubis to the vagina with the palm of the hand. This gradually (or sometimes swiftly, depending on the circumstances) leads to partial erection of the clitoris and secretion of lubrication from the vagina. At this moment, they usually begin drawing the index finger upward from the vagina toward the pubic bone to pick up some of the secretion and spread it over the labia minora and clitoris. Then using one or two fingers they slowly stroke upward beside the now-pouting labia minora, along one side of the clitoris, and back down again. (Interestingly, right-handed women usually titillate the right side of the clitoris, while left-handed ladies keep to the left.) Most women keep away from the tip of the clitoris because of its extreme sensitivity. As they begin to gather momentum toward orgasm, some girls—usually those who have already had intercourse—accompany clitoral caresses with a finger that slides in and out of the vagina. Other women will gently pinch and squeeze their nipples, although that occasionally brings on a surprise.

What kind of surprise comes from nipple-pinching?

A surprise like this:

"The strangest thing happened to me last week, Doctor. I—uh—I guess I can tell you. I mean, everybody does it and doctors are used to hearing about it—aren't they? Well, sometimes I play with myself, you know, masturbate. At the same time—you know, I didn't realize it'd be this hard to tell. Anyway while I'm doing it I play with my breasts too. Mostly I squeeze the nipples. It helps me to get excited, and when I finally come, if I pinch the nipples real hard, it feels as if the orgasm is starting right from my toes. Anyhow, my husband has been away most of last month and I've been doing it almost every night, and the day before yesterday I really got scared. When I got undressed and began playing with my breasts I discovered this creamy discharge coming from both nipples. I'm really worried about it. Is it normal?"

Not only is that "discharge" normal but it is *edible*. It's *milk*. Daily pinching and squeezing of the nipples—even in a woman who is not pregnant—often brings on the spontaneous flow of milk.

How come?

No one knows precisely, but stimulation of the nipples probably acts on the pituitary gland to produce a hormone known as *prolactin*, which then causes the breasts to secrete milk. As a matter of fact, primitive African tribes have been using exactly the same technique of breast stimulation for centuries but for a different reason—an acute shortage of drugstores.

What do drugstores have to do with it?

Well, in the jungles of Africa there's no place to buy those little prepackaged presterilized plastic bottles of baby formula. An infant whose mother dies is usually put to the breast of another nursing mother—except when all the lactating breasts in the tribe are in use. Then the baby is encouraged to suck from almost any breast—even one belonging to a virgin. After a reasonable time, milk usually flows abundantly. (Incidentally, that's good news for the woman who adopts children and still wants to breast-feed them. With persistence she can usually start her own milk flowing.) But back to masturbation.

Do women use any other techniques of masturbation?

The possible variations of masturbatory methods are only limited by the extent of the female imagination. However, in the past few years, a new trend in automated masturbation has developed. Among more sophisticated women the old electric vibrator is being replaced by more versatile and exciting devices. Probably number one on the list is the electric toothbrush. This little dispenser of dental hygiene offers an almost unlimited range of sexual sensations in the hands of an ingenious woman:

"I found out about it in the strangest way. One morning it suddenly dawned on me that my roommate at college had *two* electric toothbrushes but I only saw her brush her teeth with one of them. I asked her about it and she laughed—and then she told me. I tried it that same night and it's really something else.

"At first I kept the toothbrush in the handle and used the flat part—certainly not the brush—against my pubic bone just above my clitoris. That gets pretty wild, let me tell you. After awhile I got up the nerve to do it the way Connie— that's my roommate—does it. She lies down, spreads her legs apart, puts the handle tight up against her vagina and clitoris —like she's sitting on a rail—closes her legs tight, and turns it on. What a wild feeling! I guess it's from holding it so tight, but it makes me come and come and come until I can hardly control myself. The part I like best is that instead of turning me off, when I'm through it makes me want to have real intercourse even more."

Then there is the popular new sexual water sport.

Which sexual water sport is that?

The one that's played with the home dental jet. Originally designed for dental hygiene, the unit consists of a small pump which is attached to a slender plastic rod by a length of plastic tubing. The idea is to hold the handpiece against the gums and allow the powerful, pulsating jets of water to wash the spaces between the teeth. Simple, sanitary, and unexciting. Some time ago a dauntless female pioneer decided to see what else her dental jet could do:

"The idea first came to me because I had always found water kind of sexy. Taking a warm bath or a hot shower really turns me on. So one Saturday morning I figured it couldn't do any harm if I tried water spray somewhere else. Doctor, that has to be one of the world's most sensational feelings. The thing that makes it so exciting for me is the way the water pulsates against my clitoris. I've tried masturbation and I enjoy cunnilingus, but none of it really begins to compare with that jet of deliciously warm water going thunk-thunk-thunk as it splashes against me. Once I get started it feels as if I can have orgasms for hours and hours. Most of the time I just use it to get myself excited, but now that I'm going to be married maybe I'll let my husband do it to me before we have intercourse. He might get to like it almost as much as I do."

Are there any masturbation techniques like that for men?

Not exactly. Because the penis is so much larger, men are really at a disadvantage. The dental jet that does so much for a woman would have to be a fire hose to excite a man. Besides, that impressive looking phallus is so much less sensitive than the tiny clitoris that the more subtle sensations are wasted on it. There is, however, a kind of foam-rubber stretch-stocking with a series of tiny vibrators built in that fits over the penis. When the gentleman flips a switch his penis is alternately squeezed and released about a hundred times a minute. Some men like the feeling but there are complaints:

"I like the sensation—it's really unusual. But sometimes it feels like my penis is a hot dog in an electric hot dog bun."

There are certain risks involved as well; the following cryptic newspaper item describes one of them:

"London: A nineteen-year-old youth was found dead in his flat late yesterday by the Metropolitan Police. Certain unusual aspects of the case have caused authorities to schedule a thorough inquiry."

What actually happened to the youth?

The nineteen-year-old lad had been in the process of trying out his latest toy—an improved version of the artificial vagina. This one had inflatable rubber lips and a plastic liner that could be filled with warm water. It also contained a powerful electric vibrator. Apparently he had inserted his penis, pumped up the imitation labia tightly around the shaft, turned on the vibrator, and in his enthusiasm, punctured the waterbag. That shorted out the vibrator and provided him with the ultimate 220-volt orgasm—and no chance for an encore. Even in the Space Age, sometimes the old familiar hand-crafted ways are still the best. Besides, complex machines like the artificial water-filled vagina with internal electric vibrator are uncomfortably close to the shadowy world of sexual fetishes and perversions.

Exactly what are sexual fetishes and perversions?

Fetishes and perversions are ways of finding sexual satisfaction—of sorts—in areas farther and farther away from heterosexual penis-vagina activity. The textbook definitions themselves are not very enlightening:

FETISH: deriving erotic gratification from other than a sexual organ
PERVERSION: sexual deviation

In practical terms the whole concept of "perversion" and "fetish" is like a bikini—what it reveals is interesting, but what it conceals is vital. There is a broad range of human sexual behavior—most of it harmless—that hardly deserves to be painted with the sensational brush either of fetish or perversion. Nearly everyone—women as well as men—gets a little extra sexual zing from having his sexuality "gift-wrapped," so to speak. That's the idea behind black negligees, sexy perfume, and taking a bath together.

However, some interests are on the academic side:

"I have always found pubic hair a fascinating part of sex. Whenever I go out with a girl for the first time I always try to imagine what her pubic hair looks like. I try to guess if it's full and bushy or tightly curled around her sexual area. Usually after I have intercourse with her, I can hardly wait to turn on the light to see if my guess was right."

Other variations move farther toward the edge:

"Last week it was Hughie's turn to get a spanking. After I put on my short, short nightie, I made him take off his pajama bottoms and bring me the Ping-Pong paddle. I sat down on his big round bed and I made my naughty boy lie down across my naked lap. Was he ever excited—especially when I scolded him first. His penis got as stiff as a whip, and I started in.

"First I worked on one bare buttock, then the other. He wiggled and squirmed as his backside became a deep crimson. Suddenly he whispered to me to stop. He jumped up, pushed me backward on the bed, and gave me just what I wanted. We both had sensational orgasms—so good in fact that I can hardly wait until he puts my bare fanny across his naked knees tomorrow night."

Isn't that sort of thing abnormal?

Childish is a better word for it. Hughie and his girl friend probably both have trouble reaching a climax—like most sexual variety artists. They need a special brand of play-acting to accomplish what many men and women achieve without all those painstaking preliminaries. Sometimes the picture becomes a bit cloudier:

"I am a foot fetishist and nothing means more to me than feet. If Miss America were to stand naked in front of me right now it wouldn't excite me as much as two small feet in a pair of tight high-heeled shoes. At lunch time I can't even walk past a shoe store without getting an erection. But I have an understanding wife. Whenever we are going to have sex she always undresses, puts on the latest pair of shoes I have purchased for her and walks around until I can't hold myself back anymore. Then she quickly takes off the shoes and I masturbate against her feet. That excites her but of course she can't reach a climax that way so every *other* time I make sure to do it the regular way. That way we're both happy. By the way, I really turn on to those new platform soles."

Along with others on the fringe of sexuality, foot fetishists often have flawed potency—although in this case a sympathetic wife makes a reasonable compromise possible.

Some fellows have even more unusual tastes: "Before I got married I used to do this instead of masturbating. Every weekend in the summer I'd go out to the park and join the crowds around the hot dog stand. I would pick out the sexiest-looking girl and move in right behind her. As we got closer to the stand there would be more pushing and shoving and we'd all get squashed together. My hard penis would be jammed right up against her rear end. Every time she moved it brought me closer to a climax. By the time I was up to the front I'd usually had my orgasm and I was ready to go home until the next time. What amazes me is that I did this every Saturday and Sunday in the summer for almost four years and I never had a complaint. Maybe I was just lucky in picking girls who enjoyed that kind of business as much as I did. I think I have a normal marriage now—except, of course, I get awfully excited whenever I see my wife's naked bottom. I guess it reminds me of the old days."

Then there are situations where one partner's emotional problems surge to the surface and push across the line that separates harmless variety from pathology:

"My husband, after three years of marriage, has suddenly become a monster. He is a successful businessman, a college graduate, and a good provider. I have done everything he has asked of me sexually—including some very unusual things. But now he wants me to engage in the following:

1. parade around naked in front of other men while he watches through the keyhole
2. follow that by having intercourse with those men
3. allow him to take pictures of me playing with myself
4. have sex with other men and tell him about it while he masturbates himself

I love my husband and he says he loves me, but I honestly think he needs psychiatric treatment."

And he does need psychiatric treatment. A man or woman who is compelled to act out childish sexual fantasies that humiliate and exploit another person needs help—and right away. The whole basic idea of human sexuality is the expression of love and tenderness for another human being—sadism and viciousness belong in Nazi concentration camps, not in suburban bedrooms. Further down the road of sexual confusion are the practitioners of "D and B."

What's "D and B"?

Two innocent-sounding initials that pull back the curtain on the seamiest side of the soul—they stand for: "Discipline and Bondage." This is a quaint—and far from innocent—kinkiness that counted Hermann Goering among its devotees. The following police report gives a taste of the emotional upheaval involved:

"Responded to a routine call at 1:57 A.M., disturbance in an apartment. No answer to knock and forced door to obtain entry. A male Caucasian about fifty years old was hanging from a ceiling light fixture—a heavy black silk cord around his neck. He was wearing a white silk evening gown and a rubber gorilla mask was over his head. His hands were fastened in locked handcuffs in front of him. Subject was taken down immediately and found to be breathing. An ambulance was summoned and while waiting for it to arrive, first aid was attempted. When rubber mask was removed, subject was found to be wearing heavy female makeup, including lipstick and false eyelashes plus blonde wig. Full costume of female underwear including heavily padded brassiere, panty girdle, and pantyhose was noted. A condom was over the penis and subject appeared to have ejaculated. The upper part of his body showed extensive scars, especially around the nipple area. Subject regained consciousness before medical aid arrived but refused to make a statement. Referred to watch commander as attempted suicide."

There was only one important error in the investigating officer's report.

What was the policeman's error?

There was no attempt at suicide. "Discipline and Bondage" fans frequently play "death games" as a way of producing sexual excitement and sometimes orgasm. In the case of the "gorilla lady," the silk noose was supposed to slip loose at the last minute. It slipped the wrong way and almost cut another player from the "D and B" team. Nearly all of the bizarre suicides that are routine to veteran police officers are nothing more than grotesque fantasies of "D and B'ers" gone wrong. The notebook the officer later found in the almost-suicide's apartment gives a little more insight:

"Plans for the future:

1. try leather mask and gag
2. hang upside down in plastic bag in closet
3. eat in restaurant naked except for black leather trench coat
4. masturbate while hanging"

All the items were crossed out except number five:

"5. Gorilla lady costume, silk rope, to the point of ecstatic orgasm"

Everything else about that case was routine D and B—including the call to the police. That came from the subject's partner—who then promptly and discreetly disappeared. Many prudent practitioners of D and B are careful to have an assistant around—just in case things go wrong. And, of course, that also gives them someone else to play with.

Do women engage in discipline and bondage too?

Yes, but in a different way. Most female players take the passive role and are less melodramatic than the gentlemen:

"In order to have an orgasm during intercourse, I first of all have to become afraid of my husband. It helps a lot if he pulls off my clothes as if he is angry at me and then forces me to perform oral sex on him. When he almost—but not quite—rapes me, I really get excited. To be honest, unless he compels me to do things that I *pretend* not to like (although I secretly enjoy doing them), I just can't climax."

There are, of course, occasional ladies who enjoy slipping into a little black leather outfit after a hard day in the kitchen and gently cracking a mail-order whip over a nervously giggling middle-aged masochist. But, on the whole, women tend to be more practical about sexuality than men, and pretending that every night is Halloween just doesn't do that much for them.

Why do so many male D and B fans dress like women?

Because sexual perversions have a perverse way of overlapping. Take the field of cross-dressing for example. There are three types of men who wear women's clothes—transvestites, trans-sexuals, and homosexuals. Many members of each of these groups insist that they have an exclusive organization. That is, a lot of transvestites claim that their team is not homosexual, a lot of homosexuals insist that their boys are not transvestites, and transsexuals may admit to cross-dressing but generally deny homosexuality. That confuses everybody—including some doctors and psychiatrists.† A little research and observation however gives a clear picture —and reveals the real state of affairs.

---

†There is also a small group of people who are victims of developmental accidents. These are "intersex" individuals who are born with some sexual equipment of both sexes. Nowadays most of them are identified during early childhood and given medical and surgical treatment to assign them to the most appropriate sex. Boys are not turned into girls or vice versa—their ambiguous sexual roles are simply clarified.

What's the real relationship between transvestism and homosexuality?

This is the line-up:

1. There are some men who dress in women's clothing who are *not* homosexual. They are pure transvestites and often use ladies' ready-to-wear as a preliminary to heterosexual intercourse:

"As a transvestite, I would like to share a few thoughts with you. Under my regular clothing—a conservative pinstripe business suit—I love to wear a 'complete outfit.' That means nylon panties next to the skin, then a girdle, plus a bra and, of course, nylon stockings. (The only problem is that the smoothness of the panties tends to give me a constant erection.) I am a successful corporate executive and I presume that at least part of my pleasure is imagining how shocked my associates would be if they only knew what I was actually wearing. My wife is somewhat opposed to my proclivity, but since it stimulates me to the point where I can fully satisfy *her* sexual needs, she accepts it philosophically."

"All that I can say in my defense is that I detect a substantial feminine trend in male fashions as time goes on, what with higher heels, tighter pants, brighter colors and patterns, and more delicate materials. If this trend continues, one day I should be able to wear my 'outfit' *over* my clothes—and no one will know the difference. Is that too much to hope for?"

Many transvestites derive a certain amount of secret pleasure from the muffled rustle of lace as they go about their daily tasks. More than a few high government officials, prominent actors, and captains of industry prefer pantyhose to jockey shorts.

The next group of men who wear ladies' clothes are:

2. The homosexuals. Male homosexuals who don female attire are known to their group as "drag queens." Generally speaking, their use of female garments is basically ceremo-·

nial; that is, incidental to their sexual satisfaction. They get their real pleasure from mutual masturbation, anal intercourse, and fellatio—for them women's attire is merely a matter of gilding the lily. Most of them emphasize that they are homosexuals first and transvestites only by assimilation.

The third group is the most fascinating:

3. The trans-sexuals. These are the men—and to a lesser extent—women, who passionately believe that they should belong to any sex except the one into which they were born. They are a very small group but they have a dramatic situation that assures them front-page position whenever the matter comes up. (More than one obscure Ph.D. has rocketed to momentary fame on the shoulders of an unfortunate trans-sexual.) Some trans-sexuals are transvestites, others are homosexuals, and some are simply discontented with the side they have been chosen to play on:

"I am in my middle thirties, born a girl. However, as long as I can remember, I hated my body and took every opportunity to disguise myself as a boy. I knew down deep that wearing boy's clothes did not make me a boy but it was better than the other way. I took every opportunity to make myself as much a man as possible. Finally, by the time I was twenty, I was living as a man, working in a saw mill, and nearly happy. Then my periods began. I was almost ready to kill myself. How could I have a beer after work with my co-workers—all men—if I knew I was wearing a Kotex? Fortunately, I got a bad infection of the uterus and my doctor insisted on a complete hysterectomy."

"I don't wear men's clothes just to be stimulated sexually. I wear them because I feel right in them—I feel terribly embarrassed in women's clothes. For the past five years I have been living with an older woman and we only make love together about once a month. In the meantime, I fight a battle with the world and with myself, wondering who I am and where I belong."

Can't anything be done to help trans-sexuals?

Maybe. Virtually every trans-sexual, male and female, at one time or another has fervently wished to go to sleep at night and miraculously wake up in the morning as a full-fledged member of the opposite sex. When these unhappy folks pick up their morning paper and read how a former fighter pilot was magically transformed into a cocktail waitress they suddenly see a way out. The ones with limited means put themselves on the mile-long waiting lists at the experimental "sex-change" clinics. More affluent trans-sexuals jet to Casablanca or even suburban New York City where the surgeon's knife awaits anyone with $5,000 (no checks, please). The specific surgical procedures are standardized.

What happens in a "sex-change" operation?

Let's take men first:

After the patient is anesthetized, the penis is amputated—as close to the body as possible. Then the testicles and scrotum are removed. Some surgeons fold skin from the scrotum —and perhaps the penis—inward to form a sort of vaginal pouch. To reinforce the new image, the Adam's apple is pared away and silicone is deposited in the breast, buttocks, and hips. The beard and body hair are permanently removed and the lifetime intake of female sex hormones begins.

What does a "sex change" for women involve?

It's a lot more complicated. The operation is usually done in several stages. First both breasts have to be amputated. Subsequently a complete hysterectomy does away with the uterus, ovaries, fallopian tubes, and much of the vagina. The labia majora are brought down and filled with imitation testicles—like two plastic Easter eggs. The final stroke is to make an imitation penis out of a loop of skin from over the stomach. (The clitoris is sewn into the top of that tube so that orgasm is at least theoretically possible.) Then powerful doses of male hormones deepen the voice, darken the hair, build the muscles, and coarsen the skin. The penis, unfortunately, is usually a disappointment to everyone.

Why is the penis disappointing?

Well, first of all, an artificial penis can't become erect. Since it is no more than a flabby hollow tube of skin, the patient —and "his" partner—have to find some way of making it stiff enough to enter the vagina. The current procedure is to slip in a plastic rod which converts the flap into a skin-covered dildo. Since the imitation phallus is made from abdominal skin, it retains the same limited sensation as the abdominal skin; orgasm, if any, originates along the pubic bone at the clitoris. And, of course, most "new men" have to urinate sitting down because urine still dribbles out of the urethra. There seem to be other disappointments in store for transformed trans-sexuals as well.

What else might disappoint trans-sexuals?

Adapting to their new role. Tragically, a significant number of men who were made into "new women" have undertaken careers as professional prostitutes. Suicides, depressions, and serious emotional problems seem to intensify after the operations for some individuals. It might be—in one sense—because there is no way to go back. Once those penises, breasts, uteruses, testicles, and vaginas go into the specimen jar, no power on earth can restore them. And that, of course, is the potential tragedy of trans-sexuality.

124

Why can trans-sexuality be a tragedy?

Because of the obvious fact that no surgical technique can make a man into a woman or a woman into a man. It makes men into *imitation* women and women into *imitation* men—even if the doctors don't know the difference, the patients do. Maybe there's a better way.

What's a better way for trans-sexuals?

Giving every trans-sexual a chance to understand the emotional factors that just might be responsible for his wish to trade a real penis for an artificial vagina—or sacrifice a real vagina for a flap of skin. There are an untold number of cases —the ones that don't get into the daily papers—of trans-sexuals who are restored to normal happy sexual lives *without* science-fiction surgery. These are the ones who are guided to fulfilling their God-given sexual roles by compassionate and dedicated physicians and psychiatrists. Maybe the first few thousand dollars spent in the treatment of every trans-sexual should go to trying to help him (or her) adjust to life with everything they were born with—there's plenty of time for the operating room after that. Society has a responsibility to care for its less fortunate members. Fetishists, perverts, transvestites, and trans-sexuals may frighten some of us and offend the rest. Those who are dangerous to the community need to be isolated, those who are dangerous to themselves need to be treated, those who are missionaries of distorted and damaging sexual practices need to be restrained, and all of them need to be studied and understood. No matter how much perverts and fetishists upset us all, we must never forget that most of them are no more than confused, confounded fellow members of the human race.

7

IMPOTENCE: THE PROBLEM

What is impotence?

Impotence is a penis in rebellion—a phallus that has embarked on a life of its own—much to the dismay of its owner and operator. Impotence is a penis that zigs when it should zag, lies down when it should stand up, and sleeps when it should be wide awake. It is the sexual equivalent of a pen that won't write, a car that won't start, and a key that melts in the lock. It is the most frustrating experience that the average man ever has—or more precisely, *doesn't have.* It is, in the words of a patient who should know, "a sexual accident that's always just about to happen." And worst of all, *ninety-nine times out of a hundred, impotence doesn't have to occur.*

Impotence doesn't have to occur?

Correct. One of the most overlooked facts in the consideration of impotence is: *Satisfactory sexual intercourse is a normal response.*

The male reproductive system is so perfectly designed that it takes deliberate (although perhaps unconscious) interference to make it misfire. Few other parts of the body have as many backup systems, fail-safe mechanisms, and self-repair provisions as the male genitals. Men can ejaculate without testicles, with half a penis, and sometimes even when most of their body is paralyzed. The male equipment is fabricated to stand any assault short of the atomic bomb—except the one that comes from the inside.

How is the penis attacked from the inside?

By the organ that should be its best friend—the human brain. Nearly every satisfactory sexual experience depends on carefully synchronized cooperation between the sexual parts of the brain and the pelvic projectile that we call the penis. Except in those rare cases of physical disease, the penis is ready to be launched into Inner Space twenty-four hours a day, seven days a week. The only limitations on totally satisfying sexual performance are imposed by the reluctance of the brain to cooperate. The proof is everywhere. From a physical point of view, the genitals of an impotent man and those of a normally potent male are virtually identical. The vital difference lies in the function of a few hundred million brain cells at a particularly critical moment. The way that the vital components of the brain choose to function—or malfunction—determines which form of impotence a man will succumb to.

How many types of impotence are there?

There are four major varieties—and none of them is exactly a picnic:

1. *Absolute impotence:* In this condition, the penis acts as if it were afraid of the vagina. As soon as the man's sexual feelings begin to rise, his penis begins to fall. As the moment for intercourse comes around, erection just doesn't occur. Like this:

"When it comes to sex, I can do everything—except the most important thing—I just can't get my penis into the vagina. I'm fifty-three and I used to do it every night—and I still want to. But my penis just lies there like it has forgotten what to do—only *I* still remember *what* to do if I just could figure out a *way* to do it."

2. *Copulatory impotence:* Not quite as frustrating as absolute impotence, copulatory impotence is still no thrill—for sender or receiver. Just when things seem to be going well, the penis turns off.

"Is there such a thing as a trade union for penises? What I mean is, I can get it into my wife all right but I can't keep it in. My organ works for about four minutes, then goes on strike. Is it trying to tell me something?"

3. *Premature ejaculation:* This form of impotence is really "mini-sex"—for everyone. The man who ejaculates as soon as he starts to copulate may set new speed records, but he will soon find himself setting them alone. Imagine how a woman feels when it happens to her. It has been a perfect evening and finally the couple has found their way to bed. After passionate caresses, he is about to enter her. He leans over and whispers softly, "Now this won't take a moment. . . ." A second or two later, he adds: "Didn't it?"

4. *Retarded ejaculation:* This is the case of the penis that won't quit. Perfect erection, flawless insertion, powerful thrusting, and thrusting, and thrusting . . . but no ejacula-

tion. Retarded ejaculation (or psychogenic aspermia) is the male equivalent of orgasmic impairment in women—only men have one questionable advantage:

"I am unhappy to announce that I am the world's greatest lover. Although I am only thirty-three, I have had over 1,700 women—most of whom called me. I attract them because I can keep my erection for one to two hours or longer—something few other men can do. Everyone envies me but I would trade it all for a few simple ten-minute experiences ending in ejaculation. Any chance of that?"

One of the most annoying features of impotence is that men as a group are all victims of a sexual practical joke.

What kind of joke does impotence play on men?

The one based on the fact that *until the penis is erect, it is not actually a sexual organ.* As one whimsical patient remarked:

"Doctor, I haven't had a decent erection in six months and during that time as far as I can tell the only good thing my penis has done for me is to keep my shoes dry."

At least in theory, a woman is always capable of intercourse. The vagina, after all, is a space and on the most basic level merely needs to be filled. But unless a whole chain of events occur in precise order, the human penis remains merely a decorative accessory, an aesthetic contribution, an unfulfilled promise.

The process that converts the phallus from a modernistic plumbing fixture into Rocketship Penis is a complex one and proves once again that things are never what they seem.

You mean, sexually?

Yes. A normal man who is copulating with a normal woman centers his attention on *his* penis and *her* vagina and clitoris.

That's fine but the *real* action is taking place about three feet away from his points of interest. The success or failure of his mission depends on what happens on the surface of his brain —not the surface of his penis. Usually it starts with a mental telegram:

ATTN: PENIS
OPEN VALVES. FILL WITH BLOOD. PREPARE FOR INSERTION. FURTHER INSTRUCTIONS WILL FOLLOW. BEST WISHES.
(Signed) BRAIN

If nothing else interferes, that original telegram is followed in short order by this one:

PREPARE FOR INSERTION. REDUCE SENSITIVITY UNTIL FURTHER NOTICE.

This prevents the first contact with the vagina from triggering that unscheduled blast-off known as "premature ejaculation."

The next message, a few moments later, might go like this:

INCREASE DEPTH OF PENETRATION. RESTORE SENSITIVITY TO MAXIMUM. OPEN AUXILIARY VALVES TO MAINTAIN HARDNESS. ADJUST TO MAXIMUM SPEED.

Seven minutes later:

ADJUST ALL CONTROLS TO "MAXIMUM FOR SPEED, PENETRATION, SENSITIVITY, RIGIDITY. PREPARE FOR COUNTDOWN. BLAST-OFF SCHEDULED FOR MINUS TEN STROKES. SPERM ARE NOW MOVING AND ON THE LINE.

Five strokes later:

URGENT-URGENT-URGENT
ATTN: PENIS
THIS IS FINAL MESSAGE. POINT OF NO RETURN IS NOW.

REPEAT NOW. YOU ARE ON AUTO-PILOT. HANG IN
THERE.

(Signed) BRAIN

And another payload of 400,000,000 sperm are on their way
to the uterus.

But what if something goes wrong with those mental telegrams?

That is what we call impotence. Each form of potency failure
is characterized by a distinct failure in communication between brain and penis. For example, in the case of absolute
impotence, it might go like this:

Moments after the original "erection telegram" is received, the nervous system crackles with this message:

EMERGENCY: FOR IMMEDIATE DELIVERY
ATTN: PENIS
EMERGENCY PROCEDURES IN EFFECT. DEFLATE. PRE-
PARE TO CRASH. REPEAT. CRASH. REGRETS.

(Signed) BRAIN

Why should the brain suddenly call off sexual intercourse?

Often it happens because one of the three enemies of sexual
satisfaction suddenly appear on the horizon: *Fear, Guilt,
Anxiety.*

Frank's situation is typical. He is in his early thirties,
tough-looking, and built like the professional football player
he is:

"I never mentioned this to anyone before, Doctor, but I
guess I have to let it all hang out with you. I never had any
problem at all with sex until about a year ago. I was just

getting started in football then and I used to sell vacuum cleaners door-to-door during the summer. You know, every little bit helped. So I rang this doorbell about ten o'clock one morning and this girl answered in her bathrobe—and nothing else. She was about twenty and had one of those bodies that gets right to you, if you know what I mean. She looked at me and I looked at her and we knew right away what was going to happen. She just turned around and went into the bedroom, taking off her robe on the way. I still can't figure out why it happened but I guess sometimes you just get lucky."

Frank stopped and groaned. "I should never be *that* lucky again. So anyway, she was wild. I mean first me on top, then her on top and still she couldn't get enough. After I came the second time she was climbing all over me and sort of moaning, 'Now let me take it in my mouth. I want it in my mouth. Pretty please?'

"Could I say no? I was there to enjoy it. So I closed my eyes and lay back and all of a sudden I heard this shriek and some footsteps and when I looked up, the girl was gone and her husband was standing over me with the biggest revolver you ever saw. He didn't say a word. He just pointed it right at my testicles, from about two inches away, pulled the hammer back slow, and said, 'BANG!' "

There was sweat on Frank's upper lip now. "I didn't even stop to get my clothes. I pulled the sheet off the bed and raced for the car. I drove off looking like a ghost—all wrapped in that sheet—and I guess I felt like one."

He managed a thin smile. "I even left my vacuum cleaner behind. I wrote it up on my sales sheet as a trade-in. I suppose that was close enough to the truth."

"But that was a year ago and I've never had a decent erection again—even with my own wife. Every time I close my eyes I can see that guy with the big cannon aimed right

between my legs and I can hear him saying, 'BANG!' "
Frank shuddered.

From the moment of his symbolic castration on, every time Frank's brain sent the routine erection telegram, its automatic retrieval system recalled the threatening experience and sent instructions to "CRASH." And crash he did.

The worst part was no matter how exciting the woman, no matter how enticing the situation, forbidden sex—at least to Frank—means castration. It doesn't take much for the brain to expand that concept to include even socially approved sex —say, with his wife. But the back alleys of the human mind are so mysterious that for some men forbidden sex is the only kind that can goad their reluctant penis into action. Donna describes it:

"*Before* we were married my husband and I enjoyed a fantastic sex life. We used to have each other four or five times a day—in the shower, in front of the fireplace, out by the swimming pool at night, at the drive-in movie—anywhere and everywhere. He even had me once in the kitchen while I was leaning over doing the dishes.

"Now he's lucky (and I consider myself really lucky) if he can even get an erection once a month. Last week he tried for two hours without even getting half-hard. The next day he felt so bad he sent me a single beautiful long-stemmed rose. What does he expect me to do with it?

"Could this possibly be related? Before we were married, he loved having to coax me into giving into him. He would spend fifteen minutes unfastening my bra and half an hour pulling down my panties. That time in the kitchen—I forgot to tell you—I was doing the dishes with nothing on. It was kind of a . . . you know . . . a game.

"Anyhow, now that he can have me anytime he wants, it doesn't seem to do anything for him. *But* he can walk around with an erection for an hour if he sees some other girl bend over or stoop down in the supermarket. He says just thinking about getting into *them* drives him out of his mind."

The only unusual thing about Donna's husband is that he started early. Usually "the impotence of boredom" doesn't strike men until the age of forty or so. That's when husbands start to complain about "doing the same old thing in the same old way." They forget that when it comes to sexual intercourse, there is only one basic way to do it—the same way that has been around for fifty thousand years. The penis goes in and out of the vagina. But their underlying problem is a real one. That all-important erection message from the brain starts coming through like this:

NIGHT LETTER: ALL OTHER MESSAGES TAKE PRIORITY.
DELIVER BEFORE NOON IF POSSIBLE.
DEAR PENIS:
IF NOT OTHERWISE ENGAGED, PLZ OPEN SOME VALVE OR
OTHER. DONT XPECT MUCH. SORRY TO BOTHER. WILL
TRY TO FINISH FAST.
YR FRND,
BRN

When one middle-aged sportsman tells another in the country club lounge: "Listen, Buddy, take it from me. After you hit forty, you're all washed up," he's saying something important. He doesn't mean that on a man's fortieth birthday he can expect his sexual organs to self-destruct. He's really complaining about something else. Almost every man in the fourth decade becomes painfully aware that he needs more stimulation from his wife as a sexual partner at the same time that his own brain is less willing to provide its own particular brand of erotic electricity.

It works this way. Every erection is the combination of erotic impulses originating within the brain and erotic impulses originating in the outside world that are perceived and processed by the brain. If the two sources of sexual energy reinforce each other, the result is a penis like a steel poker. If the sources of stimulation work against each other, the penis looks and acts more like an overdone dumpling.

By the forties, the sexual voltage put out by the brain begins to diminish slightly. The testicles and adrenal glands also cut back on production of testosterone. And the wives put on weight *and* start the menopause *and* twenty years of minor squabbles settle like smog over the sexual relationship. The combination is hazardous to a man's sexual health—not to mention his potency.

Harry's experience is typical. He is forty-eight, a successful lawyer, and an unhappy man:

"Doctor, I can get anything money can buy and I want the one thing money *can't* buy. For over six months I haven't really been able to get hard enough to have relations with my wife." Harry tugged at the collar of his monogrammed shirt.

"Why not?"

He reddened. "If I knew, I wouldn't be here."

"And if you *don't* know, there's no point in being here. After all, isn't it your mind that has made the decision not to have an erection?"

"You're right, Doc."

As Harry began to describe his relationship with his wife, all the pieces fell into place. A typical night of love went like this:

[*The arena is a king-sized bed in a king-sized bedroom in Beverly Hills.* HARRY *is wearing monogrammed silk pajamas,* SALLY, *his wife, has on an imported silk nightgown.*]

HARRY: "Sally, what about it?"

SALLY: "What about *what,* Harry?"

HARRY: "You know, do you feel like it?"

SALLY: "Sure, Harry." *(She pulls her nightgown up.)*

HARRY: "Why don't you take it *off*?"

SALLY: "Because I'd just have to put it on again in about half a minute."

[*Harry immediately loses what had been the first faint suggestion of an erection.*]

HARRY: "Why did you have to say that? Now you made me lose it."

SALLY *(gets angry):* "*I* made you lose it? Sometimes I wonder if you ever *had* it! I mean, you were never really that long, were you?"

HARRY: *(defensive):* "Before you put on all that weight I didn't *have* to be that long. There was nothing in the way."

SALLY: "Listen, it isn't my fault that I married the man with the teenie-weeniest wienie in all of Beverly Hills! Why don't you go and try it out on your secretary—she collects little things!"

Every word that Sally utters is being soaked up by that limitless data bank that operates inside Harry's skull. It is filed under the heading of "Anti-Erection Material." The next ten times he tries to have intercourse with his wife, as soon as the erection message hits the wires, this telegram will override it:

PENIS: DISREGARD PREVIOUS MESSAGE. RESPOND TO FOLLOWING CODE WORDS: "TEENIE-WEENIE WIENIE," "COLLECTS LITTLE THINGS," "WONDER IF YOU EVER HAD IT." BETTER LUCK NEXT TIME.
BRAIN

If Harry is typical of men with this type of absolute impotence, there are two exceptions to his lack of potency. He tells about them:

"You know, Doc, there's something fishy about my condition. When I make it with my secretary—and by the way, my wife was right about that—about half the time I don't have any problem. My organ doesn't really get what you'd call hard but I can do something with it."

"And you don't have any trouble masturbating?"

Harry sighed. "Yeah. It's tough to admit, but the best times I have are when I play with myself. Believe me, that's not what I'm looking for."

A forbidden interlude with an accommodating secretary provides just that little zip of external stimulus that nudges the brain to produce an erection. But the magic is only intermittent. And masturbation still works because it operates on a different wavelength. The old patterns established during adolescence and reinforced thousands of times are generally the last to succumb to the ravages of absolute impotence.

What about copulatory impotence?

More often than not, copulatory impotence (loss of erection once intercourse begins) is simply a mild form of absolute impotence. Enough juice comes through from the brain to produce the initial erection, but the subsequent messages to the penis get garbled. As intercourse proceeds, the copulatory center in the cerebrum starts putting out messages like this—confused, contradictory, and self-limiting:

TO PENIS:
CONTINUE THRUST ON SCHEDULE. REMEMBER WHAT YOUR MOTHER USED TO SAY. CORRECTION. *FORGET* WHAT YOUR MOTHER USED TO SAY. INCREASE BLOOD PRESSURE TO RESTORE LOST HARDNESS. PAY ATTENTION TO BED SQUEAKING. CORRECTION. *IGNORE* BED SQUEAK-ING. CHEER UP, YOU ARE GETTING SOFTER—I MEAN,

HARDER. TOO LATE? SORRY ABOUT THAT.
TRY AGAIN TOMORROW NIGHT.
BRAIN

Few women forget their first experience with copulatory impotence. Martha describes hers:

"Looking back on it, I guess we should've waited until the next night. But Bill had been away on business for a week and he really wanted it right then. I told him he was too tired but he was all sexed up. So there we were in bed and he got hard right away—I didn't even have to play with it—you know, to get him really stiff. He put it in and we started but then all of a sudden he went soft—like when you let the air out of a tire. He just kind of fell out of me, and I tried to make him hard again. It got a little harder, and then as soon as it was in me again, it got soft. Honestly, Doctor, I did everything I could to help. I rubbed it, and petted it, and played with it. I did everything with it I could think of except roll it in bread crumbs—and I would've done that if I were sure it would've helped. Bill really got upset and the harder he tried, the softer it got. About two in the morning, he just fell asleep exhausted. But from that night on he always had some kind of trouble before either of us managed to come. It was as if failure bred failure."

Failure *does* breed failure. It's about then that as soon as the penis is in the vagina, the message goes out from Copulation Control:

TO PENIS:
CEASE ALL FURTHER RESISTANCE. YOU ARE DEFEATED.
COME OUT WITH YOUR HEAD DOWN.
(Signed)
YOUR FRIEND AND ENEMY, THE BRAIN

What about premature ejaculation?

Premature ejaculation is a kind of phallic practical joke—almost as if the mind is saying, "You want an erection? Okay, but use it quick—before it vanishes!" "Quick" usually means something like thirty seconds—or the sexual equivalent of the speed of light. Sometimes premature ejaculation starts as far back as the honeymoon—or before:

"Unlike most men, I was a virgin when I got married, and a year later, I am almost still a virgin—if you count the actual time my penis has spent in my wife's vagina. Figuring from ten to thirty seconds each time, and considering that we've had intercourse about fifty times this year, that means I've had about sixteen and two-thirds minutes of sex since I got married. That must be some kind of record."

But what causes *premature ejaculation?*

A better name for premature ejaculation might be "immature ejaculation." Men who suffer from this condition are *unwillingly* perpetuating their original pattern of adolescent masturbation. Back when they were fourteen years old, the idea was to apply friction to the penis as rapidly and as intensely as possible and then "blast off." The more immature forms of prematurity are almost a sexual version of "Beat the Clock"—with the same "game" atmosphere. It's almost as if the brain were sending this pep-rally message:

HEY PENIS!
IN AND OUT—UP AND DOWN—YOU'VE GOT THE FASTEST GAME IN TOWN!
YEAHHHH, PENIS!
YOUR OLD BUDDY, BRAIN

There was a time when masturbation was a game, too. Some men still remember it clearly. Henry is vice-president of a large machine tool firm. He is widely known as a subdued, restrained pillar of the community. He has lost some of that restraint as he speaks:

"You asked me about masturbating, Doctor? Sure I can remember it. When I was in my teens, we used to have masturbation derbies. Half a dozen boys would go out in the woods and form a circle, take out their—uh, their—organs and the first one to reach a—a climax was the winner.

"My problem, as you've probably guessed, Doctor, is that I'm fifty-four and married and I can still come in first in that kind of contest. But now that makes me a loser, doesn't it?"

Henry's wrong on that count. The one unique feature of premature ejaculation is that it is the only form of impotence where the man enjoys full sexual gratification. Things sometimes happen a little too fast for him to savor every delicious moment, but at least he is guaranteed some sort of orgasm nearly every time. That's more than the woman gets.

Are men with premature ejaculation trying to get even with women?

Not consciously. But there is no getting away from the fact that premature ejaculation resembles—more than anything else—"masturbation in the vagina." Robbie didn't think so at first. He's twenty-nine and is the hot-shot sales manager for a hot-shot rock recording label. His official uniform is a mod suit, mod shirt, mod shoes and—in a certain sense, the mod form of impotence—premature ejaculation:

"You know, Doc, like the first time you laid it on me, it was unreal. I mean, when it comes to chicks, I really know where it's at. Like, I've tried it every way there is, but it happens—you know—*right now,* man!"

"How long is 'right now'?"

He grinned. "Well, not exactly right *now,* but say never

more than, oh, three minutes. I mean, that's how it really got to me. A couple months ago this chick, I mean she was a super-chick, after I did my thing, she leaned over and said, 'You're putting me on. You mean that's all there is? Mr. Super-Stud turns out to be just another Minute-Man? Too much!'—and she started laughing. I guess that was what got to me—'just another Minute-Man'."

Robbie shook his head. Suddenly his eyes reddened: "Doctor, this is killing me." It seemed as if those impending tears washed away the mod veneer. Now Robbie was just another man with a disobedient penis.

"I know what you said about using girls to masturbate. I remember what I said at the time: 'Are you for real, Doc? I don't have to line up the foxiest chicks in town to give me what I can give myself.' That was just jive talk. The truth is that's exactly what I have to do. For sure, it's even easier for me to play with myself than to face those chicks afterward. That's the hardest part."

"What do you mean?"

"Well, remember that one I called 'Super-Chick'? She had a body that just wouldn't quit—and she knew just what to do with it. But she had a head that worked even better. After that bad scene over at her place, she sat me down and said, 'Robbie, didn't you ever think how a girl feels when you do your little number? You get me all worked up for a trip to the moon and I end up with a lukewarm douche. Listen, I hate to say this but I can get more action from one of those feminine hygiene sprays. What's a girl supposed to do—live on her memories?'

"Then she saw I felt pretty bad, so she smiled and said, 'Say, I've got the answer! Let's do the whole thing again and maybe if I try real hard *I* can come down with a case of premature ejaculation. Think of it—'Minute-Man meets Minute-Woman'!

"Well, as you probably could predict, it wasn't that easy. But that little speech got me to start really thinking about my problem and that's what finally got me to come and see you."

Robbie eventually understood and overcame his problem. On his last visit, he was more mod than ever before.

"Say, man! Have I got something to lay on you! Next week, Super-Stud marries Super-Chick! Far out!"

Then for a moment he dropped the pose and smiled:

"The best part is I think she really *is* coming down with her own case of premature ejaculation. What a honeymoon that's going to be!"

On the other hand, there are some men who would *welcome* a mild case of premature ejaculation, too—or at least they think so.

What kind of men?

The ones with *retarded* ejaculation. Many men with this condition can point with precision to some sexual experience that they believe triggered their problem:

"I had my first sexual experience two years ago with an older woman when I was seventeen. After a high school basketball game, an older woman, who I later found out was the coach's wife, took me in the back seat of her car. I guess she must have been about thirty-five, but she was really stacked. She was in a big hurry for some reason and rushed me through it all. First she grabbed both my hands and pushed them under her sweater onto her breasts—she wasn't wearing any bra. Then she took one of my hands and slid it up her legs under her dress and put it inside her panties and started rubbing up against it—hard. She was all wet down there and it kind of surprised me, but I figured this was my chance to find out what it was all about. Then she grabbed my penis and pushed it up into her vagina. It was all so fast I hardly knew what was happening and before I could come, she had her climax. That part worried me—not being able to climax myself. So I embarked on my own little research project and tried to climax with at least a dozen other girl friends in the next couple of months. They were all willing to oblige me but somehow or other I could never quite bring it off.

"Finally, last month, I had a date with this really beautiful girl. I took her in the back seat of *my* car, undressed her, and we went to it. Right after I got inside her, she raised her head up and whispered in my ear, 'Whatever happens, don't you dare come *in* me!' Little did she know *that* was my problem.

"For the next fifteen minutes or so, she kept insisting, 'Now remember, don't come *in* me!' I wasn't about to.

"Finally, she started to have her own climax and she pushed herself against me real hard and started moving real fast and grabbed me real tight and yelled in my ear, 'Now! Come *in* me!' All of a sudden I felt this erupting volcano starting to work its way up my penis and then I suddenly remembered that's how little girls get pregnant and I managed to withdraw before I ejaculated.

"Ever since then, for the next thirty times, whenever I get to the point of coming—just as my orgasm gets to the end of my penis, I feel a sudden jolt of pain—and that's the end.''

Is a bad experience like that the cause of retarded ejaculation?

Hardly. In the old days, it was fashionable to trace a specific emotional problem to an original "traumatic experience." That made life easy for psychiatrists *and* patients because all of us can draw on a vast collection of unpleasant experiences —especially during the turmoil of childhood and growing up. More important than the experience itself is what the person is willing to make of the episode. Most men with retarded ejaculation see their own seminal fluid and their own explosive ejaculation as much more than a physiological event. They often *view* ejaculation as dangerous to their partner and dangerous to themselves. Occasionally they unconsciously *think* of sperm as a precious possession that they are unwilling to part with. The fact that they deprive themselves of the pleasure of orgasm is apparently a price that they are more than willing to pay—at least unconsciously.

There is even a minor school of philosophy that feels a man is given only so much sperm to use during his entire lifetime. When that's gone, presumably he will ejaculate apple juice or maybe just plain compressed air. (Actually, sperm and the associated fluid are constantly manufactured from the available cells of the body and there is no chance of running out.)

In retarded ejaculation, the message that makes the difference is this one. About five minutes before the point-of-no-return, this mental telegram hops over the wires of the nervous system:

ALL HANDS ON DECK—ALL HANDS ON DECK
RED ALERT. CLOSE SPERM-TIGHT DOORS. SHUT OFF ALL
VALVES. DISCONNECT EJACULATION POWER SOURCE.
OTHERWISE CONTINUE AS PLANNED. CHECK BACK IN
TWO HOURS.
BRAIN

What about overcoming impotence?

Well, if impotence *starts* in the brain, it can be *stopped* in the brain. If a man really wants to play in the sexual big leagues again—or maybe for the first time—he can do it. It requires perseverence, hard work—and a little bit of luck. But it can be done.

If a man does want to get rid of his impotence, what does he do first?

He turns the page.

8

IMPOTENCE: THE SOLUTION

Can't a man with impotence just go to the doctor and be cured?

Almost every man with impotence has gone that route already. Every day perhaps a hundred thousand reluctant penises are trundled down to a doctor's office and dutifully displayed, examined, probed, and pronounced physically fit for active duty. But that night, when the big moment comes, they refuse to perform. Then it's back to see the doctor and . . . Let Tony tell what happened to him:

"I've been married seven years, I have three children, and my patient wife is about to go out of her mind—and I'm right behind her. I've had the full course.

"First, I thought there might be something physically wrong, so I went to a specialist who said I had an infection. I didn't. Next, I went to a urologist, who said the opening in my penis was too small. He made it larger—and don't think that wasn't fun. When I told him that didn't help, he acted as if he didn't believe me. Next, I went to our family doctor. He made me feel like a fool and told me to "concentrate." His face was as red as mine. Next, I went to a psychiatrist because I was beginning to feel like a mental case. He gave me every pill in existence and asked me how my job was. If all these doctors can't help me, who can?"

Why can't doctors do more for impotence?

It really isn't their fault. We live in a society that pretends that sex doesn't happen and that sexual organs don't exist. In most medical schools, more time is devoted to the study of indigestion than to the study of impotence. Entire departments are devoted exclusively to urinary conditions—how a man makes water. No department is devoted to the study of impotence—how a man makes love.

Some medical researchers are granted billions for research into cancer to make human life longer. Others are given pennies for research into impotence to make human life happier. So don't blame the family doctor if he would rather talk about the function of the pancreas instead of the function of the penis—at least the medical textbooks tell all about how the pancreas works. The doctor who tries to help his patient by consulting the medical books comes away shaking his head. One of the most respected reference works suggests that impotent men take a few drinks before attempting intercourse "to lessen their inhibitions"—and protect them from snakebite? (Even Shakespeare knew better, when he said about alcohol: "It provokes the desire, but it takes away the performance.") The same textbook has this exciting suggestion for premature ejaculators: "Have intercourse more often." That's as thoughtless as telling a hunchback to stand up straight.

146

Is there a better approach to impotence?

There sure is. It starts with making impotence and every other sexual problem a "respectable" condition—as respectable as high blood pressure or varicose veins. Then the treatment can be taught in medical schools and will be available from any doctor's office.

What can a man who is impotent do in the meantime?

For sure, he can't spend his life on the sexual sidelines waiting for the cure that never comes. If he wants to badly enough, he can attack his problem on his own, using his intimate knowledge of his own needs and desires, combined with the freely available insights of modern medical science.

You mean a man can cure his impotence by himself?

Usually he *has* to do it by himself—because nobody else is going to do it for him. (There is no way that even a fraction of impotent men can receive psychiatric treatment—there just aren't enough psychiatrists.) Besides, *he caused it.* If he would only let his penis do what *it* wants to do, it would turn in a dazzling performance every time—that's the way it's made. But when he allows his unconscious feelings and his emotional conflicts to interfere, his penis becomes nothing more than a phallic errand boy. It is reduced to carrying complaints back and forth between man and woman via the reproductive system. Then it doesn't have time to do its real job—become erect, plunge into the vagina, and set off an orgasm in the woman as it jubilantly blasts off on its own. As soon as he decides not to let his sexual organs take part in that neurotic soap opera they call impotence, a man is on his way to being cured.

How does he go about it?

First, by facing certain obvious facts about male sexuality:

1. *Virtually every man who is diagnosed as impotent is somehow potent.* His only problem is that his potency is misplaced. Most men can have an erection and ejaculation sometime, somewhere, somehow. The fact that via masturbation most men are able to go from the first genital twitch to the final surging moment of orgasm establishes their true potency beyond any doubt. Anyone who tells a man otherwise should be viewed with suspicion.

2. *A man's sexual performance can come under the deliberate influence of his will.* Copulation is a combined physical-emotional function that can be regulated by training, concentration, willpower, and understanding. The sexual organs have no mind of their own; there is no such thing as "Every Penis for Itself"—and hopefully there never will be.

Victory over impotence depends on a two-pronged attack. The first goal is gaining control over the physical responses of the penis. That requires *phallic discipline*.

What is "phallic discipline"?

Well, it's not the kind that comes from leather clothes and kinky little whips. It means re-educating the penis to *win* instead of lose. It means making the penis perform to please its owner (and his female partner) instead of going off half-cocked. The same brain that can comprehend the facts of nuclear physics, construct the Empire State Building, and launch a 300-foot rocket onto the moon should be able to comprehend the basic facts of sexual intercourse, construct an erection, and launch a six-inch rocket into the vagina. Besides, impotence is so unfair.

Unfair? In what way?

Well, it deprives a man of the beneficial use of the most enjoyable part of his own body. It is actually *physiological castration.*

While all the other men in the world are enjoying one orgasm after another, the impotent—or partly impotent— fellow sits on the sexual sidelines thinking of what might have been. Overcoming impotence translates "what-might-have-been" into "what's-going-to-be," and it all starts with two rather mundane preliminary steps.

What are the first steps toward overcoming impotence?

The most obvious ones. If a man is going to be in good sexual condition, first he has to be in good physical condition. For those carrying a few extra pounds, it means getting down to normal weight. For some reason, the heavyweight on the scales is the flyweight in bed. Maybe at the critical moment all the blood rushes to the stomach—who knows? Anyway, a man who is overweight has to choose, right at the start, between pastries and passion, between the plate and the pillow, between the delights of digestion and copulation.

Second, he has to say good-bye to drugs—all drugs. Alcohol, tobacco, sleeping pills, tranquilizers, and the whole medicine cabinet of brain-bangers with which our society is burdened. That also includes a plea to the family doctor to restrict prescription drugs to the bare minimum. The closer an individual can come to making his entire body free of drugs and chemicals that affect the brain the better his chances for sexual success.

The next step is to concentrate on attacking impotence where it originates.

Where does impotence originate?

Where all sexuality originates—in the brain. Trying to cure impotence solely by manipulating the penis is like trying to heat a house by warming the thermometer. If the phallus were the source of impotence, then a penis transplant would be the world's most popular operation—provided one could find a willing donor. A simplified description of potency problems might go like this:

The human brain is a source of electric power—like the receptacle in the wall. There are wires—called "nerves"—that travel from the brain to the penis via a big cable—the spinal cord. If the penis is plugged into the brain at one end and a vagina at the other, the circuit is complete and the current flows in that mind-bending surge of power that we call orgasm.

Following this diagram a little further, the mechanism behind each form of impotence becomes easier to understand:

In *absolute impotence,* the plug is simply pulled out of the wall.

In *copulatory impotence,* the wires are loose and the circuit sputters on and off.

In *premature ejaculation,* the penis is plugged into the brain before it is plugged into the vagina.

In *retarded ejaculation,* only about half the electricity is getting through.

Each of these "electrical problems" is simply the result of inner emotional problems. Fortunately, the human brain has the ability to repair its own circuits—given half a chance.

Can the brain really repair its own circuits?

The proof is everywhere. Virtually every man in the world at one time or another has suffered from an episode of impotence—sometimes lasting a night, sometimes lasting a week. Most of these cases of temporary impotence are cleared up because the unconscious mind straightens itself out. (Of course, if brain cells are physically destroyed, they never grow back.)

How can a man help his brain to repair itself?

Well, take the case of Frank, the vacuum-cleaner salesman, for example. If Frank could teach his brain that sex with his wife does not expose him to the same risk of castration as sex with a friendly housewife, it would quickly allow him to have normal erections. If Harry could program his mind to overcome the jibes of his wife, he could produce an erection that would stand up in a hurricane. But a man has to face his problem with honesty, determination, and an open mind if he wants to succeed.

Where does he start?

By considering two fascinating coincidences of human behavior.

The first one is:

The Compulsion to Get Even

Every human being from schoolboy to king is ruled by the compelling necessity to do to someone else what has been done to him. The third-grader who gets shoved on the playground instantly shoves back. The child who gets a shot in the doctor's office goes home and gives "pretend" shots to his little sister. The man who is bullied by his boss comes home and bullies his wife. And in more primitive societies the Biblical law of "an eye for an eye and a tooth for a tooth" prevails. The loser must become the winner, the victim must become the aggressor, and the done-to must become the doer.

The next coincidence is:

The Mystery of the Missing Breast

Every man, when he was a tiny baby, had a white liquid, *milk,* sprayed into a round opening, his *mouth,* from a long fleshy organ, a *breast,* which had a tiny erection on the end of it called a *nipple.*

Twenty years later that same boy-baby, now a man, sprays a white liquid, *spermatic fluid,* from a long fleshy organ with an erection, his *penis,* into a mouthlike opening, the *vagina.*

Isn't that just somebody's theory?

No. It's just a description of feeding a baby and a description of sexual intercourse. But there is one big coincidence. *If* that tiny helpless baby in some strange and mysterious way twenty years later makes sexual intercourse into an instant replay of nursing at the breast (or bottle), he might accomplish two things. First, he might succumb to the temptation to distort sexual intercourse to "get even" for whatever bad things happened to him when he was on the receiving end of the breast-mouth situation. Secondly, in the process he might sacrifice his normal sexual functioning. Ironically, many men are so anxious to even the score unconsciously that they are willing to sabotage their sexuality in the process.

Is there any proof of the relationship between nursing and copulation?

Let's take a look:

1. Of all the sexual activities that men enjoy (besides intercourse), fellatio probably heads the list. In this fascinating variation, the penis is used directly as a "breast" to feed "milk" to the sucking "baby." (An interesting way of "getting even"?)

2. The male equivalent of fellatio—cunnilingus—usually concentrates on the clitoris. On careful examination, the clitoris qualifies as a pretty good stand-in for a nipple.

3. The entire "underground" language of sex overflows with terms like "eat," "suck," "lick," "juicy," "hot"—expressions *apparently* more appropriate for a baby at the breast than a couple in bed.

4. Nearly all men devote a tremendous amount of sexual attention to an organ primarily designed to feed babies, the breast. They kiss it, suck it, lick it, and frequently rub their penises against it, sometimes even squirting their milk (oops!), sperm, onto it.

Okay, supposing that's true. What does it do for an impotent man?

It provides that impotent man with a way to resolve his impotence—once and for all. If his brain has hijacked his penis to get even for some real or imagined slight when he was a nursing infant, he now has the means of understanding exactly what happened and using it to regain permanent custody of this most precious organ.

In *absolute impotence,* the man is refusing to feed the "baby" by never producing a penis-breast that she can suck on with her mouth-vagina.

In *copulatory impotence,* the man withdraws or collapses

the breast-penis before the woman can get to the milk-sperm.

In *premature ejaculation,* the man spills the milk-sperm before the woman ever has a chance to "drink" it.

In *retarded ejaculation,* the man simply refuses to produce any milk-sperm at all.

This all fits in with the observation that many impotent men can masturbate flawlessly. Perhaps that's because it's only for their own amusement—there is no woman present to provide the emotional conflict and unconscious symbolism.

Then all a man has to do is memorize these ideas and his impotence goes away?

Or put his hand on the radio and he will be healed? Not quite. To insure victory over impotence it makes sense to fight the battle at both ends of the nervous system. That means supplying the right stimulus to the brain from the inside—by altering thinking patterns—and from the outside by *sending the right messages from the penis.* The first step is to understand how the penis works—from start to finish. Roy explains:

"Listen, Doctor, when you told me to go home and play with myself, I was ready to walk out of your office and never come back. But then I thought, 'I've tried every other wild idea, I might as well try this one.'

"Now that I've done it, it makes all the sense in the world. You know, I'm a film producer and I can have almost any girl I want—all I have to do is promise her a contract. But in all those thousands of bedroom casting sessions, I never got to see how my own organ operated—or maybe I should say, failed to operate. So, I did what you told me. I went home, took a hot bath, got out some lubricating jelly and stroked my penis until it got hard. And it really did get hard —harder than it's gotten in the two years since I started having my problem. Maybe it knew it had nothing to be afraid of?" Roy chuckled.

"Believe me, that in itself made me see something. For sure if I'd had some chick there in bed with me, all she would've had would have been a handful of jello.

"So, I started sliding my hand up and back—slow—like you said. My first feeling was I wanted to come right then and there—but I did what you told me. I stopped and waited a few seconds. Right away I noticed how that feeling of tension that had climbed right up to the tip of my penis started receding back down to the base as soon as I laid off. Then I began stroking again—and stopped again as soon as I began getting carried away. The same thing happened— that feeling went up and back like a yo-yo. Listen, I must have ejaculated five thousand times since I started having sex and I never realized really how it worked. If I can have that kind of control just by thinking about it, eventually I should be able to make my little friend here do whatever I want."

Roy paused and smiled.

"What are you smiling about?"

"Hmmmmm? Oh, I was just thinking about how this would all look on film. Well, that's another project."

He went on.

"I also noticed something else. I knew that if I let that sensation get past the end of my penis, I would come then and there and that would be the end of it. Another thing. Each time I let the feeling slide back down the shaft of my penis, it got stronger and stronger and my penis got harder and harder. To make a long story short, I went for half an hour just letting that feeling build up and die down. Then I finally couldn't stand it any longer and I let it shoot over the end of my penis and I came. It was easily the second best climax I ever had."

"The second best?"

"Come on, Doc, don't kid me. You know what happened.

The best orgasm was the one I had with my girl the next night—after I began to see how my penis really worked. I want to be honest—I have a lot of improving to do, but at least now I know I have a fighting chance."

During intercourse the penis is buried deep in the cavern of the vagina and every man is operating—to say the least—in the dark. Simply observing his sexual responses carefully in the light of day can be important in achieving conscious control. The next task is choosing a partner—probably the most important one of all.

Why is that so important?

Because sex isn't a game of solitaire. It takes two people, four hands, a penis, a vagina, and two minds that are spiritually entwined. If a man is going to beat his impotence, he needs a very special kind of woman. He needs a woman who is going to fight on his team, not against him. He needs a woman who is sure enough of her own sexuality to help him win back his. He needs a woman who is compassionate, understanding, and patient. All in all, it adds up to a complicated way of saying that he needs a woman who is in love with him. One woman like that is worth a thousand sad-eyed therapists in long white coats. There is another important requirement.

What's that?

A loosening of the male ego and the admission that a fellow needs a little help from a friend. Far too many men insist on perpetuating the masculine myth of sexual invincibility that unceremoniously collapses at the gateway to the vagina. And most men don't have to go too far for help—most wives are more than willing to help their husbands:

Lila was in her early thirties, with high cheek bones and blonde hair down to her waist.

"Doctor, I'm tired of *outercourse.*"

"Outercourse?"

"That's right. When my husband doesn't have an erection, we certainly can't have intercourse. I mean, he brings me to a climax by doing everything on the *outside*. You know, with his hands and his mouth. I admit that I really enjoy that but there's no substitute for having him inside me. I'm willing to do anything—and I mean *anything*—to help him be a *real* man again."

A man with a wife like that has the odds overwhelmingly on his side. But unless and until he finds a woman willing to help him, he might as well forget about overcoming his potency problem. Trying to get things together with an unsympathetic partner is like trying to copulate with a tiger—and it doesn't matter if she's the sexiest tiger in town.

How about getting down to the practical steps in curing impotence?

Everything up until now has been a *practical* step. The chap who's looking for something he can strap onto his penis and use to crank out one erection after another is wasting his time. Electronic devices like that have been manufactured but they are more appropriate for reluctant rams and stallions than for sensitive, civilized human beings. A man who wants electronic sex might as well put his penis in a light socket—that's really the ultimate love affair with electricity anyhow.

Once a man understands the emotional basis of the various forms of impotence, he is ready to come to grips very directly with his problem.

Let's look at absolute impotence first. The key to solving absolute impotence depends on the lucky accident of *spontaneous erections.*

What's a spontaneous erection?

A desperate attempt on the part of the reproductive system to save itself. The penis, testicles, and all the rest of the male sexual apparatus are vital dynamic structures—not just a tangled jumble of plumbing. They refuse to die without putting up a valiant fight. Virtually every man who complains of absolute impotence has spontaneous "wildcat" erections —*sometimes.*

"Doctor, I'm sixty-one and almost every morning I wake up with the kind of erection I used to have when I was eighteen. But by breakfast time it melts away."

Or, "I just can't figure out what's wrong with me. When I ride home on the subway every night, I sit across from all those young secretaries with their miniskirts pulled up. I'm ready for action by the time we pass the first station. But they don't allow sexual intercourse in the subway—at least not yet. By the time I get home, all I have is a wet noodle."

Or, "I haven't been able to have intercourse with my girl friend for six months now. But every time I take a hot shower, it gives me a great erection. What am I supposed to do, put on baggy pants and try to smuggle it over to her house?"

The first step on the road back to normal sexuality is to seize these "wildcat" erections and use them as the lever to pry control of sex away from the negative forces that cause impotence. The male sexual organs never wear out—they only rust out. Men with absolute impotence should carry every possible erection through to ejaculation and orgasm— that applies especially to those wake-up-in-the-morning erections. The fellow who wants to save it for after supper soon

158

discovers that erections are perishable—there is no way to pickle or preserve a rigid penis. So with a cooperative wife, many men have found that the best guarantee of having a nice night is to have a nice morning.

What if there's no woman available?

Then a fellow has to do the best he can. That's the time for therapeutic self-induced orgasms. Many men with absolute impotence—for obvious reasons—often have trouble finding a woman who's willing. Then it becomes a matter of putting the cart before the horse—or the penis before the vagina.

Nearly every man with absolute impotence can bring himself to a climax successfully. By using his spontaneous erections this way, he can restore his confidence, exercise his sexual reflexes, intensify his sexual desires, and make real progress toward his goal of successful intercourse. As a fringe benefit, this self-induced orgasm proves to the sufferer —once and for all—that his impotence is emotional. Generally, orgasm produced this way is conclusive proof that all the sexual circuits are *physically* intact.

Doesn't that sort of thing waste a man's sexual strength?

Like lifting weights wastes physical strength? Potency isn't like that—something to be hoarded for that gigantic super-colossal orgasm that may be lurking in some dark corner of a singles bar. Male sexual power is a bottomless resource— the more you spend, the more you have to spend.

What about the man who can't even have an erection?

There is an almost foolproof method available to him. It

starts with one of those small pistol-grip vibrators that plug into the wall. He uses the attachment that looks like a suction cup, lubricates it well with surgical jelly, and applies it gently to the head of his penis—erect or not. Then he turns on the vibrator.

Phil described it this way:

"Doctor, as you know, I'm a newspaper reporter and somehow I always considered myself sophisticated. My wife died about four years ago when I was fifty-five and it seems as if my potency died with her. I've tried out—or maybe I should say I've *tired out*—a dozen women since then. The last two fell asleep after a couple of hours of trying to help me raise a half-decent erection. I just haven't had the nerve to impose myself on anyone else. When you told me about the vibrator for men, frankly I didn't believe you. But I followed your instructions anyhow—I certainly had nothing to lose, because I had nothing to begin with.

"I used one of those pistol-grip jobs with the rubber suction cup on the end. I smeared some surgical jelly on the tip of my limp penis, put the cup over it, pulled the trigger, and began vibrating. For about two minutes it was what you might call an interesting sensation. My penis got about half-hard and then all of a sudden, I came—and came, and came —like I hadn't come in four years—or maybe forty years! The only thing I can compare it with was an experience I had in Burma during the Second World War with a couple of sixteen-year-old temple dancers—but that's another story. Anyhow, it works. That's for sure! The first few times I only had a weak erection but it gave me the confidence to try intercourse again. Now I start with the vibrator, then after about half a minute I'm hard enough to get it into the vagina. What a difference!"

Once a man with absolute impotence has accomplished the feat of making his sexual organs perform on command— whether it's from spontaneous erections or by means of the vibrator—he's halfway to his goal. Then it's back to the brain to see what's going on there. Absolute impotence has some fascinating emotional implications.

What are the emotional implications of impotence?

To start with, in relation to the woman in his life, a man has a monopoly on sperm-milk. Since she can't produce her own, she must look to him for her supply. That's where the revenge comes in. Instead of providing an abundance of free-flowing "milk-sperm" from an erect "nipple-breast" to a hungry "mouth-vagina," the gentleman in question may simply become the victim of a sudden mysterious attack of impotence. In a few short moments, in the privacy of his own bedroom (ironically, the place where his mother used to feed him), he has begun to even the score. If he has unconsciously chosen absolute impotence as his method, it's just a matter of the breast failing to appear—because he doesn't want to produce it. No erection means no breast, and no breast means no milk.

Well, if that's true, what can the man do about it?

First of all, he can decide not to do it. It's not quite as simple as merely saying, "From now on, I'm not going to be impotent any more." To be effective, he has to resolve to stop using his penis as a weapon of revenge. It is much better to use it as a lover's magic wand. If fear can be replaced by tenderness and love, limpness can be replaced by rigidity. Ironically, the phallus that is used like a sword becomes a feather, and the penis that is used like a feather performs as if it were forged of steel.

Once he makes that decision, he can say to himself: *"I'm all through refusing milk (sperm) to get even for what might have happened to me as a baby."*

If he constantly thinks of his sexual relationship in those terms and tries to understand his behavior toward his partner with that in mind, he will go a long way toward helping himself. If he concentrates on understanding that idea just before intercourse, and more importantly, in the early stages of copulation, his decision not to refuse sperm-milk may become a reality.

What if a fellow doesn't believe in that?

He doesn't have to—because it doesn't matter whether he "believes in it" or not. Nobody has to "believe in" penicillin to make it work. Besides, if it's right, it will take effect like magic. If it's not right, he's just taken some free-of-charge mumbling lessons.

Is that enough to resolve impotence?

In some cases. But to be doubly sure, it pays to reinforce the encouraging messages from brain-to-penis with equally effective communications from penis-to-brain. It's called Positive Sexual Reinforcement.

How does Positive Sexual Reinforcement work?

Like this:

Few men can have an erection simply by wishing for it. Once their brain is receptive—that is, when they have solved the Mystery of the Missing Breast—they still need as much point-of-contact stimulation as they can get. That's where Positive Sexual Reinforcement (or PSR) takes over. Things like an indifferent partner and clumsy caresses can be an anchor tied around the end of the penis. On the other hand, an exciting woman and inspired preparation can send a pulsating phallus unerringly to its target.

As one patient—who happened to be a professor of physics—expressed it:

"The angle of the dangle equals the heat of the beat times the mass of the lass."

The man with wavering potency has to tip the balance of power in his favor as much as possible by bombarding the penis with all the stimulation it can take.

Later on, when his potency is fully re-established, he should be able to have intercourse, as the Italians say, ". . . in a tree, under water, or with a jealous husband knocking on the door." But until that exciting moment, Positive Sexual Reinforcement can be a big help. There are five techniques of PSR that can help a man with absolute impotence. The first and most important is:

Titillation

Passionate and enlightened petting of the penis is the simplest and most effective method known for producing an erection. In addition, it reinforces the lifelong reflexes every man has established during adolescent (and later) masturbation. It requires good lubrication to distribute the sensation over all the nerve endings—saliva is a good choice, although everything from olive oil to hair tonic has been used. The penis itself is like a thermometer—the closer one gets to the tip, the hotter it becomes. Gentle stroking with the fingertips from the base to the tip followed by a circular massage around the mushroom-shaped cap (known as the corona) gives good results. At the point where the tip meets the shaft, there is an area like the brim of a hat which is extremely sensitive to vibration. The classical method of forming a ring with the thumb and index finger and rapidly flicking that tense ring of tissue can often produce a satisfying erection.

Frequently, alternate squeezing and massaging of the shaft will trigger the erectile response. Titillation is one area where experimentation is rewarded. If the woman accepts her task as a friendly challenge, everyone will benefit.

That's the direct physical side to titillation. There is also the emotional part of Positive Sexual Reinforcement which is just as important. It depends on bringing out all the latent male images of a sexually aroused woman—images which have a powerful ability to arouse every man. At this stage if a woman rubs her pubic area against her partner and then takes his hand and gently slides it over her vulva and clitoris, both of them will be rewarded. If she will take one of her breasts in her hand and slip the nipple into his mouth while she jiggles the breast gently, the brain—and the penis—will get the message at almost the same time. She can also intensify the Positive Sexual Reinforcement with words. The simplest and most effective way to do that is to tell the man honestly what she wants and why she wants it:

"I want to make it good and hard so I can feel all of it when you put it in me."

One man whose wife was finally determined to try PSR testified: "Doctor, I don't know what you told my wife, but those things she did to me last night could put an erection on an iron lamp post."

But isn't it unladylike to act that way?

Maybe at the opera but not in the bedroom. The man who needs an erection doesn't need lessons in etiquette—he needs a woman who can turn him on so he can turn her on.

The next technique is:

Fellatio

As the woman continues her bombardment of PSR, she can take the penis in her hand, kiss it and lick it with her tongue as she strokes the shaft. Under the most difficult circumstances gentle intermittent suction with the woman's lips pressed tightly around the tip of the penis can be dramatically effective. In resistant cases, sometimes *very* gentle nipping of the loose skin on the undersurface of the penis can be rewarding.

Perineal Stimulation

For some men stimulation of the area behind the testicles, (called the "perineum") can provide just the extra boost that nudges the sexual reflexes into action. The exact explanation is not clear, but from a practical point of view it seems to work for many men. If the woman strokes and tickles this area at the same time she is caressing the penis or performing fellatio, the chances of a good hard erection are increased. For some men *gentle* use of the vibrator at that spot gives better results.

The next technique of PSR hinges on stimulating the "Third Sexual Organ."

Is there such a thing as the "Third Sexual Organ"?

Yes, there is—and it's the most neglected one of all. Men rarely use more than 2 percent of their third sexual organ, while women use about 6 percent of theirs. The average person has about 2,800 square inches of this largely unexploited sexual organ and it goes under the name of *skin.* For sexual purposes, most men use only the 56 or so square inches that cover the penis and testicles. Women, being more versatile, take advantage of the sexual potential of the cutaneous covering of the breasts as well as the clitoris, labia majora, and labia minora—that gives them the 4 percent edge. From the erotic point of view, for most people the rest of the skin is just something to look good in. But for those men who want a way out of impotence, the "Third Sexual Organ" has possibilities.

What kind of possibilities?

Well, just because the skin is *non-genital* doesn't mean it's *non-sexual*. As every high school girl who has spent any time in the back seat of a car will testify, there is plenty of erotic excitement available from the inner surfaces of the thighs, the ears, the lower abdomen, the lips, the buttocks, and nearly every other area of the human skin. (Even the *male* breast can be turned on as a sexual receptor.) A powerful weapon against absolute impotence is PSR directed toward getting the most out of the skin.

How does a woman go about it?

By using the favorite methods of the ancient Greeks and Romans—not to mention the proprietors of modern massage parlors. All it takes is a simple lubricant—mineral oil is fine —a warm place, and an eager and inquisitive pair of feminine hands. There are no specific instructions—under the magic spell of massage, every one's erotic zones will quickly stand up and cheer. One word of warning: the amateur masseuse is exposed to the same occupational hazards as the professional lady massager. They include lustful thoughts, wandering male hands, and the risk of being suddenly invaded by a throbbing penis. But then, that's the whole idea, isn't it?

Is it really worthwhile going to all that trouble just for an erection?

Ask the man who can't have one. In these overautomated times so many of us have come to think of *human* responses as being cook-book responses:

Get into bed, place your left hand on your husband's penis, he places his right index finger at the entrance to your vagina. Wait fifteen seconds.

Then place penis *in* vagina and agitate continuously for three minutes or less. Allow penis to overflow. Remove, set aside, and let cool a week to ten days. Then repeat. Guaranteed to work every time.

Maybe it works with cake mixes, but not with the fragile sexual responses of living human beings. Anything (within reason) that contributes to the sexual happiness of men and women is worthwhile. Allowing a man to have an erection seems to be one of the items at the top of the list.

What else can help an erection?

Stuffing

In recent years a dozen models of external splints for limp penises have appeared. For all practical purposes, a man might as well encase his penis in a plaster cast. Actually, there's a safer, more effective way. It's called "stuffing." It works pretty well.

This remedy for impotence depends on two often-over-looked facts of sexuality. First, *the most powerful sexual stimulant is sexual intercourse itself.* And secondly, *the penis doesn't have to be erect to enter the vagina.* Stuffing is so simple—and effective—that almost everyone who tries it has the same reaction:

"Doctor, it's so easy. Why didn't I think of it myself?

"My wife and I did it just the way you described. To start, I made sure she was sexually aroused enough so that she wouldn't lose interest while I was getting ready. Then I got in position above her and she helped me stuff my soft penis carefully into her vagina. We found that it helped if she kept her legs wide apart and we used a *little bit* of lubrication. Then she closed her legs tightly, pulled me close to her, and started slow rhythmic pelvic thrusts. It was amazing!"

"What do you mean?"

"As usual, when we started, my organ was as limp as canned spaghetti, but the heat and the moisture and the friction of her vagina slowly brought on an erection. I mean, it wasn't hard like a rock but it was the best I've had in months. But that's only half the story."

"What's the other half?"

"I didn't manage to reach a climax that time—I guess it was all too new to me. But maybe because I had half an erection or maybe because she did all the work herself, my wife had her first orgasm in more than a year. And things keep getting better as time goes on. My erections get firmer and my wife responds a little more each time."

What can a man do who has copulatory impotence?

Plenty. First of all he is halfway to his goal—and that's a big improvement. He has an erection—he just can't make it stick. He can insert his penis into the vagina but he can't keep it rigid long enough to bring on either his climax or his partner's. Predictably, a lot of copulatory impotence occurs in young men. Their inner emotional conflicts are not quite strong enough to completely extinguish the roaring sexual fires of the early twenties. Tim is typical:

"Doctor, I thought sailors were supposed to be great lovers. I've spent three years stationed in Hawaii and I might as well be in Greenland for all the good it's doing me. Am I finished at the age of twenty-two?"

"That's not very likely. What's the problem?"

"It goes like this. I meet a girl in a bar, for example. Just talking to her or looking at her body gives me a super-hard

168

erection. Later on when we're getting into bed, I masturbate myself a little bit just to feel the end of my penis wet. Besides, it seems to get them excited seeing me do it. But—and this is the *big* but—as soon as I·slide up inside her, I lose all my hardness in a few moments. Then when I pull out, I get hard again. Then I slip it in again and I go soft. It's like I want to do it but my penis doesn't. Half the time I end up masturbating myself right then and there just to calm down."

Tim has related the inner story of copulatory impotence. He wants intercourse but his penis doesn't. Everything is fine until the moment when he is going to *feed the baby*. If he wants his penis to perform like it should—where it should—there's one thing he has to do. He has to understand the *emotional* reason for its misbehavior.

What's the emotional reason for copulatory impotence?

Back to that penis-breast relationship that is engraved in the unconscious mind of every adult male. In copulatory impotence the man-baby is not quite so eager for revenge. He is willing to deliver a big fat breast-penis to the eager mouthvagina—until halfway through the process of feeding-copulation he remembers what may have happened during the first six months of his life. He hurriedly deflates his penis to avoid the risk of giving milk-sperm. He gives up his pleasure, but more important to him, he deprives his woman of orgasm —and milk. Every man with impotence is a sexual kamikaze —deliberately (but unconsciously) crashing his chance at sexual satisfaction against the pubis of his dismayed partner.

What does he have to do to **overcome** *copulatory* impotence?

He has to take the self-destruction out of sex by giving up the baby game of penis-vagina revenge. A good start might be to tell himself—from the first moment he meets his girl of the evening: *"I am not going to snatch away the penis-breast just as my 'baby' is getting ready to drink."*

Will that work for sure?

When it comes to the abstract realm of human emotions there is no such thing as "sure." In great measure, medical and psychiatric treatments work if the recipient wants them to work. That decision is buried deep, deep within the twisting byways of each individual's mind. However, these self-applied psychiatric interpretations have a better chance of closing the emotional gap and restoring potency than anything else short of full-scale psychiatric treatment. They have helped thousands of patients and have the potential for helping millions more.

Since copulatory impotence is virtually the second cousin to absolute impotence, Positive Sexual Reinforcement can help prolong and strengthen the erection. For some men, that's all it takes. Simply proving to themselves that they have the potential for flawless performance acts like a sexual tonic that lasts and lasts and lasts. Mike describes it:

"Well, I'm not as young as I used to be. I was forty-nine last month and I've been starting to have the problem you describe. I can start intercourse okay but I can't always finish it. I just seem to run out of gas—or whatever you call it. My wife, Marcia, has been watching me go through it, although she never said anything—that's the way she is.

"Last night she said she wanted to go to bed early. I didn't think much of it and when I went in the bedroom to get undressed, she was just coming out of the bathroom. She had on this shorty nightgown and her hair was all let down and she was wearing this perfume. Well, I hadn't seen her that way in about fifteen years.

"When we got into bed, it was a brand new Marcia. Why she had tricks up her sleeve I never even imagined she knew about. Let me tell you, I went back three times for more and I barely got up in time to make my appointment with you. Impotence? Not as long as I have a wife like that!"

Mike is lucky. Other men will have to deal more directly with the emotional elements in copulatory impotence before they will be able to do sexual handsprings again.

In impotence, the physical function of copulation has been commandeered by the pirates of inner emotional conflicts. Attacking them with their own weapons aimed at the specific conflict is an effective way of becoming captain of the sexual ship once and for all. That particularly applies to premature ejaculation.

What about premature ejaculation?

Prostitutes love it, most wives and girl friends hate it, and a lot of men who have it suffer from mixed feelings. As one unhappy young lady summed it up:

"The only good thing you can say for premature ejaculation is that it doesn't take too long."

Sexually speaking, premature ejaculation is too much of a good thing. A hard erection, a lot of excitement, a penis plunged into the waiting vagina, instant orgasm (ten seconds to one minute, average), a self-conscious smile, a mumbled apology, and another lovely evening splashed down the drain.

What's the treatment for premature ejaculation?

There are plenty of treatments—most of them unexciting. The classical approach is to anoint the overanxious penis with an anesthetic ointment. This is supposed to cut down on sensation and postpone ejaculation. One chap who tried it reported:

"Doctor, I used some of that ointment the druggist recommended last night for my premature ejaculation. I wouldn't exactly call it a complete success. I followed the instructions exactly; as soon as I got an erection I squeezed some of that salve on my penis. That was my first mistake. The minute I began to rub it in—I came."

Putting the penis to sleep isn't the solution—waking up the brain makes more sense.

Another common treatment for premature ejaculation is using extra-thick condoms to dull sensation and delay orgasm. A disappointed user remarked:

"Doc, I've tried everything. I've used condoms so thick they made my penis bulletproof. The only thing I haven't tried is aluminum foil because I can't find a girl who'll hold still for it."

Armor-plating the penis doesn't seem to work because the instant ejaculation comes from the brain—not the skin of the penis. Some of those dauntless sex researchers who toil endless hours in gleaming laboratories have come up with probably the most unexciting treatment for premature ejaculation yet developed. It consists of instructing the lady to masturbate her premature partner almost to the point of orgasm, then suddenly grab the tender end of his swollen penis and squeeze—*hard.* Instead of curing the terrified male of premature ejaculation, it may cure him of *any* ejaculation. Even less exciting is the prospect of haunting side streets looking for women who get their kicks from penis-pinching.

Far more humane—and much more effective—is the ancient Chinese technique for indefinitely delaying the explosive moment of ejaculation. Used properly, it can allow even the most anxiety-ridden instant-ejaculator to prolong intercourse almost indefinitely.

How is it done?

Gently. From the first moment of erection, the woman grasps her partner's testicles carefully—and avoids touching his penis in any way. She then slowly steers his erection toward and into the vagina, using the testicles as a "handle." If he gives any sign of an impending orgasm, she simply pulls downward—slowly and tenderly. After the crisis passes, she lets up and he begins pelvic thrusts again.

How does the man feel about this maneuver?

Listen to what one of them says. Mark is a young dentist who has been married for six years, five and a half of them unhappy:

"Doctor, when I first heard you describe that cure for prematurity, it sounded to me like that sadist-masochist scene you wrote about. You know, girls in leather suits, whips, and all that sort of thing. I couldn't even get my wife to try it—I guess she felt the same way I did.

"Finally I said, 'Listen, Karen, you don't want me to be a "hot-shot" all my life, do you?' And it was really that bad, Doctor. Things had gotten to the point that the harder I tried to hold back, the faster I would come. I'll never forget the night that made up my mind."

Mark winced, then shrugged, and went on:

"I'd finally resolved that I just had to control myself. I got all psyched-up long before bed time. I was going to overcome my problem once and for all. I had a good erection. Karen was as quiet as could be, I put it in, and we both held perfectly still for about a minute. I whispered to her, 'I think this time's going to be different!' She whispered, 'I hope so!' and squeezed my arm."

"Then what?"

"Then, I came." He smiled grimly. "But the very first time

we tried that testicle technique, it really worked! Even if I'd been a bull elephant in heat, I couldn't have done a thing. I just couldn't believe it the way I kept from climaxing for thirty minutes until Karen was on the brink of having her first orgasm—the regular way—since we were married. When she felt it coming on, she let go of my testicles, grabbed me real tight and whispered in my ear . . ."

Mark paused, flushed, and then went on:

"Well, anyhow we both came at the same moment—like two sweating volcanoes. Wow! I never imagined sex could be that good!"

What about the emotional basis of prematurity?

The chap who ejaculates too soon is engaging in an ironic variation on the mother-baby-milk-sperm theme. Only in his case the unconscious logic is flawless—apparently. He says, "Look, I'm not refusing to feed that little mouth-vagina. I'll give it all the milk-sperm it can drink."

Then with a sly smile he adds: "Uh, it's not *my* fault if it spills before she can lap it up."

The antidote to premature ejaculation is to make the following decision: *"I will no longer insist on spilling the milk before my 'baby' can drink it."*

If the man can get this concept clearly in his mind a few minutes before intercourse—and make sure it stays in focus as his penis enters the vagina—he will go a long way toward overcoming prematurity. If he adds the testicular maneuver, his chances of normal intercourse increase immensely.

What about the fellows who take too long to ejaculate?

You mean the ones who believe it's "more blessed to give than to receive" orgasm? A man with retarded ejaculation typically begins with a rock-hard penis and keeps it that way. Even after an hour or two, it's as if he just got started. In fact, these men with semipermanent erections may become professional copulators. Society ladies with orgasmic impairment, wealthy widows who can afford the best of everything, and discerning nymphomaniacs all beat a path to their beds. But it isn't so much fun for the gentlemen. Sexually speaking, they operate a nonprofit enterprise. To make matters even more frustrating, most delayed ejaculators climax promptly by masturbation. It's as frustrating as the baseball player who has no trouble hitting a home run—as long as it's during batting practice.

What's the solution to his problem?

Intensifying the stimulation by PSR usually doesn't do much good; it may increase the force of the erection but that's rarely a problem. The most effective approach is to deal with the underlying emotional problem directly. The delayed ejaculator is playing this unconscious game: *"I refuse to feed milk to any 'baby.' Period."*

The message that every man with retarded ejaculation needs to get to his brain—and ultimately his penis—is this one: *"I will eagerly feed milk to my hungry 'baby.'"*

Thinking about this idea before intercourse is not quite enough for the delayed ejaculator. He must remind himself over and over again throughout the entire sexual experience that bestowing his milk on his partner is the most important thing in the world to both of them. He should also keep in mind during copulation that by giving up a little sperm, he gets a gigantic orgasm in return. In that sense, ejaculation is only a small investment that pays a 1,000 percent return—nontaxable. If he is willing to deal conscientiously with his problem at this deepest of all emotional levels, he has an excellent chance of success.

Then any man can overcome his impotence?

Almost any man can overcome his impotence. There is a minority whose problems are basically physical and there is a small group who wear impotence like a badge—and wouldn't give it up for anything. But for the majority, restoration to vigorous satisfying sexual performance only depends on their personal decision. With determination, hard work, and the love of a devoted woman 'virtually any man can become *and remain* dramatically potent to the age of seventy, eighty, and beyond. Most men, if they had the choice, would want it that way. The good news is: most men *have* that choice—all they have to do is exercise it.

9

HOMOSEXUALITY

Why does anyone decide to become a homosexual?

That's the fascinating part of it—hardly anyone ever *decides* to become a homosexual. It just happens. Often a teen-ager slowly develops the vague awareness that he or she is "different." For many of them it is unsettling, confusing—even frightening:

"I'm sixteen and I think I might be going crazy. Whenever I go out with girls, I always get really excited by watching the rear ends of the other guys. Is this a common problem?"

And, "My name is Sandra and I'm fifteen and I have a homosexual problem. I wish I didn't want girls to touch me. I wish I could fall in love with boys again the way I did in the sixth grade."

Then what happens to young homosexuals?

Then the incipient homosexual stands at the cross roads of his (or her) sexual destiny. Some of them select that moment to "come out"—to make the dramatic decision to undertake life as a practicing homosexual. It's a hard choice for most:

"I'm a freshman in college and something weird is happening to me. When I was nine I had a grown-up cousin who used to sleep with me and masturbate against my body. I never told anyone because I was scared of him. Then in high school I had one or two homosexual experiences with a friend but I immediately regretted them. I was in love with this wonderful girl and we planned to get married, but now here's my problem.

"There's one guy in my fraternity who's like a brother to me. We've had a lot of physical contact—you know patting on the arm or knee and wrestling matches. One day his roommate was out and he said, 'Come on, lay down with me.' I did, and pretty soon we had our hands all over each other. Then he climbed on top of me and before we knew it we had made a mess. The next morning we sort of looked at each other and smiled and said, 'That was quite an experience.' Then I broke up with my girl because I found out what real love for a person was. It's not that we just loved each other's penis, but we loved *each other.*

"Now after vacation he says he's met someone else and he feels different about me and we hardly speak. We used to kiss like lovers, and he even gave me a hickey and I was proud of it. Even though he hurt me, I still love him and I even sucked him a couple of times after that but I never got a satisfying reaction on his part. This experience with him has shattered me."

Do female homosexuals start the same way?

They can. For some young lesbians it goes like this:

"I met this girl at work last summer and we had this crazy relationship. Her husband was away and she asked me to stay with her because she was afraid to be alone. She only had one bed so we slept in it together. The first night she tried to get close to me but I told her 'no' and she didn't try it again. But gradually we fell in love, and one night when she was asleep I couldn't control myself and I made love to her. I put my finger inside her and ate her and everything I had been dying to do, but she pretended to be asleep all the time.

"Finally we went to a drive-in movie one night and in the next car we saw this girl sucking on another girl's breasts and she hugged me and said, 'I know that's what you like.' I was embarrassed but I knew she was right. Then we went right home and she sucked me and gave me the finger and sucked my breasts and I did all that to her and we told each other how much we loved each other. And this time she didn't pretend she was asleep. But the next week her husband came home and she got afraid. I can't see her anymore and my boy friend left me because he found out I was sleeping with her. I can't live not seeing her—she's like a goddess to me. That may sound stupid to you, but she has a beautiful soul inside.

"I guess I'm a homosexual but I live with pain all the time. It's worse than having a knife in your heart. The thought of holding her kills me because she held me so softly and kissed me so softly."

What causes homosexuality?

And What Is the Meaning of Life? The question of why men copulate with men and women copulate with women is among the most elusive riddles of human behavior. To begin with, there are some things that homosexuality is *not:*

1. Homosexuality is *not* a hereditary condition. A hundred years ago medical science explained most complicated situations by putting the blame on the genetic defects of Great Grandpa and Great Grandma—who were never around to defend themselves. These days enough is known about genetics to confirm that homosexual traits are not transmitted from parents to children. Besides, since homosexuals engage in heterosexual intercourse so rarely, it would be hard to produce enough little homosexuals to replenish the supply.

2. Homosexuality is *not* a hormonal or glandular problem. That was another popular nineteenth-century explanation. Any condition that baffled the experts was called "glandular" since no one knew anything much about glands anyway. In spite of years of tinkering with male and female sex hormones by researchers no one has been able to significantly stop or start homosexual behavior by giving or taking away sex hormones.

3. Homosexuality is *not* what everybody should be in the first place. There is a small but dedicated group of ladies and gentlemen who insist that everyone is fundamentally homosexual and only those of us who "deny our true nature" become heterosexual. By identical reasoning all of us are fundamentally cannibals and only those of us who deny our true nature eat hamburgers and hot dogs instead of each other.

But then what causes homosexuality?

As in every other complex human problem, all the returns aren't in. However, there are some compelling clues drawn from the common experiences of many homosexuals that point to a common emotional pattern. So many homosexuals, for example, absorbed more suffering and rejection as children than ten heterosexuals experience in a lifetime. The stories many of them tell are truly heartrending:

"These are some of my thoughts on my homosexuality for whatever use you might have for them. Being a homosexual is not so good really—I just don't know what to do about it. Tomorrow I start with my fourth psychiatrist, but I'm just going because my mother is forcing me to. If I don't go they'll hassle me until I have to go out of self-defense. They never allow me to disagree with them or even contradict them. I can't leave my mother because somehow I still love her."

"But I hate and despise all women! I'd like to put them all in a concentration camp so they couldn't emasculate me anymore."

"I can never remember being straight, and I knew I had to satisfy what was there. Even though I was scared and ashamed, I finally got up the courage to do it. I even enjoyed the 'whore stage'."

What's the "whore stage"?

When they finally "come out" into the "gay world," many (but not all) homosexuals become eager contestants in the Erotic Olympics. Since they are usually young and in demand, they swing from one partner to another and set new records for ejaculations-per-day (or occasionally per-hour). Generally they settle down to a more sedate level of sexual consumption, although a minority never lose their youthful enthusiasm. But let's go back to that letter.

"The only trouble was that it passed and I became more discriminating. I wanted a lover but I wanted one that looked like the Marlboro Man. When I finally found him it was great—while it lasted. After eight fantastic hours he said:

'This is just a one-night-stand, kid. Now smile, or I'll hit you . . .' Later on he got serious with someone else himself and I had to laugh when the same thing happened to him. But I'm getting older—I'm thirty now and I still look good. I've started to wear a lot of leather and I'm still as passionate as I am lonely. And whenever a woman touches me I feel like I should take a bath. *C'est la vie! Au revoir.*"

Lesbians can have the same experience:

"I think you might want to know about how I became a lesbian—now that I am forty-four and can look back on it. My mother always told me that sex was dirty, and when I was seven my grandfather proved it to me. Whenever I was alone with him he undressed me and masturbated me and once or twice tried to put his penis in. When I started to menstruate my mother told me to stay away from boys. By then I was so terrified I would have anyhow. When I got to be seventeen I met a wonderful teacher in high school who taught me the meaning of love and sex. Even though she was twenty years older than I was, I still loved her. I always thought of her as rescuing me from my mother and grandfather, although there have been several other women who did the same thing for me. Sometimes I feel guilty, but then who doesn't?"

Is it true that homosexuality is caused by dominant mothers and weak fathers?

Yes and no. This is the "yes" part:

"When I got married I never expected to deal with a problem like this. My younger brother is a homosexual and I sort of 'grew up' with his gay friends. I always thought I was more tolerant as a result, but then a few months ago my seven-year-old son was molested by a homosexual. Since then I've thought of homosexuals—rightly or wrongly—as 'filthy perverts.' Whenever I saw one of my brother's friends I found myself wondering whose innocent child they had defiled. Now I am terrified that my own boy—the one who was molested—is becoming a homosexual. He seems effeminate and insecure, and I am a domineering mother. The obvious answer is for me to change, but that's part of my make-up and I don't think I can do it. I am noisy and bossy and my husband is quiet and introverted. I don't want my son to go the way of my brother and I just hope I can get myself under control in time."

Other mothers are less profound:

"I just found out that my twenty-two-year-old son is a homosexual. His brother, who is twenty-eight, also went the same way. I know that I am to blame, so to prevent him from ruining his life I know what I have to do. I am sure if I just get him interested in girls and normal sex he will see the light. Tonight I am planning to seduce him, if possible, and in that way try to lead him to a normal heterosexual life."

Is that a good solution?

Substituting incest for homosexuality? Hardly. It simply illustrates the pattern of thought and desperation of one mother of a male homosexual. What's the "no" part about dominant mothers causing homosexuality? Just this. A lot of heterosexuals have tough, overpowering mothers—and cream-puff fathers—and they never waver for a moment from penis-vagina sex. Even in the same family one child may grow up straight and another homosexual. It's like mixing up two cakes at the same time, using identical ingredients. When they come out of the oven one turns out to be a coffee cake and the other one is a lemon meringue pie.

Can psychiatrists help homosexuals?

Yes, no, and maybe. On any given Monday morning of the year there are about as many concepts of psychiatry as there are psychiatrists. Some of them insist that homosexuality is an emotional problem, then go on to classify it as an *incurable* emotional problem. That doesn't leave a homosexual much to look forward to. Other psychiatrists offer to treat homosexuality rather energetically—some homosexuals complain it's too energetic. These are the practicioners who recommend electro-shock treatment to the brain, lobotomy (removal of certain pieces of brain tissue), and aversion therapy.

What's aversion therapy?

Basically it consists of taking the fun out of homosexuality. They take the penis of a homosexual and hook it up to an electric shock machine. Then they provide him with homosexual pornography. When his penis stiffens, he gets a shock —and a *big* one. After enough experiences like this, most homosexuals develop homosexual impotence. To many with the problem it sounds more like punishment than treatment and has few fans among the gay guys. On the other hand, one homosexual with a sense of humor insisted that after taking the treatment, every time he pays his electric bill he gets an erection.

But, in general, these are techniques of desperation. Psychiatric treatment of *any* kind can only help the homosexual who wants to be helped. That boils down to two categories of homosexual: those who suffer as a result of their homosexuality, and more importantly those who are anxious to give up their homosexual way of life. But no homosexual can be "converted" against his will—there is no magic way to make a man's penis stand up for a girl and lie down for a man. In the same way, lesbians cannot be involuntarily programed to develop palpitations for a football player and become indifferent to the girl under the next hair dryer.

Besides, there are some homosexuals who are apparently delighted with things the way they are:

"Most psychiatrists tell us that we are emotionally mixed up or some other idiotic statement. Didn't it ever occur to you that some people prefer Fords to Cadillacs and that some men prefer other men to women? Homosexuality can no more be cured than heterosexuality because there is nothing to cure. Both are natural."

And there are others who *aren't* so delighted:

"I am a homosexual. Moreover I am a closet queen, as you so candidly note. To say that I am miserable would be an understatement. Three suicide attempts have only brought me to the realization that the escape I am looking for is happiness in married life with wife and children. My only sexual outlet is now gone, but I no longer have to live in the make-believe homosexual world—a place that I don't belong. I am ready to do better than that."

And, "I don't know where I ever got the nerve to write you but I want to be a normal man. Every night when I go to sleep I hope that I will wake up in the morning desiring a girl."

The ingredients for successful psychiatric treatment of homosexuality are these:

1. a homosexual (male or female) who desperately wants to renounce his (or her) homosexuality
2. an experienced resolute psychiatrist who is dedicated to do better than make his patient more than a "happy homosexual"
3. a lot of hard work
4. a sizable dose of good luck

But even if every homosexual in the country decided he wanted to become a card-carrying heterosexual, there would still be problems.

What kind of problems?

Well, there are an estimated eight million active homosexuals in the United States. There are probably less than one hundred psychiatrists who are motivated to devote themselves to specializing in the treatment of homosexuals. Even if only half the homosexuals wanted to give psychiatry a try, each doctor would acquire a patient load of approximately forty thousand patients. Assuming they saw each homosexual for only five visits for evaluation, each psychiatrist would get to the last patient on his list *one hundred years later.* A one-hundred-and-fifty-year-old psychiatrist treating a ninety-six-year-old homosexual is probably the classical exercise in futility.

All in all, the homosexual's lot is not a happy one. He faces massive rejection by heterosexual society, exploitation by other members of the homosexual community, and from time to time, oppressive inner conflicts. The net result can be a heavy burden of guilt, anxiety, and depression. Some of them try desperate solutions, like an impulsive switch to heterosexuality:

"I've been going with this boy for two years and at first we got along real well. But for the past seven months he gets really mad if I even kiss him. Last night he confessed that he was homosexual. Should I still go around with him or would it hurt my reputation?"

Other girls are somewhat more sympathetic:

"One day I found some passionate love letters in Tom's, my fiancé's, car. I got very angry to think he had another girl friend—until he admitted that they were from his *boy friend.* He told me he had been homosexual since he was fourteen and really wanted to change but just couldn't make it. All along I had been telling myself how lucky I was that he never insisted on sex before we got married. Now I don't feel so lucky. I want to help Tom more than anything else, but now he's gone to live with his boy friend. I guess that's better than losing him to another girl, but I just don't know."

Fleeing to a hasty marriage can be even more disappointing:

"I don't even know how to describe the nightmare I find myself living. I am in my early thirties—married seven years with four children. Last Saturday I came home from the supermarket early and found my husband in our bed with another man. They were masturbating each other. I staggered out of the house in a daze and when I came back two hours later he and his 'lover,' as he calls him, were gone. Thank God, because I had a gun and I was planning to kill them both."

"My husband confessed that he has been 'gay' since he was fourteen and has never stopped even after we were married. He is willing to see a psychiatrist but he insists that he doesn't want to give up his homosexuality. I wish I had never met him or had his children. As soon as I mail this letter I am going to take the children and leave him to all his faggot friends before his sickness poisons us all."

From a practical point of view it makes sense to put aside old debates about homosexuality and get down to the real problem: helping homosexuals find whatever happiness is available to them.

What's the best way to help homosexuals?

It all begins by understanding what life as a homosexual is like. Once the average homosexual "comes out," goes through the "whore stage," and recognizes the reality of his sexual destiny, he gets down to the business of finding his place in the homosexual community. That isn't as easy as it might seem because there are, if anything, too many choices.

How many choices does a homosexual have?

Enough to meet the tastes, aspirations, and resources of virtually every homosexual. Starting from the bottom up:

Homosexual prostitutes

Generally mistrusted and feared by homosexuals, they offer customers an array of instant sex. Most hustlers, if they had a list of services, could offer:

"Masturbation to your order."
"Anal intercourse, your place or mine."
"Fellatio, 'do' or 'done'."
"Anilingus (oral-anal sex)."

Some homosexual prostitutes style themselves as "trade." They offer the "john" two choices: he can fellate the hustler or be anally penetrated by him. That makes some male prostitutes feel better about what they're doing because they don't really consider themselves to be homosexuals—they tell themselves they're just making some "easy money." But dedicated homosexuals know better—or as the saying goes, "Today's Trade [masculine-appearing homosexual prostitute] is tomorrow's Queen [ultra-effeminate male homosexual]." And only too often it comes true. "Love affairs" between prostitutes and customers are extremely rare—unlike heterosexual men, when it comes to commercial sex, homosexuals are hard-headed realists.

A step up from frank homosexual prostitution is the "tearoom."

What's a "tea-room"?

First of all it isn't a place where a weary homosexual goes to sip a warm cup of tea and nibble on a crumpet. "Tea-rooms" are public toilets where homosexuals meet each other for a few moments of rather frantic activity. And a lot of things can go on in the typical tea-room.

Some men go there simply to suck penises, while others are on hand to be sucked. A smaller number visit the public toilet to engage in anal intercourse, either as the donor or recipient. Some men go just to watch the festivities and masturbate in the process. (Although a few of those become so excited that they later take part.) Others are simply Peeping Toms of the homosexual variety who look but don't touch—themselves or anyone else. And, of course, there are always those solid citizens, the heterosexuals, who keep dropping in to answer the call of nature—and incidentally interrupt the proceedings.

Don't normal men get propositioned by the homosexuals?

Not deliberately—at least not by any homosexual in his right mind. Engaging in homosexual acts in a place as public as the comfort station in the park is about as hazardous as having heterosex on a tightrope over Niagara Falls. The police department does its best to make it even more hazardous, and homosexuals have a complex unwritten security system. It works like this:

A homosexual who wants to be fellated walks up to one of the urinals and in an obvious way fondles his penis. If a homosexual at another urinal is willing to fellate, he responds by playing with his own penis. A homosexual who wants to *perform* fellatio sits down on one of the toilets and waits impatiently until he is approached by another man with an erection.

Ironically, the public washrooms where the doors are removed from the toilet compartments have made life somewhat more hazardous for those who are there on strictly gastrointestinal missions. So, gentlemen, if you don't want any surprises, stride in resolutely, do your business expeditiously, and leave briskly. Or better yet, make sure you go before you leave home. The next source of homosexual gratification is "cruising."

What's cruising?

Cruising is a way of letting the world of homosexuality know that you are ready, willing, and able to play the game. The "cruiser" roams the streets, parks, and bars, offering his sexual resources to his companion for the evening. And like everything else, cruising goes on at many levels simultaneously. Some homosexuals, known as "bush queens," cruise in the park for a fast fellation in the shrubbery. Others cruise the beach for an instant orgasm on the sand, weather permitting. The mainstay of those who cruise is the "gay bar." Just as there are "straight bars" for every taste and pocketbook, there are gay bars for every level of homosexual—from the alcoholic derelict to the affluent businessman.

Each homosexual bar is its own little world. Some specialize in "rough trade"—the homosexual ideal of super-masculinity—complete with big muscles, tattoos, grimy work clothes, and lots of leather. Milder-mannered homosexuals are often attracted to these bars primarily to fellate and be anally penetrated. Other gay bars attract a nucleus of young effeminate-appearing homosexuals who play host to "rough trade" or those who would like to *think* of themselves that way. There are homosexual motorcycle bars, homosexual bars that cater to self-styled sadists and masochists, gay bars that cater to transvestites, and, of course, lesbian gay bars.

What are the lesbian bars like?

They are much like any other all-girl bar. Generally there are two types of girls: the "femmes," or feminine lesbians, and the "butches," "dykes," and "bull dykes" (in order of ascending masculinity). The femmes are ultrafeminine, the butches are ultramasculine. In some ways lesbian bars seem to be less tense and more sedate than the typical gay bar. Occasionally there are arguments between two butches over a femme, but in a sense the atmosphere in the tavern mirrors some of the differences between male homosexuals and lesbians.

What are the differences between male homosexuals and lesbians?

Aside from the obvious ones, lesbians tend to be less flamboyant than their male counterparts. With the general exception of those who hold court in women's prisons—"jailhouse mamas"—the *average* lesbian maintains a low profile. Her relationship with her partner tends to last much longer than the male homosexual equivalent, since most lesbian relationships are not as overheated as other homosexual encounters, with more emphasis on emotions and less on specific sexual acts. For example there is less cruising and virtually no sex of the tea-room variety. (No sedate matron who stops in at the ladies room of her department store is likely to find one fellow-shopper copulating with another among the shopping bags.)

What exactly do lesbians do with each other?

The best they can under the circumstances. In contrast to male homosexuals, most lesbians begin their careers with the emphasis on hugging and kissing and, say, minor fondling of the breasts. As time goes on they graduate to mutual masturbation and cunnilingus. The use of the dildo—as dramatically featured in pornography—has declined lately among most lesbians. Mutual pubic rubbing is still very much in fashion, however. Anal interests, which loom so large in male homosexual circles, are small change in the currency of most lesbians.

How does a homosexual find a gay bar?

In most large cities, a better question is: "How does he avoid them?" Los Angeles, Chicago, San Francisco, Miami, and New York are the headquarters for gay establishments of all kinds. To get established as quickly as possible, all a homosexual newcomer has to do is consult the local "trade journal."

What's a "trade journal"?

There are several major homosexual tabloid newspapers that keep gay guys right up to date. Besides spotlighting the latest oppressions and raids against homosexuals, reporting homosexual weddings (but not homosexual divorces), and serving as a sounding board for homosexual opinion, they feature display ads of major homosexual bars. Just as important, they offer a wide selection of "health clubs." Of all the homosexual establishments that exist, the "health club" is one of the most popular.

Why is it so popular?

Not because homosexuals all want to stay so healthy. Our society being what it is, there is only one situation where men can associate with each other absolutely naked without getting arrested. If two gentlemen, or a dozen, get together for the purpose of swimming, massage, sunbathing, or sauna, no vice squad in the country is going to lift a finger. So, a certain proportion of Turkish baths, athletic clubs, and locker clubs are exclusively homosexual territory. Homosexuals can usually go there in absolute safety, the police ignore their existence, and obviously straight gentlemen are tactfully turned away.

Shouldn't those places be closed down?

Some people think so. But homosexuals will be homosexuals, and if they don't copulate and fellate in private clubs they will do it on the beach, in the park, in tea-rooms, and in even more obvious places. Harrassing homosexuals in the name of morality is a tempting sport but hardly pays any long-term dividends. On the other hand, it seems only fair that the same rules of discretion apply to all members of society. A man and woman who have intercourse in a public toilet (Ladies *or* Gents) are asking to be arrested. Female prostitutes who solicit are still violating the law—and offending the sensibilities of a lot of people. But arresting homosexuals who dilly-dally with each other behind the locked doors of their private clubs seems a waste of police resources that could be put to better use protecting the streets.

What goes on in the homosexual "health clubs"?

Everything. Typically, a homosexual enters, pays a fee (ranging up to $5) and gets a towel and a key to a tiny room. He undresses and then gets down to business.

He may simply lie naked on the cot in his cubicle and wait for some action. If he leaves the door open and lies on his back, that's a sign he wants to be fellated. If he lies on his stomach, he wants anal penetration. More actively inclined members cruise the halls selecting partners that appeal to them. Some "clubs" have "orgy rooms"—larger rooms with wall-to-wall mattresses for group sex. Other establishments feature such exotics as shallow heated pools, tropical gardens, and "Oriental massage." A few establishments have become classics among the homosexual community and acquire pet names like, "Our Lady of the Mists," "The Tubs," and simply, "The Baths." There are even special events. For example, the busiest day of the year at steam baths seems to be "Mother's Day." Most relationships that homosexuals strike up in "baths" are short-term, limited to an orgasm or two.

That's another contrast between lesbians and their male equivalents—relatively few male homosexuals establish exclusive sexual-emotional relationships that can be measured in years. Many male homosexuals insist that they "know of several," but the actual parties to the relationship are somewhat rarer. So far, lesbians have not flocked to "health clubs" and still tend to live together in their equivalent of "marriage." But gay bars and "baths" aren't right for every homosexual. Some meet their sexual objects at parties, in stores, and even are introduced by friends. For those who want to do it another way, there are homosexual computer dating, homosexual pen pals, and homosexual lonely hearts clubs. And of course there are the want ads. A few minutes spent perusing the gay classified columns opens up new worlds.

What are they like?

Like nothing else in the world. Here are a few examples, verbatim:

DID YOU EVER TRY IT? Joy Juice would have made the job easier. Totally safe for use anywhere on or in the body. Swallow it with no side effects. Order it today.

The same product column has something for lesbians too:

Ben-Wa—as featured in All Time National Best Seller. Women drift from orgasm to orgasm . . . Only $10.95.

But it's the personal columns that really let it all hang out:

EX-MARINE STUD MASTER—His Most Arrogant Masculine Majesty has lowly positions of boot and water slave open. I am longer than one foot. My slave must be young, tough, and dig on levis, dirty sex. Write in awe and respect.

What does that all mean?

Yes, a little translation is in order. This last is an ad by a "sadist" who wants a "masochist" to do little chores like lick his combat boots, pose in dirty levis, and allow himself to be teased with water, all as a preliminary to homosex. And there are fellows out there ready to play that role:

SPANKING AND PADDLING—Cute young white male likes good-looking butch guys who dig spanking and paddling, old bluejeans, boots, and dominance.

In the ads, most homosexual sadism and masochism is all in fun:

SADIST with leather toys and rack seeks male under 35 for pain and pleasure. Your limits respected. No fats, prudes, one-wayers, oldies, or trade.

The chap that answers that ad can look forward to a little foreplay out of the Marquis de Sade—without real blood being shed. But he will find a cold welcome if he is fat, prudish (yes, there are homosexual prudes too), insists on only one form of homosexual orgasm ("one-wayers"), is too old (or even *looks* too old), or qualifies as "trade."

Moving on, we find a fetish or two cropping up:

RUBBER CLOTHING LOVERS ATTENTION!—W/M loves rubber boots, raincoats, scuba wear, and ponchos.

That's probably the closest thing to the old joke about the fellow who fell in love with his galoshes. And speaking of footwear:

BAREFOOT GUYS—unusual desire to go barefoot in dirty streets or apartments then make love. Will worship young dirty bare feet.

Things can also get pretty heavy:

ORTHOPEDIC BRACE FETISH—I am looking for long leg and body braces for an S/M trip. I also need young guys who are paraplegics or amputees with similar interests.

Some of the ads are more conventional:

ATTRACTIVE white male seeks black male, effeminate ok, for fun with silk and satin clothing.

A few columns away someone else seems to be giving up their hobby:

SACRIFICE: Long white and gold sequin satin gown with matching feather boa. You won't believe the price. Not a mark on it.

Some of the ads might almost fit into straight publications:

I'm blond, slim, early thirties, attractive, intelligent, shy. I enjoy dancing by moonlight, evenings by the fire, sincerity. I want to be a friend to someone.

At the other end of the spectrum are a few ads that cause the mind to whirl:

GOOD-LOOKING SNOB seeks affluent male patron to create bizarre life, body, face; for example, 17th-century costumes, whole-body tattoo, Iron Boots and Iron Mask, I want to live a Gothic Tale.

Then too:

Young guinea pig available for experiments with steel, rubber, vacuum, hot wax, ice, and forced feeding.

With another mind-boggler for a finish:

LIKE your slaves cuddly, sir? Affectionate masculine dog-slave is ready to be collared and caged.

Does that mean all homosexuals are like that?

No, it doesn't. It does mean that some homosexuals are like that. And some are as conventional as the retired lady school teacher who lives down the block. There are so many separate "scenes" or subcultures available to homosexuals that it is hard to find one who has been in every possible homosexual role. However, in the course of their lives many homosexuals play many different parts in the drama of homosexuality. They may begin as young passive-effeminate boys—or as tougher-looking homosexuals called, "trade." A few years later they can casually switch roles as "trade" becomes "queen" and passive becomes less passive. (The second possibility is rarer, since the "queen" of super-feminine identification is usually considered the end-of-the-line among male homosexuals. "Aunties" have a tough time going "butch" again.) There is one near-constant in male homosexuality, however. As a man gets older he finds it harder and harder to find another man to suck his penis—without paying him for the service. Most middle-aged homosexuals find themselves forced into the role of sucking the penises of younger members of the clan—whether they like it or not.

Lesbians, as usual, have their own variations. Many of them are relatively stable in their unconsciously selected "roles," although occasionally a butch type will "drop the belt" and become a femme. Often lesbians find a position midway between butch and femme where they can straddle the sexual fence. They seem to be happiest there.

What about bisexuals?

It's hard to consider them a special category for obvious reasons. Most so-called bisexuals are people who copulate basically as homosexuals. On some occasions they do what the typical homosexual *doesn't* do—they have heterosex. For most of them their hearts are basically committed to homosexuality—and their genitals as well. If they feel better sailing under the flag of "bisexual," that's probably their business.

Is there any way a parent can tell if a child is developing into a homosexual?

That's always been a knotty problem and current fashions don't make it any easier. A sixteen-year-old boy with shoulder-length blond hair and tight pants makes many parents wonder which direction their son is pointed. And a seventeen-year-old daughter with short hair, no make-up, denim trousers and hiking boots, has given more than one mother sleepless nights. But that's not the real problem. Superficial styles of dress, hair, and footgear are just the frosting on the cake. A true fledgling homosexual (of either sex) can be homecoming queen or captain of the football team.

Actions speak louder than accessories. In evaluating incipient homosexuality, one of the key points to consider is intersexual relationships.

If a boy or girl over the age of sixteen or so has *no* budding socio-sexual relationships with the opposite sex, there is every *possibility* that a homosexual conflict is beginning to erupt.

Then every teen who gets along well with the opposite sex is free from the risk of homosexuality?

Not by a long shot. The *quality* of the relationship is just as important. A budding homosexual—and an acknowledged one as well—may maintain superficial heterosexual contacts. Especially with teen-agers, the boy who has a free-and-easy acquaintance with a lot of girls without the slightest emotional involvement with any one of them may well have an underlying homosexual problem. In the same way, a girl who is friendly with many boys, but relates to none of them, may not really be interested in boys. Another clue is age discrepancy.

What does age discrepancy reveal?

Sometimes it's the first hint of homosexual pairing-off. A fifteen-year-old boy who suddenly becomes attached to a twenty-three-year-old gas station attendant may be striking out in a new direction. A high school senior who spends all her free time with a forty-two-year-old widow just might have made the choice of her lifetime. There are other clues too.

What are some of the other clues to early homosexuality?

The most obvious ones. Homosexual books and pictures in the bottom drawer of the youngster's dresser and homosexual love letters under the mattress are obviously undeniable evidence. But most parents don't have to go that far—there's a simpler, more humane way. It consists of simply asking the question.

How does a parent phrase it?

Like this: "John, have you ever been concerned about homosexuality?" or "Judy, do you think you might be in love with another girl?" A son or daughter who is homosexual will rarely be embarrassed by honesty and directness about the subject—a teen-ager who doesn't have that problem ordinarily shrugs off the inquiry. In the case of the budding young homosexual who denies his situation, opening up the subject may be the first step in bringing everything out into the open.

Why is it important to "bring everything out into the open"?

Let Arthur answer that:

"Last night I finally came out, Doctor, at least as far as my parents are concerned. I had my first full homosexual experience about three years ago—let's see—that's when I was about sixteen and a half. Since then I've been terrified

200

that my mother and father would find out. I had all kinds of ideas about what they'd do to me, you know like calling the police or beating me up." Arthur smiled sheepishly.

"I guess that was all in my mind. A couple of weeks ago they sat me down for a 'little talk.' Mom said she found some gay magazines in my room, and they wanted to know if I was really that way. Boy, I started sweating and I denied everything. I said that the magazines belonged to a friend and I told them how sick I thought homosexuality was and all that. They didn't say much and we just all went out for dinner."

"And that was the end of it?"

"You know it wasn't. After that it was really on my mind and a couple of days later I just told them the truth—all of it. I told them about my chemistry teacher in high school, about the track coach at college, about what goes on at the beach in the summertime, and even about my few ugly experiences in the tea rooms. I think they took it pretty well —considering."

"Considering what?"

"Considering how hard it is for straight arrows to know how a gay person feels."

What can parents do to help a homosexual child?

It depends. Sometimes not very much—let Arthur continue:

"Well, of course they wanted to 'help' me and all that. But I don't particularly want to be helped—if that means giving up the gay life. I know it's not perfect, but that's the way I am, and I kind of like the excitement and the exotic feeling that I'm different from everyone else."

Helping a homosexual requires the active and enthusiastic cooperation of the helpee. The most Arthur's parents can do is exactly what they did—assure their son that they still love him and are willing to do anything within reason to help him.

What about the young homosexual who wants help?

That's a different problem, though not necessarily an easier one to solve. The basic task consists of finding a dedicated and understanding psychiatrist who is willing to devote the enormous amount of time and energy that the project requires. Then all the parents have to do is find some way to pay the bills, encourage their child when the going gets rough, and hope for the best.

What's the solution to homosexuality?

Homosexuality has been around a long time. It was considered enough of a problem in the Old Testament to merit the death penalty: "If a man also lie with mankind as he lieth with a woman, both of them have committed an abomination: they shall surely be put to death; their blood *shall be* upon them." (Leviticus 20:13)

Even that didn't seem to solve the dilemma. And in modern times putting homosexuals in jail simply for being homosexuals is also going out of style. There is an added touch of irony to that approach. Prisons are notoriously homosexual, and the homosexual prisoner is condemned to an exclusive diet of just that kind of sex he was put in jail for engaging in.

Every homosexual who seriously wants to renounce his or her homosexuality should be given the chance—and at a reasonable cost. Those homosexuals who are satisfied with their roles still deserve an opportunity to be treated for the unavoidable emotional hazards of the homosexual way of life. That includes their vulnerability to suicide and excessive exposure to the risk of VD. Homosexuals also need protection from other homosexuals who prey upon them, including blackmailers, robbers, and even murderers. The majority of homosexuals—both male and female—lead otherwise respectable and sedate lives. To persecute them for the way they are—or for the bizarre and disruptive behavior of a homosexual minority—doesn't seem to make sense.

At the same time, two hundred million heterosexuals have their rights too. Public homosexuality, seduction of children, and homosexual displays deliberately designed to offend others need to be discouraged and punished.

Most homosexuals who are honest will agree that homosexuality isn't exactly "Heaven on Earth"—and never will be. But homosexuals, as fellow human beings, deserve all the understanding we can spare.

10

VENEREAL DISEASE

***What's the number one health problem in the
United States?***

Gonorrhea. *Every year more Americans come down with
gonorrhea than any other contagious disease* (except, of
course, the common cold). In spite of our superhygienic
ultrasanitized obsession with cleanliness, we are infecting
each other with one of the nastiest of all known diseases
at a record rate. According to the Surgeon General of the
United States, who ought to know about those things,
*"Gonorrhea ranks first among reportable communicable
diseases and is out of control."* There are nearly *four million cases of gonorrhea every year*—but that's not the
worst part.

What's the worst part?

Just this: *the rate of infection is increasing 12 percent each year.* If that keeps up (and the population remains stable) *in less than eight years every man, woman and child in our country will be blemished with gonorrhea.* (We won't be the first—there are already some tropical nations where the VD infection rate runs over 90 percent.)

Where do these statistics come from?

The U.S. Public Health Service, The American Social Health Association, The American Medical Association, and other august bodies. And of course, the Surgeon General, who estimates that barely 15 percent of the cases of gonorrhea ever find their way into the official statistics. (That means that there is up to six times as much VD around as the official reports show.)

Why isn't something done about the problem of gonorrhea?

That's what a lot of people want to know:

"Doctor, please answer this question for me. I know that venereal disease is ravaging our young people. I read yesterday that a teen-ager comes down with gonorrhea every sixty seconds. I also know that so many men and women have gonorrhea that the government can't even count them. What I don't know is why are billions of dollars spent every year on such relatively rare diseases like cystic fibrosis, muscular dystrophy, and multiple sclerosis? Why not concentrate on stamping out a disease that sooner or later is going to infect all of us—*before* we all get infected?"

That's a good question, particularly since gonorrhea is a "simple" disease.

What's "simple" about gonorrhea?

"Simple" in the sense that there is an effective way to diagnose it, to cure it, and to prevent it. It can be diagnosed by a smear and/or culture from the penis or cervix, and there are a couple of one-dose antibiotic treatments that effectively cure it. But there are also some big obstacles that stand in the way of the battle against this form of VD.

What obstacles?

For one thing, the kind of people that get the disease. The three biggest targets for gonorrhea in our nation are teenagers, non-whites, and male homosexuals. Not by coincidence these are the three groups with the least clout in our society:

"I don't pretend to represent all non-white citizens, but many brothers and sisters agree with me. Instead of all this jive about welfare and all that, how about getting rid of all the VD that's around? When we were brought here as slaves we were clean people—now make us clean again."

Is VD that common among non-whites?

Take a look at the figures:

According to the Metropolitan Life Insurance Company's Statistical Bulletin (updated yearly), the comparison goes like this:

YOUNG *WHITE* MALES: about *5 percent* have gonorrhea
YOUNG *NON-WHITE* MALES: about *60 percent* have gonorrhea

Young non-white men also have about 25 times as much syphilis as young white men.

206

Why do non-whites have so much more VD than whites?

First of all, they don't actually have *that* much more VD. The statistics always show less gonorrhea and syphilis for whites because they generally go to private doctors. Non-whites are often treated in public clinics—where *every* case gets into the record books. To make matters worse the bulk of VD education programs are aimed at the obsessively clean middle-class white consumer—where the rate of VD is the lowest. That's like selling refrigerators to the Eskimos—who, incidentally, have VD problems of their own.

What kind of VD problems do the Eskimos have?

According to recent figures from the *Journal of the American Medical Association,* about 6 percent of all Eskimos are infected with gonorrhea—that's one situation where a parka gives no protection. And the Virgin Islands apparently have lost their virginity too, since over 7 percent of the residents are gonorrhea-ridden.

Atlanta, Georgia, takes the honors as the VD center of our nation, with approximately 15 percent of its citizens afflicted with gonorrhea. Our capitol, Washington, D.C., isn't far behind with an 11 percent rate of infection.

What about teen-agers and VD?

Because of fear of discovery many teen-agers avoid getting treated:

"I am thirteen years old and VD is a very frightening thing to me. Even if I am rather young, a little necking and petting now and then isn't entirely unknown. Last week I noticed this teeny-weeny bit of discharge right at my opening. Is treatment for VD available to everyone? Do I have to have my parents' consent? Would it be worth my trouble to get examined?"

Adult attitudes are not always reassuring:

"Doctor, it is difficult to understand how a man of your intelligence and learning can fail to see the connection between the present high incidence of VD and sexual permissiveness. Venereal disease is a *punishment*. It is nature's retaliation for man's desecration and pollution of a body which is meant to be kept clean."

That brings up the fascinating question of punishing the unborn infant with congenital syphilis, the innocent wife whose husband brings gonorrhea home from the sales convention, and those rare folks who get VD without sexual intercourse. Is the unborn baby collecting his "punishment" in advance?

Why do male homosexuals have so much VD?

For several reasons. First, male homosexuals are among the most sexually active members of our society. It is not unknown for a single male to have twenty or more sexual contacts in a given week—all with different partners and all men whom he has never met before. Of course, there are also homosexuals who confine their attentions to one or two partners at a time—but one extremely energetic homosexual can make up for a dozen less flamboyant brothers. Consider the mathematics. If an infected man has anal intercourse with twenty partners a week—and each one has contact with twenty more—at the end of the week, *there are four hundred new cases of gonorrhea*. If the same rate continues, the following week there are eight thousand new cases. In three weeks, there would be (theoretically) one hundred sixty thousand men infected with VD—all from one dedicated individual. (Fortunately, there are some natural barriers to that kind of dissemination. Some men have built-in immunity, others will treat themselves promptly, and a few will get sick and drop out of the chain.)

The second problem with homosexuals is that many of them are afraid to seek treatment. Barely 10 percent of active male homosexuals publicly admit their sexual tastes. The other 90 percent "pass" as heterosexual. That makes treatment difficult. There is no way that a professional football player can go to his coach with a case of rectal gonorrhea and still conceal his homosexuality. If a homosexual school principal in a small town, or a homosexual minister in a farm community, or a homosexual physician anywhere seeks treatment, he runs a high risk of being exposed. To make matters worse, gonorrhea of the rectum can be a relatively mild disease—and the pus that drips from the penis eventually goes away by itself, even without treatment. But the disease lingers on.

Physicians with the most experience in treating homosexuals estimate that anywhere from 10 to 77 percent of all male homosexuals have VD at any given time. The accurate figure probably falls somewhere in between—about 45 percent. In analyzing the figures it's important to remember that their high rate of VD is not a form of moral judgment—it is simply a reflection of their particular life-style. But there is one bright note on the homosexual VD scene. Some Gay Liberation clubs offer free VD testing at each of their meetings. Certainly "liberation" from VD is an important step on the road to progress. But the worst aspect of the raging epidemic of VD is that nothing effective is being done about it.

Isn't anything being done about the VD epidemic?

Oh, sure. It's an interesting exercise in futility known as "case-finding." It's something like looking for a black cat in a dark room in the middle of the night—after the cat has run away. It works something like this:

A man with gonorrhea goes to the doctor to be treated. The doctor then sends a form to the Public Health Department. A day or so later a fellow from the department comes out to interview the patient and ask him the name and address of each of his sexual partners and the date that intercourse took place. (Imagine how many gentlemen develop instant amnesia at that moment.)

Then the case-finder goes around to each of the sexual partners and asks them the same questions—and advises treatment for their diseases. He follows up a week or so later by making sure that they get treated.

What's wrong with that approach to VD?

Everything. Although the men and women who do this work are among the most dedicated of all public health workers, they are beaten before they start. Look at it this way. Barely 15 percent of cases of VD ever get reported to the Public Health Department. That alone makes case-finding a guaranteed failure. Then, married men and married women are reluctant to get the story of their extramarital escapades into *anybody's* files. And prostitutes, although only a minor factor in VD these days, don't rat on their customers.

The final blow to the case-finding technique for VD is the cost. Official estimates put it at $6.16 for a female case and $12.32 for a male case of VD. (Apparently the gents are more elusive than the ladies—or more active.) That averages out to about fifty million dollars a year for gonorrhea alone—and remember for that kind of money, no one has gotten treatment yet. Fifty million bucks just buys you a mailing list.

Even the U.S. Government seems to be getting the message, since the federal funds for case-finding have been cut dramatically.

What else is being done against VD?

The latest head-in-the-sand approach to the problem of syphilis and gonorrhea is the fruitless attempt to develop a vaccine. The theory is that everyone will some day line up for their VD vaccinations and then the disease will be no more. It's a beautiful theory but it overlooks one simple scientific fact.

Which fact is that?

A person who gets infected with syphilis or gonorrhea *rarely* develops immunity. A person who gets infected with polio, measles, whooping cough, and all the other vaccine-prevented diseases almost *always* develops immunity. That's the sole purpose of a vaccine—to trigger the body's immune defenses and erect an antibody wall against the disease. If an individual can't become immune to gonorrhea after exposure, there is virtually no way for the vaccine to work. Of course, that doesn't keep the researchers from trying—and every minute they labor, the meter is running. Recent estimates put the cost of a vaccine against gonorrhea alone at *two billion dollars*—and several more years.

That's another problem: what happens to the four million cases a year of gonorrhea while the vaccine is being researched? Do those millions and millions of people go on the waiting list?

The concept of a vaccine for VD is cumbersome, hazardous, expensive, and designed principally because of our prudish notions of sex.

What does prudishness have to do with venereal disease?

A lot. Syphilis and gonorrhea are unique in several ways.

They can be diagnosed easily, treated simply, and cured permanently. Vaccines are usually developed for diseases that cannot be easily diagnosed or effectively treated. Diseases like rabies, small pox, and polio *may* justify vaccines since they are potentially fatal and do not respond to antibiotics. The main purpose of an anti-VD vaccine seems to be extrascientific. With a vaccine, no one would have to go to the doctor, admit something as shocking as sexual intercourse, and be treated. With our breath already deodorized, our body hair chemically removed, our genitals sprayed with gardenia perfume, the ovulation of our women blocked by birth control pills, a plastic gizmo floating in each uterus, and men discreetly vasectomized, vaccination against VD is the last step to chemically prepare us for absolutely sanitary sex —if we can cough up two billion bucks and sit around watching our kids get infected for the next five years. And remember, the vaccine won't cure a single one of those four million cases. There's an easier way.

What's the easier way?

Virtually wipe out gonorrhea in *one* day. It's as simple as the National VD Day that was proposed in *Everything You Always Wanted to Know About Sex.* It consists of every American over the age of puberty taking an effective antibiotic on the same day. Several one-dose antibiotics with nearly 100 percent cure rates are available, nearly everyone infected on that day would be cured, and overnight gonorrhea would become virtually a medical curiosity. The idea got two kinds of reviews:

"Everything you said on the subject of VD made sense— especially National VD Day—but four years later VD is still going strong. What can I do to help stamp out this scourge? For awhile I toyed with the idea of walking to Washington as a protest, but somehow the image of a plump middle-aged housewife walking for the eradication of VD doesn't quite make it."

And, "Doctor, I am a fifteen-year-old girl and I think your solution for VD is perfect. I just want to know why National VD Day is not being done? Is it because people are afraid that if teen-agers are protected they will 'mess around' more? Most of my friends and I agree that we would not lower our standards just because we were safe from infection."

And, "Maybe your idea for a National VD was just a witty thought but it's really fantastic. You ought to go ahead with it. If you need any staff, I'll be there to help."

A local commander of a national veterans organization wrote to the national commander:

"I've known for some time that the national image of our organization has been deteriorating and have felt something must be done to get us back on the plane we should be in the public eye. I'm sure the best way to accomplish this is by giving service to our fellow Americans.

"If an organization as strong as ours backed National VD Day and took care of the necessary publicity and arranged for the clinics, antibiotics, and personnel, we could do the country a great service and at the same time raise the image of our organization.

"Incidentally, our chief of police is very enthusiastic about the idea and suggests that all prisoners be given the same type of treatment."

And finally a doctor put his finger on the real obstacle:

"Please don't laugh. What was the highest level in the chain of command that your recommendation reached in the Federal medical hierarchy or Public Health Service?"

What was the highest level National VD Day reached?

The President of the United States. It went like this:

"I followed your suggestion and wrote to President Nixon requesting him to inaugurate a program to eradicate VD through mass inoculation with penicillin. A reply came from the Assistant Surgeon General of the United States which I herewith enclose in the event that you would like to reply to him. . . ."

The letter concludes:

"I have written to politicians in the past concerning various issues and more often than not I received some printed pamphlet having nothing to do with my statements or questions, and I have vowed not to repeat my same old mistake. . . . This letter differs from others in that it is a direct and personal reply by an apparently qualified individual. Will you carry the ball the rest of the way?"

The reply follows:

"President Nixon has asked me to reply to your very thoughtful letter of October 20, 1970. The President and we in public health share your concern over the threat of venereal diseases.

"Many positive measures are being taken to find cases of both syphilis and gonorrhea, get them treated, and stop the spread of these diseases. However, despite the fact that proposals for widespread or universal injection of penicillin into the population have been made from time to time, this simply is not a practicable solution for a number of reasons, some of which follow:

1. Cost. While the penicillin cost alone might be relatively low, costs of mass administration of it would be prohibitive.

2. Sensitivity. Many people are allergic to penicillin, and a few persons have very serious or even fatal reactions to it. For this reason, each patient about to receive penicillin must be evaluated by the physician, who

must make a professional judgment as to the patient's penicillin tolerance.

3. Differential treatment. The recommended treatment for syphilis requires one kind of penicillin, while that for gonorrhea requires another. It is seldom feasible to administer both at the same time.

4. There is also the problem of convincing any large number of Americans that they should be treated for such a socially unacceptable possibility as gonorrhea. The vast majority (the at least 195 million *uninfected* persons) have every right to ask 'Why should I submit to this?' What answer would you give them?

"I hope that this explanation has been of some value to you. We are most appreciative of your interest and concern in the venereal disease control program."

Unfortunately, that self-assured Assistant Surgeon General forgot to do his homework. *At the very moment that letter was written the U.S. Government was conducting its own National VD Day!* But American taxpayers were not invited.

According to the prestigious *New England Journal of Medicine,* American Navy doctors were using all the techniques of National VD Day to protect the health of 396 Filipino "bar and restaurant hostesses" (prostitutes) by giving each of them two drugs (at the same time) and eradicating gonorrhea among them. The drugs used were ampicillin, 3.5 grams, and probenecid, 1 gram. Ampicillin is a form of penicillin and probenecid is a drug that raises the blood level of the penicillin. *One hundred percent of the patients were cured of gonorrhea with this one-dose combination.* The side effects consisted of itching of the skin in two patients.

But that was only one example, wasn't it?

No. If the President had asked the Assistant Surgeon General to check with the Navy he would have found out some other exciting news. Between 1967 and 1968 the same ampicillin-probenecid treatment was given to U.S. sailors with gonorrhea. *Ninety-six percent were cured in a single dose!* Side effects? The article, published in the *Journal of the American Medical Association,* says: *"No allergic reactions to any of the drugs administered were noted."*

And there's more. The Los Angeles County Health Department has used another antibiotic, doxycycline, to prevent infection with gonorrhea. Estimating that 20 percent of the gonorrhea and 50 percent of the syphilis in that part of the country is transmitted by homosexuals, 115 males were asked to take a single dose on the day of intercourse. In four months and 5,400 acts of homosexual intercourse only *two* cases of gonorrhea developed. (Maybe somebody forgot to take their pills?) The drug apparently also provided protection against syphilis.

It doesn't stop there. In Nevada, where commercial-sex-for-pay is legal, 324 women who worked in licensed houses of prostitution were treated daily with Progonasyl jelly—an ointment that is inserted into the vagina like contraceptive cream. After forty-eight days of hard work—up to twenty customers a day—only one positive case of gonorrhea was found. (A nice project, but ironically the rate of gonorrhea is much higher in teen-agers than it is in professional prostitutes.) What kind of mad medicine is it that saves the whores and sacrifices the kids?

With that question in mind, let's take another look at the objections of the Surgeon General:

I. "Cost. While the penicillin cost alone might be relatively low, costs of mass administration of it would be prohibitive."

    I. *Cost: about one dollar per person or a total price equal to twenty jet fighters to save the entire nation. Mass administration of drugs to combat national epidemics is invariably done by medical volunteers —at no cost.*

2. "Sensitivity. Many people are allergic to penicillin, and a few persons have very serious or even fatal reactions to it. For this reason, each patient about to receive penicillin must be evaluated by the physician, who must make a professional judgment as to the patient's penicillin tolerance."

   2. *Sensitivity: "No allergic reactions to any of the drugs administered were noted": remember the AMA article?**

3. "Differential treatment. The recommended treatment for syphilis requires one kind of penicillin, while that for gonorrhea requires another. It is seldom feasible to administer both at the same time."

   3. *Differential treatment: Let's eliminate gonorrhea now. Then we can use all our resources against syphilis. (Incidentally, by comparison, syphilis is a minor hazard. There were only an estimated 125,-000 actual cases in the latest year.)*

4. "There is also the problem of convincing any large number of Americans that they should be treated for such a socially unacceptable possiblity as gonorrhea. The vast majority (the at least 195 million *uninfected* persons) have every right to ask 'Why should I submit to this?' What answer would you give them?"

---

*Although the combination of oral ampicillin-probenecid has been used on a mass basis with gratifying freedom from serious side effects, the theoretical possibility of penicillin allergy always exists. However, according to the U.S. Department of Health, Education, and Welfare (Publication No. (HSM) 73–8195), a five-year study of penicillin administered in mass VD clinics revealed only one death attributable to a penicillin reaction. So, although the risk exists, it is a notably small one.

4. *You give them this answer: they have a choice—
they can take their two medications now and crush
the disease. Or they can wait until they are inevitably infected and take the medicine later—unless
it's too late.*

How can it be too late?

Well, that's another little bit of reality the Assistant Surgeon
General left out. He forgot to disclose the fact that every
physician knows—as each day of bungling and inaction goes
by we come closer and closer to losing the battle once and
for all. That's because as we get weaker the bacteria that
cause gonorrhea get stronger. First, the types of gonorrhea
imported from Southeast Asia are more resistant to penicillin
and other antibiotics. According to the *New England Journal of Medicine,* the number of strains of gonorrhea that
laugh at normal doses of antibiotics has increased 300 percent. Secondly, more and more patients are becoming infected with a "body-guard" variety of bacteria—gonorrhea
plus a harmless bug that destroys penicillin and protects
the gonorrhea germ from its effects. Third—and right out
of science fiction—the gonorrhea germs are learning to
change themselves into a new form (called L-form) that
sneers at antibiotics. Fourth, there are now over 198 separate strains of gonorrhea, with more developing every day.
It all boils down to one chilling conclusion: unless we de-
stroy gonorrhea fast—and decisively—the disease could become as common as the common cold *and* as hard to cure.

So National VD Day is inevitable—it's only a matter of
when. Now, when it's easy. Or later, when we all have it. Oh,
yes. There's one other little terrifying detail that makes that
approach the *only* way out.

What's that terrifying detail?

Eighty percent (or more) of all women who get gonorrhea have *no overt symptoms at all.* They just spend their days like Typhoid Mary dispensing sickness to all comers. At the same time, the disease is corroding their own bodies from the inside. (The fallopian tubes, cervix, and uterus are primary targets, with permanent sterility as the payoff.)

But now there's a new menace on the horizon.

What's the new menace?

It seems that, according to some experts in VD, *as many as 20 percent of men with gonorrhea show no overt symptoms.* They don't seek treatment, never initiate case-finding, and innocently infect their partners. But in their case too, the disease continues to ravage their bodies. And unless the people we trust our bodies to get on the ball, we will become the world's leading reservoir of sexual disease.

Isn't the government doing anything?

Well, it continues the flood of pamphlets that warn that gonorrhea and syphilis are hazardous to your health. But if it's any consolation, the Russian approach isn't much better. Faced with their own epidemic of VD, they have responded in a predictable manner. It used to be that anyone there who infected another person with VD got a year in jail. Now he gets two years. (Two pills would be more sensible.) There's also a group rate available: anyone infecting two or more people gets five years. If it sounds a little heavy-handed, it is.

Is there something a person can do in the meantime to protect himself and his family against gonorrhea?

There are a couple of things. First of all—know your sexual partner. The more sexual contacts he or she has with others, the greater the chance that you will become infected. And as the number of victims increases day by day, the odds against you go up. Men can get excellent protection by wearing a condom every time they have intercourse. Strangely enough, using vaginal foam as a contraceptive gives some protection against germs as well as sperms. It seems that gonorrhea, at least, doesn't thrive in the foam.

Women should have a smear *and* culture each time they visit the doctor—every three months isn't too often. Men should get medical attention the same day they develop that creamy discharge from the penis. Tomorrow may be too late.

Why does a man have to go to a doctor the same day if he doesn't have sexual intercourse until he is treated?

Because he can infect his family and friends *without sexual intercourse.* Children are particularly vulnerable and in one set of cases seven children from families who often shared the same bed came down with the disease without sexual intercourse.

Some mothers even insist that you *can* get gonorrhea from the toilet seat:

"At the age of five years I contracted gonorrhea from my mother who was ill at the time. I got it from contaminated bathroom facilities—a toilet seat. The doctor who was treating my mother at the time didn't tell the rest of the family what I had and some of my friends—other small children—also got the disease."

And:

"I never believed that you could get gonorrhea from a toilet seat either until I spent three years living in Europe. We had a maid, and our seven-year old daughter sat down on the toilet seat as soon as the maid had finished. A few days later she had gonorrhea—and so did the maid."

Can you really get gonorrhea from a toilet seat?

It's hard to say. The gonorrhea bugs can live for several days in contaminated creams and perhaps for hours on moist skin. Besides that, little girls are especially susceptible to the infection because their tiny vaginas are thin-walled and vulnerable. But there are other places that VD strikes as well.

Where else?

Almost anywhere that human ingenuity can insert a penis or volunteer a vagina. Syphilitic and gonorrheal infections of the lips and tongue are possible—usually from careless cunnilingus and feckless fellatio. (These structures become the "ports of entry" for the diseases to enter the body.) Homosexuals tend to come down with syphilis and gonorrhea at both ends—tonsils and rectum. Ironically, almost half the women with gonorrhea of the cervix have rectal gonorrhea.

Do that many women have anal intercourse?

Probably not. But it does tell something about female anatomy. The same lymph glands that drain infection from the vaginal area also protect the rectal area. It's possible that the vaginal infection can spread to the rectum from *within* the body rather than via an invading penis. Besides, gravity works against a woman—any gonorrheal discharge from the vagina tends to drain directly onto and into the anus. Of

221 VENEREAL DISEASE

course, some women do have anal intercourse and get their infections that way.

How do you tell which is which?

It's not easy—although physicians have a rule-of-thumb: "If a doctor's wife comes in with rectal gonorrhea, it's always from the lymph glands." Women also can get syphilis of the breast—from the affectionate caresses of an infected penis. And notwithstanding the old joke, you *can* get syphilis of the big toe.

How do you get syphilis of the toe?

In the same way the famous case that got into the medical journals came down with it. A lesbian lady used her toe to masturbate her partner for the evening. The partner had active syphilis and the masturbatrix caught the disease between her fourth and fifth toes.

Lately a new venereal disease has surfaced which adds a sinister dimension to the whole VD problem. In addition to infecting the reproductive organs there seems to be strong evidence that *this new disease can transmit cancer via sexual intercourse.*

How can that happen?

Three harmless initials tell the story: HVH. They stand for: "Human Virus—Herpes." That's the name of the innocent little virus that causes embarrassing and annoying cold sores on the lips of men and women. So far no problem. But HVH has a cousin called "HVH—Type 2," and if there ever was a black sheep in a family, "Type 2" is it. It's the virus that's responsible for ugly little pimples and blisters on the penis, labia, vagina, and other important sexual intersections. A

222

man with HVH-2 can give it to his female partner—and vice versa. (Homosexuals also pass this disease back and forth.) That's bad enough—but recent studies indicate that a woman who has been infected with HVH-2 has up to 800 percent more chance of developing cancer of the cervix than a woman who has never had the disease.

Can't a woman protect herself?

It's not that easy. Of course, no fastidious lady is going to copulate with a man who has a pimple on his penis—at least until she knows exactly what his problem is. But that's not much help in HVH-2. As many as 15 percent of apparently uninfected men may have the virus in their seminal fluid— when they ejaculate, the cervix is flooded with millions of little viruses. Wearing a condom helps but nobody likes to do that all the time.

What about treatment?

As they say, it is still on the drawing board. Several types of therapy are being investigated, but as of now HVH still deserves to be considered an unsolved crime. And crime seems to be the right word. You see, infected mothers pass it on to their newborn children as they travel through the vagina on their way to the outside world. In newborns the disease is serious and sometimes fatal. Of course, that's the darker side of VD.

Why is that?

Well, theoretically, adults who get crummy diseases on their sexual organs are supposed to be able to take care of themselves. But an hour-old baby is helpless. And sometimes we haven't kept up our responsibilities to them.

Gonorrhea is a good example. As a newborn's face is dragged through the cervix of a gonorrheal mother, the virulent germs are rubbed into his eyes. The result is almost certain blindness unless he is treated promptly. For years babies were given a drop of silver nitrate solution in each eye within moments of being born and the incidence of gonorrheal blindness slid almost to zero. Then things got more "modern" and penicillin ointment was substituted for "old-fashioned" silver nitrate. The result was predictable—the bacteria got tougher and more resistant to penicillin and gonorrheal blindness started showing up again. Now more and more doctors are going back to using silver nitrate for the newborn.

Syphilis also infects unborn babies—and destroys their lives. That, incidentally, is the reason nearly every state requires a blood test for syphilis before a marriage license is issued. (By the way, Assistant Surgeon General, that's another example of people cooperating to win the battle against a "socially unacceptable disease.")

Syphilis is a bad disease—it ravages the brain, the heart, and the spinal cord. That makes it all the more urgent to defeat gonorrhea so that we can turn our resources against syphilis.

Although it is much less common than gonorrhea these days, syphilis has the potential of being a thousand times more destructive. Its most terrifying symptom is the relentless destruction of the human brain. Not so long ago, as many as half of all the patients in mental hospitals were suffering from syphilitic insanity. Like every other bad actor, syphilis is always waiting in the wings to make its dramatic comeback. And in a frightening way, the deadly germs of syphilis have more than once changed the course of history.

How did syphilis change the course of history?

By slowly driving important world leaders mad. The cork-screw germs of syphilis produce two major types of delusions, both familiar to students of history—and readers of the daily newspaper. The number-one delusion is that of grandeur: "I alone can save the world!" Next is the delusion of persecution: "We must attack them before they can attack us!" All too often the ruler with blazing eyes finds it easy to make his germ-generated schemes sound plausible to the majority of citizens who are not wracked with venereal disease. For example, one of the things that made Ivan the Terrible so terrible was the syphilis that he picked up as a lad. Henry VIII of England, a notorious syphilitic, not only murdered several of his wives but wantonly executed many thousands of Englishmen as well. Napoleon Bonaparte and Kaiser Wilhelm were *relatively* benign rulers who apparently acquired their VD late in life. Mussolini, on the other hand, got both syphilis *and* gonorrhea long before he became "Il Duce." Adolf Hitler slipped three cents to a Viennese whore in 1910 (that was the going rate for street girls then) and she slipped him a few million bacteria of syphilis. Ironically, that one case of syphilis besmirched a cultured and civilized nation with depravity and sadism previously unknown in the history of the world.

Syphilis of the brain also causes bizarre images and thought patterns which can occasionally produce works of art. Renowned syphilitics included the poet Keats and the composer Schubert. Among the painters, Gauguin, Goya, and van Gogh suffered from the disease. Some of the brightest stars in the literary world wrote under the burden of their disease—Nietzsche, Schopenhauer, Molière, De Maupassant, and Oscar Wilde. And it is only poetic justice that Casanova should finally have succumbed to the invisible stiletto of syphilis.

Do any modern leaders suffer from syphilis?

That information is locked in their secret medical files. However, the danger always exists. Washington, D.C., has the highest rate of syphilis in the nation—up 31 percent from the last year. (It ranks fourth in gonorrhea, up only 16 percent.)

Fortunately, all important U.S. Government officials undergo regular exams for VD so Americans are protected against such an unfortunate turn of events.

What's going to happen as far as venereal disease is concerned?

Ultimately we are going to come to our senses and face reality. Then we will swiftly make our nation free of VD. We already know how. We've known why for a long time. The only question is—WHEN?

11

TEEN-AGE SEX—A CRISIS FOR PARENTS

What's the difference between adult sex and teen-age sex?

The basic difference is the age of the equipment. Although most adults don't like to think about it that way, a fifteen-year-old penis engages a fourteen-year-old vagina in the standard way. Teen-age erection (of the penis *and* clitoris), copulation, ejaculation, orgasm—and conception—are virtually identical with the way "grown-ups" do it. By the age of fourteen or so, most teens are grown-ups—at least from a sexual point of view. Of course, some of them are more grown up than others:

"Please tell me if you think I'm doing the right thing. I have a boy friend named Gregg and we've been going together for about six months. He's sixteen and I'll be fifteen next week. We haven't gone all the way yet but we mess around a lot. For instance, we'll go to the drive-in movie and he'll play with me and lick me between my legs and all, and I'll play with him and blow him. He's able to come but sometimes it takes longer than other times. (I don't always talk like this but I guess I should tell you everything.)

"I found out what an orgasm was accidentally. I was taking a bath about a year ago and I decided I'd like to get real clean so I turned on the water and spread my legs way apart and let it run on my clitoris and vagina. Well, as you probably know, it felt real good, and even though I never had an orgasm before, I had one then. So I started doing it a lot because I liked it so much. At first I would run the water full blast but lately it's been quicker and feels better to have the water just going a little. My boy friend doesn't know I do this but he says he used to jack-off when he was little so maybe he'd understand about me.

"There was only one time when we tried to go all the way. It was in Gregg's backyard one night when no one was home. Before we started he asked me if I wanted him to wear a rubber because he'd bought some. I said, 'I guess so.' I was a little disappointed because I wanted it to be more romantic. He put me on my back in the grass by the pool with my knees up, but he couldn't get in. I guess I must have been pretty tensed up because later on he told me he couldn't even get his little finger in."

Do all teen-agers start that young?

No. Some start much younger:

"I am twelve and when I was in seventh grade, at the age of eleven and three quarters, I had intercourse with a boy just to see what it was like. No one had ever told me anything about it and my brother kind of played it up and my mother played it down, so I decided to see for myself. Do you think I did the right thing?"

228

Others are just getting ready to start:

"I'm a thirteen-year-old girl and I've experienced a strong desire to have sex with the guy I'm going with. I haven't given in as yet, but I'm afraid I'm weakening. Am I normal? What should I do? If it'll help you to give me the right answer, I've always been a 'nice' girl and an outstanding student."

What should she do?

By now she has probably done it, felt guilty about it, and then done it again. Hopefully someone got to her in time and cleared up some of the confusion by assuring her that:

1. The desire for sex in girls after puberty is normal.
2. If she was a "nice" girl before sex, she will be a "nice" girl after sex. There is nothing about normal sexual intercourse that makes people nasty.

But there is more to her plea than appears on the surface. Few adults have any notion of the intense pressures that drive teen-agers toward sex: For example:

"I have a little problem. I know a lot of boys that like me —I am an attractive girl. They always ask me, 'Come on, how about having some sex with me?' I always answer, 'No, I'm going to wait until I'm married.' So the boy will say, 'It's all right, let's just make a little love.'

"But see, I'm only fourteen years old and I'm scared to have sex cuz I might get pregnant. So what should I do when a boy wants to have a little sex? Doctor, do you think every lady needs sex? Why? If parents can have sex, why can't teen-agers?"

Do all teen-agers give in?

Not by a long shot. But all of them are caught in the sexual squeeze play. On the one hand, society tries to keep the kids in cast-iron underwear. On the other hand, teens' powerful sexual feelings insist on some release.

Ronnie is sixteen, dressed in the current uniform of his clan: white bell-bottom denims, red and blue striped undershirt, and sandals. He slumps low in the chair, one foot thrown over the arm rest:

"Like, you wouldn't believe it, Doc. Around my house they have the 'Original Family Do-It-Yourself Anti-Sex Program.' "

He paused and laughed:

"No, it really ought to be called, 'The *Don't*-Do-It-Yourself Program.' It comes in two unexciting flavors: one for me and one for my sister—she's seventeen. I guess I get off easier. Oh, they try to scare me with VD and 'getting a girl in trouble.' That's a laugh! Half the girls in my class have been taking the pill since their periods started—there's no way they're going to get into trouble. And even if they do, their folks'll get them an abortion and they know it. But my Mom really comes on strong with Connie, my sister. Like, whenever she goes out on a date, she goes: 'Remember, we brought you up to be a nice girl. Don't let us down.' "

Ronnie sat up in his chair.

"Unreal! Far out! I mean, you should see the look on Mom's face! It's like sex was super-bad! I mean, if they can do it, why can't we? Do you have to have a note from your doctor or something?"

Are parents to blame for teen-agers' sexual difficulties?

Not really. For ten thousand years it has been fashionable for kids—and everyone else—to put the blame on Mom and Dad, not only for their sexual problems but for everything else. That's a neat and easy way out but it overlooks one little detail. The parents of today are the teen-agers of yesterday and the teen-agers of today are the parents of tomorrow. (Although those who are a little clumsy may well become the parents of *today*.)

If Mom and Dad are tempted to deny and reject their teen-ager's feelings, it is only because their parents denied and rejected them in the same way.

Let's give a little truth-serum to a few selected parents:

MOTHER *(self-righteously):* When I was growing up my mother wouldn't even let a boy who was "fast" into the house.

QUESTIONER: Where did you meet them?

MOTHER: Over behind the railroad station.

FATHER: Listen, my daughter's going to be a virgin when she gets married!

QUESTIONER: Like your wife?

FATHER *(blushing):* Well, a guy's only human.

MOTHER: When I used to date, my mother knew where I was every minute of the time.

QUESTIONER: *Every* minute?

MOTHER: Except that time on the hayride and, well, do I have to count those times in the rumble seat?

The combination of resentment at being overcontrolled when they were young, and guilt over their "forbidden past" when they were teen-agers, can blind parents to the reality of their children's need for constructive sexual guidance.

Whether he likes it or not, no parent can repeal the laws of physiology. No matter how much parents complain, teen-age testicles and teen-age ovaries don't get the message. They continue to flood the body with sex hormones and rush the penis and vagina and breasts toward adult size and capability. At the same time, teen-age thoughts uncontrollably begin to focus on fulfilling the accompanying new and strange desires. Listen to this appeal for information on how to cope with the problem:

"I'm fourteen years old—almost fifteen. Can a girl of my age have sexual desires? I have these urges to make love and have frequent dreams of me in sexual intercourse. Personally, I don't think a girl of my age should have dreams like that. The main reason I wrote was to find out if it's normal or if I need psychiatric help."

In their anxiety to preserve their daughter's hymen, some parents may forget that there is another more perishable sexual organ to preserve—her brain. If their fifteen-year-old thinks there is something wrong with her mind because she has sexual urges, they may have done their job too well. Perhaps they need to be reminded that one of the prominent signs of emotional sickness is the *loss* of interest in sex. "Urges to make love" are a gift bestowed on the most fortunate of men and women. The ones who need psychiatric help desperately are the unlucky few who *never* have sexual feelings. Boys are sometimes caught in the same trap:

"I'm a fifteen-year-old boy and I know this letter may sound kind of babyish but I am all mixed up about sex. Mostly I am afraid to make a mistake. What should a boy *not* do to a girl so the boy and girl will not get into big trouble?"

The answer is clear: If you don't want to make a mistake, don't do *anything*.

But then there's another problem. If a boy *never* does

anything to a girl, both of them will be in big trouble of another kind. So it looks as if teen-agers can't win, either way.

Then teen-agers should have sex anytime they feel like it?

Hardly. Even mature adults can't have sex anytime they feel like it. Venereal disease, unwanted pregnancy, abortion, orgasmic impairment, and impotence are big problems for married adults—they are often overwhelming for frightened and timid teens.

No one in his right mind recommends unlimited sex for young people. But, sex does happen to teens and when it does, parents need insight and understanding so that they can do the best for their children. Most kids want—and need —their parents help when it comes to sex:

"I'm a boy eleven years old and afraid to ask my parents about sex. I would like to know how old I should be before I start doing anything? If you think I am too little, don't tell me."

A thirteen-year-old girl:

"Can you tell me what happens to a guy when a girl sits on his lap? My Mom says it's wrong for a girl to do that but she won't tell me why. She says that kids are so open about sex these days that I should know. Well, it seems as if none of the girls in my class are *that* open."

Should her mother tell her?

Probably. If she doesn't, her thirteen-old daughter may puzzle about the riddle until she solves it by *sitting* on a boy's lap. A moment or two later when she feels his erection driving against her, she will know—and wonder why her mother was afraid to discuss this universal sexual reflex. There are a lot of other things that teen-agers need to know —things that nobody is telling them:

"This boy I know—the same age as me—fourteen—he and I have something going. We're not very serious yet but we like to make out.

"Whenever we're alone, the next thing I know I feel his hand going down into my pants. I admit that I enjoy it when he does 'feel me up' and 'plays inside my pants,' but there is one thing that he does that puzzles me.

"I don't always let him, but here's what he does: he unbuttons my blouse, lifts my bra, and starts to "suck" at my breasts like a baby would. After he finishes sucking me and playing in my panties, I feel much better. But as I get older, will this always fulfill my sexual needs? Is there something wrong with me if I continue to let him do these things? I would appreciate your answering me—cause I'm too embarrassed to ask my own doctor. Don't forget."

This young lady might have been spared a lot of anxiety if her parents had simply explained to her that "playing inside her pants" and "sucking her breasts" are normal preliminaries to sexual intercourse. It might also be a good idea if they explained to her that often these preliminaries swiftly lead into the main event—full sexual intercourse. And few fourteen-year-olds are ready for that.

But boys and girls can have normal intercourse by the time they're fourteen, can't they?

Most of them can do the mechanical part all right, but that's the least of it. Sex—between two people who care about each other—sets off an explosion that reverberates throughout an individual's entire personality. Most teens aren't ready to cope with the conflict and they need parents who are. But

234

parents can panic too. Some of them fall back on chemical warfare. A mother asks:

"Years back I heard they gave college students saltpeter to keep their minds on their studies instead of on sex. Is this still being done anywhere? If not, why not? Don't you think if they did it there would be less raping and unwanted pregnancies?"

Even if one could find a group of students who didn't mind having yet another chemical added to their already doped-up food, there is still a problem. Most experts agree that saltpeter or potassium nitrate doesn't depress sexual performance. (The only dissenters are a few old professors who insist that the saltpeter they got back in college is just starting to take effect.)

Then there are some mothers who seem sincerely concerned about their daughters and sex:

"To me it seems as though you approve of sex before marriage. Our seventeen-year-old daughter has just started dating and she feels she can tell me anything and we can talk about it—like the boy who tried to get fresh.

"I told her that's the only way a boy can tell what kind of girl she is and that it is the girl that has to put a stop to it. I'm trying to teach her to keep herself clean and pure for the man she'll marry someday. I want her to know that sex is not to be played with—that it is really a wonderful thing."

Is she right?

Yes and no. She's right for herself and wrong for her daughter. Her refined advice to young ladies has the unmistakable ring of "Rules for Conduct" at the Girls' Reformatory. It also converts an innocent Saturday night date into some kind of freaked-out ritual:

[SCENE: *A boy and girl, about seventeen years old, are sitting in a car watching the movie at a drive-in.*]

GIRL *(to herself):* It's been five minutes already. I wonder when he's going to try and find out what kind of girl I am?

BOY *(to himself):* Well, it's been five minutes. I guess it's time to find out what kind of girl she is. *(He slowly and gently places his arm around her shoulder.)*

GIRL *(indignantly):* My God! What do you think you're doing?

BOY *(cheerfully):* I was just getting fresh.

GIRL *(businesslike):* Well, young man, I'm just going to put a stop to it. *(Pulls his arm off and slaps his face— hard.)*

BOY *(obviously relieved):* Thank goodness! I wasn't sure that you were clean and pure but now I know. Let's not play with sex and maybe some day we can get married —but not to each other.

[*They slide quietly to opposite sides of the front seat and with serene smiles lose themselves in the Walt Disney movie on the screen.*]

This little test also gives high marks as marriage material to schizophrenics, man-haters, and girls whose ovaries never developed. It flunks any girl with a normal interest in sex.

However, it is a great cop-out for a mother who doesn't care. It shifts all the responsibility onto her kids: "I did my part—I told them not to have anything to do with sex. They disobeyed me and now I'm not responsible."

Are there many mothers like that?

One is too many, but here are a few samples:

"I am sixteen and all my mother ever says about sex is,

'Don't spread your legs apart for any man unless you've got a ring on your finger,' or 'Don't give up your virginity for any reason or you'll end up with nothing or a baby.'

"When I try to ask my mother about it she doesn't tell me what I need to know. She only says I better be married first and then she starts fussing about what I better not do with a boy when I'm out on a date."

And, "I am a fifteen-year-old high school girl and I think I may be pregnant. My parents are always telling me that I should come to them when I have a problem, but I know if I tell them that I am pregnant, my mother would make my father run after my boy friend (he is fifteen too) and try to harm him in some way."

And, "How can a girl tell if she's still a virgin? I have to ask you because I am very poor in my vocabulary and thus I don't know how to ask my Mom."

And, "What should people like me in the thirteen- to seventeen-year-old group do about sex? If I talk about it to my parents they will just get mad and tell me 'Don't think about that kind of stuff!' "

Why do parents act that way?

Certainly not because they intentionally want to fail as parents. But teen-age sex stirs up a lot of internal emotional conflicts for Mom and Dad. They are torn between their own moral principles and the apparently reckless behavior of their offspring. A father who may be having sexual problems of his own is confronted with the *apparently* flawless performance of his son. A mother who is concerned about getting older sees her daughter as the young sexy woman she still longs to be. Love for their children on the one hand is tempered by anxiety and discomfort about the whole sexual situation on the other.

What's the solution?

The *start* of a solution is for parents to recognize that sexual feelings in human beings start earlier and are more insistent than most adults realize.

Nearly every child has a supercharged sexual life long before most parents are aware of it:

"My daughter is eight years old and I have seen her many times putting her hand on her vaginal area and rubbing it hard. I have also seen her sitting on a log and moving back and forth to rub her vagina against this. It was a little shocking the first time but I suppose it is just normal."

And, "A little boy in the neighborhood taught our five-year-old girl how to masturbate. Now whenever she has nothing to do, she starts playing with herself. What can I do?"

Some children even go farther:

"I was the only girl in a neighborhood of about ten boys. When I was about five years old we were playing Cowboys and Indians and I had to pee. The boys watched me just like I used to watch them. Next, one of the bigger boys, about thirteen, asked me if I wanted to touch his penis. I did!

"From then on until I was nine every boy had me. I was with some one or all each day. Then one day Mom found out. From that time on I wasn't allowed to call her Mother. To be honest, I missed the sex and I used to do it to myself with my finger."

The sooner parents recognize that children have strong sexual urges, the sooner they can begin to help their kids deal with them. Sometimes facing reality is the hardest part: Richie is fifteen; he puts it this way:

"Doctor, I just don't know how my Mom and Dad think. I mean, I guess they know what sex is and I guess they still do it with each other—although they're getting a little old for it—they're almost fifty now. But they expect me to be some kind of a eunuch or something. I can level with you—I get erections all the time—sometimes even in English class. All my friends do, too. What are we supposed to do about it? You know what the coach says? He says, 'Fellows, when your dingus gets hard . . .' " Richie laughed.

Still chuckling, he continues: "That's unreal! Coach calls it 'Your dingus'! Why doesn't he just say 'pee-pee'? Anyhow he says, 'When your dingus gets hard just do a few fast laps around the track.' If we followed his advice, all the guys at my high school would be jogging twenty-four hours a day. And all the girls would be crowding around yelling at us to stop before we got too soft."

"I don't know if I should say this, but it's true. Most of the time my Dad is too tired to have sex with my Mom— I know, my room is across the hall. But sex is OK for him. Me, I'm never too tired—I could do it ten times a day and I'm not supposed to do it at all. Is that fair?"

Grown-ups don't always play fair when it comes to kids and sex:

"I am an eighteen-year-old woman and I have had the most unbelievable experience with sex. I am engaged to a wonderful man but our marriage has to be put off for a year because of financial and job problems. But we're sure we're right for each other and we have begun to have sex—because we consider ourselves spiritually married already.

"Soon after we started, I went to my family doctor, who has taken care of me since I was born, and asked for birth control pills. He looked at me like I was a slut and said, 'Why don't you just make another appointment *after* you're married?' But, Doctor, *now* is when we need the pill. When he turned me down I stopped having orgasms and now I'm afraid I'll really get pregnant."

But aren't doctors supposed to help people?

Yes, and most of them do a pretty good job, but occasionally their own sexual hang-ups get in the way. Withholding treatment to enforce the physician's personal moral code may make the doctor feel good, but it doesn't do much for the patient. That brings up another problem:

In most parts of this country it is still against the law for those under eighteen to buy contraceptives—although there is nothing in the law books that makes them immune from pregnancy. The dilemma becomes: does exposure to VD and unwanted pregnancy act as a deterrent to teen-age sex? According to the VD and pregnancy rates among teenagers the answer seems to be a resounding, as they put it, "No way!"

Would freely available contraceptives increase teen-age sex?

It doesn't seem to have. In those few areas where teens can get the same protection from VD and pregnancy available to adults, no upsurge in teen-age orgies has been reported. To make matters worse, in some states, teens who are stricken with VD can't even get treated without their parents' consent. That results in little dramas like this one:

A sixteen-year-old boy, obviously nervous, is sitting in the doctor's office.

DOCTOR: What can I do for you?

BOY: Well, Doc, I think I've got a dose of . . . I mean, you know, there's this discharge coming from my. . . . Listen, you won't tell anyone will you?

DOCTOR: Certainly not. Of course, I will have to mention it to your mother. What's her phone number? *(Doctor turns to pick up phone)* Hey! Where are you going? *(Door slams behind patient)*

The reasoning behind these laws seems unclear—is the idea to make the kids so terrified of pregnancy and VD and they'll just stay home and masturbate? But it doesn't work: the teen-agers still copulate, they still get pregnant, they still get VD—but what a lot of them don't get is orgasm.

Are teen-agers supposed to have orgasms?

Almost everybody agrees that human beings are supposed to have orgasms—the only problem is *when?* Adults want kids to wait until they are married; kids want to do it right now. Guess who wins?

Who wins?

Nobody. The final result is an old-fashioned standoff. The kids copulate but don't climax. And sometimes they can't even copulate:

"I am seventeen years old and a boy of better than average physical condition. Occasionally I go on 'masturbation benders' where I masturbate every day until I can get my mind off sex and onto something more creative. I always vow to cool the habit, but my penis is such a strong influence on me, I can honestly say I have not been able to quit it yet. Maybe this has caused my problem.

"I have this wonderfully brilliant girl friend who functions quite well during sex—but I have some hang-ups. *I cannot reach an orgasm at her hands.* No matter how long she masturbates me even though I stay hard, I cannot reach a climax. When she gives me a short fellatio, I don't even feel it. Yet I can—as I mentioned—masturbate myself easily.

"The other problem is that I can't keep a hard-on when a rubber is put on me. Once a few years ago, I went out with a prostitute and tried to become devirginated with a rubber on, but I lost my hard-on. (The only consolation is that I can honestly tell my new girl friend that I am still a virgin.).

"We can't get married for at least a year and neither of us wants pregnancy. If she could only masturbate me like I do her, or if I could come in her mouth, or if I could learn to keep a hard-on with a rubber, we could work out some kind of sex life together."

What's this young man's problem?

Here is a classical example of a boy who was frightened by a penis when he was a child—his own. He now believes that sex—and masturbation—are simply "bad habits" that can be "cooled." (When men and women succeed in "cooling sex" they will also succeed in cooling the entire human race.) Now he thinks of his penis as a dangerous weapon and he tries to disarm himself by shooting it off in the privacy of the bathroom where it can't hurt anyone—except himself. But the penis is a clever organ and it learns quickly—now it has been trained not to discharge within fifty feet of a female hand, mouth, or vagina. It's about time that someone explained to him that his phallus is not a tool of mass destruction and that there is literally nothing more *creative* than sex. Once he (and his penis) get that message, life will be better for him and his future wife.

What does this have to do with his future wife?

Everything. Successful sexual intercourse is an extremely demanding and complex endeavor. It requires the endurance of an athlete—as most newlyweds will testify—the sensitivity of a poet, and the technical skill of an astronaut. After all, copulation is, in its own way, a space shot. The missile is a little smaller, the target is inner space rather than outer space, the passengers are a few hundred million microscopic sperm, but the logistics of launching are just as challenging. Space men must train for years for one lift-off. Teen-agers are forbidden any training at all to prepare for a lifetime of lift-offs. It doesn't make much sense. If our astronauts were prepared for space the way our young people are prepared for sex, they wouldn't be able to shoot their rockets two inches and would probably impregnate every woman at Cape Kennedy in the process. Their preparation might go something like this:

[*Project Director, addressing assembled astronauts, both male and female:*]

DIRECTOR: Okay crew, listen carefully. In a couple of years you're going to be called on to do the most important job in your life.

FEMALE ASTRONAUT: What job, Chief?

DIRECTOR: Are you crazy? I told you never to ask me that!

ASTRONAUT *(mumbling):* Gee, I'm sorry, Mom—I mean, Chief.

DIRECTOR *(still angry):* All right now. This is crucial. I've seen some of you men and women sneaking out there and touching those . . . uhm . . . rockets. I have to warn you about that. You'll spoil it all unless you wait until the big day. When it happens, I want it to be beautiful —I mean, it should be perfect. Don't dirty your mind with thoughts like, "How will it feel?" or "Will I like it?" That's not the point.

MALE ASTRONAUT: What *is* the point, Chief?

DIRECTOR *(furious):* Now you're talking dirty again! How many times do I have to remind you that when you're sailing through space at twenty-five thousand miles an hour, it'll all come to you at once. You don't need to understand how the equipment works. Knowing what you're doing would just inflame your minds and make you lust for blast-off before you're old enough to appreciate it. And anyhow, you're not supposed to enjoy it. Remember that! I mean, forget that! And don't let me catch you thinking about anything—if you know what I mean.

It just isn't possible to turn teen-agers off sexually for ten years or so and then suddenly catapult them into a perfect sexual orbit ten minutes after they cut the wedding cake. Girls suffer as much as boys:

"I am an eighteen-year-old girl and I am getting married in three months. My fiancé and I have been going with each other for three years; but now we're both worried. We both intended to save ourselves for marriage, so for the first two years we only had oral sex and I came almost every time— and so did he. This past year we lost control and started having sex the regular way—and I stopped coming at all. I love to feel his mouth sucking on me—it's really exciting. But I just can't respond to his penis.

"I wonder if subconsciously I feel guilty about having regular sex—and that keeps me from my climax. Besides the oral way doesn't have any danger of getting pregnant. I don't regret not waiting but I'm just worried that our wedding night will be a failure. Do you think I did right? Please let me know?"

Did she do right when it came to sex?

Well, she did what a lot of other teen-age girls do. By rigidly condemning copulation, well-meaning parents drive teen-agers into each others mouths. "Save your virginity for marriage!" is the battle-cry, and girls soon find their own private loophole—the vagina. Once the penis penetrates the hymen, virginity is gone forever. But after an hour of fellatio, a fast swish with iridescent mouthwash and the teen-age mouth is "kissing sweet" once more. There is another fringe benefit—

244

as the letter-writer points out—no one ever got pregnant by swallowing sperm.

She is probably right about something else too. When mouth-vagina brings orgasm and penis-vagina brings frustration, it often means guilt about sex "the regular way." It's a tough spot to be in! By obeying her parents—who aren't even there in the motel room—she has to give up orgasm. Obviously her next thought is, "Will my orgasms be there on my wedding night?" The answer is, probably not.

Why won't the orgasms be there?

As a social event, the wedding night is vastly overrated. Most newlyweds expect something like New Year's Eve at Disneyland—including half a dozen reruns. After all the stress and strain of the wedding, it usually turns out to be more like Ground Hog Day. But that part shouldn't matter—there will be plenty of other chances. If the young bride will devote her energy to overcoming her guilt about sex, the wedding night will tend to take care of itself.

Then teen-agers should be allowed to have any kind of sex they want to?

That's not really the issue because not even the most emancipated adult can have any kind of sex that he or she wants to. The most important question of all is: What can parents do to help their teen-agers convert those primitive sexual stirrings into a productive and rewarding use of their God-given sexual and reproductive endowments. There are four approaches that *don't* work—and don't have a chance of working.

What approaches don't work?

The sanctimonious approach doesn't work:

"It would break your mother's heart if you ever disgraced us!"

And, "Your father and I hope that you will bring yourself to your wife *absolutely* pure."

These exciting pronouncements create a credibility gap that makes the Grand Canyon look like a crack in the sidewalk.

Threats of retaliation are equally futile. They only drive teen-agers into cheap motels, parked cars, and worse places. One the other hand parents who prepare a canopied bed with satin sheets for Junior and his date—and then go out to a movie, don't solve the problem either. And pretending that the problem doesn't exist only succeeds in ultimately complicating the lives of everyone involved.

What is the solution?

It's called "sexual reality" and it consists of facing the following facts:

1. Nearly all teen-agers are capable of sexual intercourse.
2. Many of them *want to do it*—very badly.
3. A lot of them *are doing it*—very badly.

Facing these three basic facts of teen-age sex sweeps away all the little self-delusions that so often paralyze effective action. That prepares the way for the next step—*sexual accident prevention.*

What's sexual accident prevention?

Just what it sounds like—helping teens to sidestep the three biggest hazards of pre-adult sex: disease, pregnancy, and emotional turmoil. What good is it to vaccinate a girl against German measles and deny her protection against a far more hazardous condition—unwanted pregnancy? Every mother makes sure her son is protected against whooping cough—a relatively insignificant disease. Many mothers neglect to guard their boys against syphilis—a deadly crippler. Patting a sixteen-year-old on the shoulder and mumbling, "Stay out of trouble," doesn't ward off sperms *or* germs.

From a practical point of view, every child from the age of twelve on needs to know *at least* the following:

1. What the major sexual diseases are, how they manifest themselves, and how to avoid them.
2. Every girl who is capable of becoming pregnant should know precisely how it happens and how to avoid it.
3. Every boy who can can impregnate a girl should know how to avoid accomplishing it—in detail.

Pretending that sexual accidents don't happen—and withholding the basic safety information is cruel, thoughtless, and unrealistic. In sex, more than any other human endeavor, truth is vital for happiness.

What's the truth about premarital sex?

The truth is that the majority of people in our society engage in premarital sex in some way—although they may not rent billboards to advertise the fact. The truth is that most of them don't suffer any serious or lasting damage from it—provided they know enough to avoid VD, pregnancy, or mental suffering. The truth is that most parents themselves engaged in sex of some kind when they were teen-agers—and they grew up to raise a family of their own. Pretending that men and women don't touch each other below the belly button until they're twenty-one just doesn't fool anyone— not even a thirteen-year-old.

There's the other side of the story, too. Sex outside of marriage has the potential for a lot of unhappiness. Unwanted pregnancy, abortion, VD, and sexual exploitation do exist and they are nasty things for teen-agers to be involved with. They are generally less likely to happen within the socioeconomic shelter of marriage. And in spite of what the cynics may say, there is a better chance for true love to blossom and flourish when a couple has the emotional and sexual security of a happy marriage.

If love and sexual fulfillment are the ultimate achievements, teen-age sex is one of the important challenges along the way. Maybe this young lady expresses it best of all:

"I am a young girl, sixteen years old, and I have done a lot of thinking about teen-agers and sex. I think this time of life is so important for carving a healthy sexual relationship. Take my case, for example.

"My parents set certain guide lines—the time to come home from a date, telling them where you are going to be, etc. They tell me this is their way of showing they care. But now that I am becoming an adult, I have to break off and find my own world. It wasn't so long ago that I was sweet and innocent and I even put down kissing boys. But my ideas have changed a lot, and now I believe that sex is something beautiful between two people and I want to use it to express my love to my boy friend. At the same time I know that a lot of what teen-agers call 'love' is really a strong friendship and companionship.

"My parents still say things like, 'Don't let him touch you!' and that kind of foolish talk. I look at it this way—setting up your own system of morals is a big responsibility and a

248

sign of maturity. I think most parents underestimate their children today. Maybe that's why so many kids reject their parents and rebel. If our mothers and fathers could just accept us the way we are, we would all be a lot happier. Please think about it."

Maybe we should all think about it.

12

SEPTEMBER SEX

What is the menopause?

The menopause is an illusion and a delusion. It is an accident of evolution misused by a guilty society that equates sexual satisfaction with stealing from the collection plate on Easter Sunday. According to some experts who should know better, the menopause is a sort of "Sexual Day of Judgment"—"You've had your fun, and now it's over." All too many women—and men as well—have been given the idea that when the "change of life" begins, everything from the pubic area downward turns to dust. Passion, lust, and the midnight orgasm have to be traded in for daytime television, sensible shoes, and an advance reservation at a modest nursing home. Maybe that's the way it used to be, but that's not the way it is now.

Has the menopause changed?

No, but a woman's *defense* against the menopause has changed. Now any woman who really wants to can sail through the menopause almost as if it were a fast luncheon on a big shopping day. The only thing she has to give up is her monthly menstrual periods—and she can even have those back if she wants them.

What made the outlook better in the change of life?

Some smart doctors finally started listening to their patients. Until about fifty years ago, the menopause was a disaster area for most women. When that little pair of ovaries stopped putting out their daily drops of female sex hormones—basically estrogen and progesterone—the curtain went down on femininity. The most obvious event of the menopause was the gradual end of menstruation. (That's why they call it the "menopause": "meno" = "month" and "pause" = stop.) But that's not the only thing that stopped. Also canceled for many women was most of their sexual feeling, the majority of their orgasms, and a lot of their interest in the opposite sex. This coincided with the gradual wasting of everything that made a lady a lady—the vagina, clitoris, labia, breasts, and uterus. Menopausal women gradually retraced their sexual pathways—first to little girls—and then to something worse.

What could be worse than retracing their sexual pathways?

Turning into a semi-man could be worse:

"Doctor, I just can't believe it. I'm fifty-seven and my

periods tapered off about twelve years ago. Not only did I completely lose interest in sex and get those awful hot flashes but now I see black hair on my face, my voice is getting deep and husky, and I can't believe what's happening. Last night I got out some old pictures and even the look of my face is changing. My features are beginning to look like a man's. Help! Help! Help!"

Can a woman really go through that?

She *can*—and does. Just take a look around your local supermarket some afternoon. There are always a sprinkling of overweight, over forty, overburdened ladies who are obviously creeping over that invisible line that separates masculine from feminine. It works this way:

In a woman the adrenal glands are a source of many hormones, *including that vital male sex hormone, testosterone.* When the supply of estrogen, the main feminine hormone, slacks off at the menopause, the relative amount of testosterone in the blood skyrockets. That's what can make a fifty-year-old woman begin to look like a seventeen-year-old boy—unless she fights back.

How does she fight back?

By doing something about the "Great Hormone Robbery." Day by day her most prized possession—her alluring intoxicating exciting femininity—is being drained out of her. She has to put it back. Theoretically it's easy. All she has to do is have her doctor replace the fleeing hormones with a tablet or a monthly injection. That's it. By harnessing the miracles of modern medicine, nearly every woman can *virtually* stop the clock. Enlightened hormone replacement keeps the vagina supple, the clitoris plump and responsive, and the breasts as firm as possible. It also keeps those vital sexual wheels spinning in that little corner of the human brain that plans what's going to happen when man and woman crawl under the covers and snap off the light. Replacement hormones turn back the threatening tide of masculinity and keep a woman *a woman*. But in practice it isn't so easy.

What's hard about hormone replacement?

Getting started:

"Hot flashes and sexual despair are not the biggest problem that we women in the change of life have to suffer—although those are bad enough. The problems of insecurity, panic over small situations, nervousness in driving the car and the fear that if these symptoms aren't resolved that we will actually lose our minds are what worry us most.

"I am forty-five and have had those symptoms for about five years. Instead of giving me the hormones I beg for, my doctor gives me endless prescriptions for tranquilizers. He keeps telling me that I will just have to 'ride it out.' "

And, "Doctor, I have a problem involving sex that I am desperately struggling with. I am forty-eight years old and in the change of life. In recent months I have experienced what I would call a 'sexual death.' I can barely tolerate having my husband touch me. In the past sex has been a wonderful experience for me so that is a very frightening change. I can't bear to think that I will have to live the rest of my life not wanting to be touched. I went to my doctor and he said that I shouldn't mess around with hormones because they would make me retain water. Doctor, at this stage I wouldn't mind retaining all of Lake Erie if it could bring back those old feelings again."

Other women find the going just as tough:

"I am a woman, forty-three and single. The gynecologist I consulted seemed so busy—he could not care less. He answered my questions in the shortest possible way: 'Change of life is not a disease!' and 'I wouldn't touch anything like *that!*' By 'that' he meant female sex hormones that women can take in order to stay young or to avoid those awful hot flashes and headaches. I would like to do something positive —in time—before I get to look like a cooked apple. Is there something I can do?"

Is *there something she can do to keep from becoming a "cooked apple"?*

Sure there is. She can find a physician who recognizes that the menopause is a disease. All he has to do is check the medical dictionary: "Disease: A disturbance of structure or function in any organ or part of the body."

The truth is that the change of life is a hormone deficiency disease caused by lack of estrogenic hormone. And the treatment—and often the cure—is simply replacing the missing hormones.

"Why does my doctor deny that the change of life exists? If I had gone to him last week and complained of a failing thyroid gland, he would have examined me and immediately given me those little thyroid tablets to make up for it. But just because my *sex* glands are failing, he gives me a lecture and some nerve pills. I felt like screaming, 'No, you idiot! It's my *ovaries*—not my head—that need the help!' I just wish that every doctor in the United States could have just one hour of hot flashes—all at the same time. You know what would happen? They would all call up every one of their patients in the 'change' and *beg* them to come in for some hormone treatments."

Do all doctors feel that way about sex hormones?

Not by a long shot. But too many influential ones do. A noted male gynecologist had this to say recently:

"Women who at the age of fifty-five truly expect the degree of libido and sex activity they had at thirty-five, are, in my opinion, simply being unrealistic. To some degree, women create this problem by unrealistic expectations. I think this is due to modern overemphasis of the importance of female sex satisfaction. . . ."

A woman who read this solemn pronouncement asked:

"I wonder if that distinguished doctor is willing to cash in his 'libido and sex activity' on his fifty-fifth birthday. I'd also like to ask his wife—in private—how she feels about the 'modern overemphasis of the importance of female sex satisfaction.' "

Why do some doctors take that attitude toward women and sex?

It's not their fault. In any society, physicians only reflect the social and moral values of the times. The official position in our culture is that sexuality is a necessary evil—and the less said from that point on, the better. The battle against sexual expression and satisfaction starts in the nursery, continues in the schoolroom, and eases up only slightly during marriage.

Isn't sex encouraged during marriage?

Barely. Remember that most states still have laws regulating the position and variations of intercourse that a married couple may engage in. Although they are rarely enforced, recent attempts to repeal these laws have been resisted in most areas. So officially, in Kentucky, for example, you are encouraged to have sex with your husband or wife as long as it is "Official Kentucky Sex." Presumably anyone who wants to get fancy has to slip across the border to Tennessee for the night.

When the menopause comes along society interprets it as

the final bell. Actually the menopause is just a bad warranty situation. The body is good for a million miles and the ovaries wear out at 400,000. Imagine how a car owner would feel if she simply wanted to replace the battery on her car and the mechanic insisted that she turn in her driver's license instead. During her lifetime, the average woman's vagina travels about two hundred miles.

How does a vagina travel two hundred miles?

Well, assume the length of the penis at six inches. Each thrust during copulation carries the vagina a foot—six inches there and six inches back. Let's say the average woman has intercourse two hundred times a year with one hundred thrusts each time. That allows her twenty thousand feet of penis-travel yearly. Assuming sexual life expectancy of fifty years—from the age of twenty to the age of seventy—gives a distance of about one million feet or approximately two hundred miles. If she is involuntarily detoured to the sexual junkyard at the age of forty, there are only eighty miles on her erotic speedometer. A tragic waste in every sense of the word. The doctor who declines to provide the hormones that sustain a woman's sexual capacity abandons her to less appealing alternatives.

Are there any alternatives to sex?

No, only unsatisfactory *substitutes* for sex. In sexual intercourse a woman is "fed" with love (and spermatic fluid), she gets "high" with orgasm, she is "rewarded" with a man, a penis, and a feeling of satisfaction. When sex fades away, she still has to fulfill those needs. She "feeds" herself by eating too much, she gets "high" with amphetamines and alcohol, and she is "rewarded" from the local department store. Compulsive Eating, Compulsive Drinking, Compulsive

Medicating and Compulsive Shopping are the Big Four with women who allow their sexual organs to self-destruct at the menopause. The risks of alcoholism (or semi-alcoholism), "pill-freaking," obesity, and twenty-years of aimless trudging through the aisles of the local shoppers' emporium can usually be minimized by solving the problems of the menopause.

What can a woman do about it?

First, find a doctor who understands that the "change of life" is a disease.

Second, have him perform a complete physical exam.

Third, take the hormones he prescribes religiously.

Fourth, forget that the menopause ever existed.

Can women who have had cancer take estrogens too?

The majority of MDs agree that there is no convincing evidence linking cancer of the breast or uterus to replacement hormones. If a woman has previously had cancer of these organs, most doctors are willing to give these hormones within three to five years after the tumor is removed. If a woman has been treated for cancer of the cervix, many doctors are ready to begin hormone replacement immediately. If a woman has fibroid tumors of the uterus, it's up to her doctor. As a matter of fact, there is some strong evidence that keeping the estrogen levels right up there *provides protection against cancer of these organs.* Even more sensational is the tentative finding that once they pass the age of forty, *women who take estrogens have a lower death rate than women who don't take the hormone.* That would give estrogen the distinction of being the only drug that simultaneously makes life longer—and nights shorter.

But if it's dangerous for a woman to take estrogens in birth control pills, how can it be safer for her to take them for the menopause?

The answer is right there staring us in the face. Birth control pills are taken during the reproductive years—when the ovaries are producing great amounts of estrogens on their own. The hormones in the birth control pills are simply piled on top of the massive hormone load a woman carries. Once the menopause begins, hormone tablets or injections are designed to bring a woman up to her normal hormone level—and no more. Ice cream makes you fat only if you eat too much of it. Estrogens cause serious problems—if they are taken in the wrong doses under the wrong circumstances. That why taking hormones—like taking any other drug—is *not* a do-it-yourself project.

Why do so many doctors give women in "the change" tranquilizers?

Because they recognize the mental changes that come from a shortage of hormones. Even someone without medical training gets the message:

"My wife is forty-seven now and for the past five years our marriage has been going down the drain. She nags, cries, complains, and goes out of her way to pick arguments with me. For twenty years before that she was what every woman hopes to be but never attains—poised, charming, graceful and absolutely ravishing. Our family doctor, a fine well-meaning fellow somewhat trapped by his own puritanical upbringing, told her: 'I could put you on estrogens if you think that would make you happy—but you're going to have to take it for the rest of your life!'

"I told him: 'Listen, Doc, *I'd* take it for the rest of *my* life if it would put our marriage back together again.' "

Ironically thousands upon thousands of those marriages that collapse after twenty years or more are destroyed as much by two withered ovaries as by any actual personality conflict between the parties. If every woman who wanted a divorce were required to restore her sex hormone level to normal—under a doctor's supervision, of course—the number of divorces would fall dramatically.

Why pick on the women? Don't men go through the menopause too?

Ahh, a most delicate subject. Although technically there is no "menopause" for men, since there is no menstruation to "pause," every man eventually goes through a "change of life." Although, in medical academic circles, the male change of life is like the bumblebee.

How is the male menopause like a bumblebee?

According to the proven principles of aerodynamics and aeronautical engineering, the bumblebee has a problem. Because of its heavy body, short wing span, and slow take-off speed, it has been scientifically proven that bumblebees absolutely cannot fly. However, nobody ever told a bumblebee that, and those perverse little gatherers of pollen can be seen doggedly dive-bombing every flower in sight on a given summer's day. Male researchers, most of them over the age of fifty, have proven (at least to their own satisfaction) that there is no such thing as the change of life in men. But in men the testicles gradually atrophy, the production of testosterone by the adrenals slows down, and the relative amount of estrogen (also produced by the adrenals in males) continues to rise:

"Must I be considered a 'dirty old man' because of the questions I ask here? To me—and many men I know—the lack of manliness has become quite a problem. I believe it needs the careful and encouraging consideration of trained men such as you represent.

"My wife and I are both seventy. She is still beautiful and a delight to know. (I should add that she takes hormone tablets regularly.) Beyond that, she is as capable sexually as when we were married forty-two years ago. On the other hand, while I am very healthy and active I have dried up sexually. I suppose the gland which produces the sperm has quit its function. Will you write something about what science is doing for this lack of male sexual vigor?"

A woman gives her point of view:

"I am a forty-eight-year-old woman and my friend of twenty years needs your help! Yes, we've been lovers for years and I like to think that I'm better in bed now than he thought I was twenty years ago. Unfortunately he is going down hill. He is now fifty-six years old and getting more depressed each day. He worries about everything—money, his job, and his health. Worst of all, he has given up on sex. I spent a weekend in the mountains with him last month and for three days he didn't even touch me. And that from a man who could give me three or four climaxes a night—night after night after night. *(Sigh...)* All he could keep repeating is, 'I'm not the man I used to be, honey.' I know he needs hormones—because that's the way I felt before I got started on my own hormones six years ago. But what do I tell him when his own doctor laughs and suggests that he's just 'over the hill'?"

If it's bad for lovers, it's worse for wives:

"I am forty-four and my husband is forty-eight and what I kiddingly refer to as my 'lustful feelings' for him are more intense than ever. But now he'd rather sleep than—well, you know what I mean. I spend a fortune on beautiful sexy transparent bikini nighties—which I daintily drop to the floor before I get into bed. I drench myself in perfume and I stay so clean it hurts. To make it worse he is so good to me and so thoughtful—except in this one thing. I have talked, pleaded—even begged. I have offered to do anything anytime —any position or variation. But he still sleeps on."

A pharmacist sheds a glimmer of light on the problem:

"I am particularly interested in possible treatment for the male menopause. My wife is undergoing treatment for her kind of menopause by our local doctor but he seems to be quite uninterested in giving treatment to me. I asked him about the effectiveness of methyltestosterone and he just gave me a blank look. Perhaps it might be a good idea to write out some details of testosterone therapy. I can remember that it wasn't too long ago that doctors wouldn't even consider female sex hormone treatment for women suffering from hot flashes during the menopause."

Is the pharmacist right about sex hormones?

Yes. Testosterone replacement therapy for men is still in its infancy. That means some doctors are still saying that the male change of life is all in a man's head. Actually the problem is about thirty-six inches *below* the head. And the proof is right there for everyone to see.

Just as women become masculinized by lack of hormones, men become feminized by that deficiency:

"I can't imagine what is happening to my husband. He's only sixty-one and his skin is getting softer, his voice is getting higher, and now he only has to shave every other day. He even has trouble changing a tire on the car. Incidentally, our sex life has gone down to less than zero."

Most men with that sort of situation respond dramatically to male sex hormones.

How are male sex hormones given?

Carefully. It is definitely *not* a do-it-yourself project. Basically there are two forms of testosterone—injectable and oral. The oral form tends to be inactivated by the liver and is therefore somewhat less reliable. A few oral preparations are designed to resist liver deactivation but they may possibly damage the liver in the process. Injectable forms of testosterone come in two varieties—short-acting and long-acting. Long-acting hormones last for a few weeks—short-acting forms must be injected about every other day. That can cause problems:

"I'm seventy-two and I am starting to peter out—if you know what I'm trying to say. I went to my doctor and he gave me a shot every two weeks for a couple of months. I had just noticed a flicker of response when he decided it wasn't working and quit. Is there no hope for me?"

There is, of course, hope. One of the major causes of failure with male sex hormones is "too little." The doctor who persists is likely to get the best results. Another cause of treatment failure is "too late." The testicles and the penis *and the sexual centers of the brain* are the target organs of testosterone. The situation is comparable to watering a lawn. If you let the grass get dried out and parched by withholding water too long, then no amount of soaking will bring it back to normal. The ideal time to begin male hormone therapy is when a man's copulatory powers *begin* to slack off—not when the sexual crabgrass has taken over.

How can you tell the difference between a sex hormone deficiency and impotence because of emotional problems?

You don't have to—because both of them can exist at the same time. Generally speaking, by the time most men are fifty years old, they begin to suffer from testosterone deficiency. Their erections are weaker, their interest in sex slacks off, and they begin to gain weight, become gloomier in their outlook, and "resigned to their fate." A reasonable trial on *injectable* hormones, say eight weeks or so, is worth a try. (The injectable form is better for trial purposes because absorption is more certain.) If the patient improves he should continue. If he doesn't improve, it's time to look deeper.

Isn't taking sex hormones dangerous for a man?

Only in certain circumstances. If he has good testicular function, administering hormones from the outside can cause atrophy of the testicles—but then no man with well-functioning testicles should need hormones. If he has cancer of the prostate—or very rarely, cancer of the breast—then it's no male hormones for him. And in some older men enlargement of the prostate may occur from hormones. But that's what the doctor's for—to evaluate the patient and guide the treatment. Few doctors would deny treatment simply because there are remote and foreseeable risks involved. After all, having your tonsils out is far riskier—and much less rewarding—than having your hormones replaced.

Can't a man live without those testosterone shots or pills?

He can exist. But after the age of fifty why should a man be forced to bury his penis—anywhere except in a vagina? Instead of offering men in the male menopause hormones, our society all too often offers them golf as a substitute for sex. The middle-aged male is supposed to turn his back on an erect penis, throbbing testicles, and an eager vagina. Instead he is given an erect putter, a golf ball that is like a petrified gonad, and condemned to be constantly frustrated by that vaginal opening that sits in the center of the grassy pubic hair known to golfers as a green. He spends three hours, ten dollars, and massive amounts of energy trying to do what he could do in thirty minutes at home in bed with his wife—if society would allow him to. (Of course there is room for golf *and* sex—but the vast armies of menopausal men that swarm over the nation's golf courses each week-end are too rarely given the choice.) For many men, the fiftieth birthday brings another painful discovery.

Another painful discovery?

Right. The fact that *there is no satisfactory substitute for sex.* No material possession—from a color television set to the world's largest diamond ring—can compete with the physical and emotional sensations of copulation. No amount of money—up to and including a *million* dollars (ask any millionaire)—can hold a candle to the intoxication of a pulsating penis intersecting with an eager vagina. No title on the door can ever mean as much as a few words of appreciation from a satisfied woman. And tragically, nothing more than a few dollars worth of time-tested medication stands between most men and successful sexual satisfaction until seventy—and beyond.

"I know this may sound crazy to you, but I discovered the Fountain of Youth. Last year I celebrated my fifty-second birthday—and I felt more like a hundred and four. I'm in a tough business—where youth counts. They say in the ad agencies that if you're any good you burn out at forty. Well,

I was a senior vice-president in a top agency and was still burning brightly at fifty. But, Doctor, let me confess that the only thing that kept me going was my manhood. No matter how much heat I had to take on the job every night there was my wife waiting for me with an ice cold Scotch, a warm hug, and a couple of great hours in bed. Then I started coming home to a warm Scotch, an ice-cold hug, and three-quarters of a double bed. It all began when I lost my erections. Shortly afterward I lost my drive, and I almost lost my job. At the advertising agency they were understanding. They offered me a chance to "move laterally" back to account executive. That was *one* offer I could refuse. I went to my doctor instead—mainly because my ulcer started up again— and he talked me into taking hormone shots. I told him I didn't believe in hormones. He told me it wasn't a faith cure and shoved that sharp needle into my tender skin. Four weeks—and six injections—later I started having erections, the ice went out of the hugs and back into the Scotch and I was able to flex my muscles at work again. I also felt about twenty years younger. The Fountain of Youth? That little plastic hypodermic syringe my brilliant doctor wields in his office."

Then all a man needs to maintain his potency is a dose of testosterone every so often?

Not quite. That's only half the story. He also needs the love and understanding of a devoted woman. Sexual happiness isn't a one-way street—or even a two-way street. It's a traffic circle. All a hormone can ever hope to do is restore sexual interest and ability—the rest depends on love and under-standing. But just as every woman past the age of forty should be required to have her hormones up to par before getting a divorce, every man in the same age group needs to have his hormones certified as adequate before he folds up his marriage. The change can be so dramatic that only someone who experiences it can describe it:

"I could see my husband getting old before my eyes, Doctor. First he was overworked, then he got overweight, then he got overbearing, and then he got undersexed. It got to the point where I thought I was living with a senile teen-ager. Every evening I'd set out two double martinis on the kitchen counter and retreat into my sewing room and start sewing like crazy. If I was lucky he'd get the gin down before he started looking for me. No, not what you might think. We hadn't had sex in so long I was *wishing* he'd ravish me. All he wanted to do was fight. I finally read about the "male menopause" in an article in the paper and decided it was hormones for him or the laughing academy for me. The first doctor I went to—to make the appointment and discuss the problem—thought I was crazy. But then, *he* was fat, overworked, and about as irritable as my husband. I figured *he* needed a little testosterone. I finally found a woman doctor about fifty who was in the menopause herself and knew the score.

"I finally got Jeff—that's my husband—to her office, and it wasn't easy. Then I dragged him back for his shots every week for two months. And nothing much happened.

"Last night I laid out the martinis as usual, retreated into my sewing fortress, slipped behind my barricade of zippers, remnants, buttons, and buckram and held my breath. The door opened, and there was my husband with lust in his eyes. I couldn't believe it! Well, everything went on the floor, and —I guess you can imagine what happened. Anyhow we don't call it the 'sewing room' any more. We have another name. We call it the—I guess you can use your imagination for that too."

The only magic of hormones for men is that they once again make possible an erect penis that can bridge the gap between a man and the woman he loves.

Isn't there a time when an individual just gets too old for sex?

Yes. There is no doubt that a person's capacity for sexual fulfillment dramatically diminishes with death. But while there is life, there is the potential for sexual enjoyment. One of the most essential points to keep in mind is that as a person gets older sexuality should play a progressively *more* important role in his life.

Why should sex get more important with the passing years?

Because there isn't that much else to look forward to:

"I hope you will understand my sentiments even though I cannot express myself as eloquently as I would like to. I rose from shipping clerk to Chairman of a "Fortune 500" company. I would say the years from twenty to sixty were the most exciting of my life. There were promotions to be earned, new products and new projects to launch, and the undeniable thrill of building a sizable estate. But now I'm seventy-one, and as they say, 'I've done it all . . .' The only real enjoyment I get out of life is the pleasure of the indoor arena, the bedroom. My wife passed away four years ago and I've been fortunate to find—after diligent searching—a woman who is as eager as I am for the satisfactions that only —if you will excuse my frankness—orgasm can bring. Every morning I wake up eagerly anticipating the enjoyment that a new day promises. How many men in their seventies can say that?"

Not enough of them, I'm afraid. Back in medical school, fledgling doctors learn a little aphorism: "From twenty to thirty, the most important thing to a man is making love. From thirty to forty, it's making money, and from forty to fifty, it's making water." And from fifty on, making love should take the center of the stage again. As one gentleman of seventy-five said, "I can do everything I could do when I was twenty-five. I just have to start earlier, stick with it longer, and hold on for dear life when it happens." But that, of course, can be an advantage.

How can sticking with it longer be an advantage?

Except for advanced cases of premature ejaculation, orgasm usually does take longer with each passing year. Many a man at fifty or sixty can continue pelvic thrusts twice as long as he could at the age of twenty-five or thirty. That makes each act of intercourse "Double the pleasure, double the fun . . ." for everyone.

And especially for women, the sexual taboos of a lifetime somehow don't seem as binding:

"I think by now I've paid my dues. I've had two husbands, five children, two abortions (one legal and one before that) and a hysterectomy. I'm sixty-one and I'm living with my lover—he's fifty-eight and comes on like ten years younger. I can't get pregnant, I don't have a 'reputation' to lose, VD isn't a problem, at his age no other woman is going to steal him from me, and if one does, I'll find a better man. I have sex every day of my life—no more periods, remember. And now I do every sexy thing I've ever dreamed of doing. I haven't missed a climax in six months and all I want to do is improve my record. I've thrown away all my pills—I even stopped smoking. I never felt so relaxed and 'together' in my life. I only wish I'd paid as much attention to the most important thing in life thirty years ago. But I'm making up for it now."

For so many men and women after the age of sixty, sex is consolation, stimulation, a tonic, exercise, and vitamins all rolled into one exciting little package. But the secret of success for a man who wants to enjoy sex as the years go by is to plan ahead.

How does he plan ahead to enjoy sex?

Like this. One of the obstacles that literally stands in the way of sexual enjoyment for older men is an enlarged prostate gland. This little plum-size organ sits astride a man's sexual thoroughfare and adds its secretions to the sperm that pass from the seminal vesicles to the penis. When the prostate becomes inflamed, sexual activity becomes downright painful. As the inflammation increases, even the ability to urinate may be impaired. (There's nothing like a full bladder to take a man's mind off sex.) If the prostate becomes large enough to shut off the flow of urine completely, the obstruction has to be removed surgically. Although the operation can be a relatively simple one, there is some risk that important nerves can be damaged, dealing the final blow to sexual potency. The best way to avoid all those problems is to avoid those things that enlarge the prostate in the first place.

What enlarges the prostate in the first place?

Nobody is exactly sure but there are some clues. About 40 percent of all men over the age of sixty have enlarged prostates. But only half of those have difficulty as a result. That means about 20 percent of older men will have actual prostate problems. That's one clue. The other interesting fact is that the first stage of prostatic enlargement is inflammation —later followed by scar tissue and fibrosis. Inflammation is reversible—but scar tissue invading the gland is there to stay. An effective treatment for inflammation is massage of the swollen prostate—the doctor inserts a gloved finger into the rectum and "milks" out the retained prostatic fluid. It's not much fun.

A more effective prevention is prostatic massage—self-administered.

How does a man massage his own gland?

The easy way. Each time a man has sexual intercourse, the prostate vigorously contracts and efficiently massages *itself.* Regular and frequent sexual intercourse throughout life is the best-known defense against enlargement of that vital structure. It just might be that the same 20 percent of men who have serious prostate trouble are the same 20 percent who suffer from chronic lack of sexual satisfaction. For some men that concept can open up a whole new world:

"Honey, I'm sorry you've got a headache again tonight but, gee, you wouldn't want me to get prostate trouble, would you?"

Isn't a hysterectomy the end of sex for a woman?

It doesn't have to be. Like the old hospital joke, hysterectomy only takes out the baby carriage—it leaves the playpen intact. Most hysterectomies, even if the ovaries are not actually removed, bring on a "surgical menopause." Since the ovaries are such delicate structures, the cutting and crushing that goes on generally puts them essentially out of business. The most important step in maintaining good quality sex after a hysterectomy is to replace the estrogens *promptly.* (Unless, of course, the operation was for cancer of the uterus, which requires that three- to five-year waiting period.)

What's the rush to start sex hormones?

A woman's unique femininity is a precious and fragile flower. Unless it is constantly nurtured, it quickly wilts. Ten doses of estrogen at the beginning of the "change of life" are worth a thousand doses six months later.

Can old people really enjoy sex?

If they want to:

"I am forty-nine and a few months ago I married a man who is seventy. He is just full of sex. He wants to have intercourse every day and sometimes twice a day. Is it healthy for a man that age to have it that often? He also likes me to run around the house naked and he always wants to suck my breasts. I surely didn't expect this much but I'm really not complaining. As long as he wants me, I'm available."

Another woman tells her experience:

"I am seventy years old and my husband is sixty-five. As far as sex is concerned, we are still very much in love with each other—as we were when we were twenty. He is very patient and considerate of my feelings but there is only one drawback. Occasionally I fail to reach a climax as easily as I used to. (I haven't told him about this.) But when it does happen, it is so satisfying and relaxing. We continue to think of ourselves only as devoted lovers."

The foundation for enjoying sex at seventy is established in the twenties. Those who carefully nurture their mutual love and sexuality over the decades harvest the fruits in their more mature years:

"I am seventy-five years old, in good health and still with a keen interest in sex. I was married at twenty-two and when I found my mate, sex was not passed around as freely as cupcakes at a church social. I picked the man I was going to marry years before we were wed. When the proper time came, I lovingly broke the news to him in a way that only a woman can."

"Personally I believe that Adam and Eve in wrestling in the clover in the Garden of Eden over that tempting apple stumbled on all the known techniques of sex as well as a few that are still undiscovered. (I think my husband and I discovered a few ourselves over the years.)

"There is one other ingredient for a happy sex life—which to me is everything. It is the ability to love deeply at all times and in all circumstances. I would compare the pleasures of intercourse with the pleasures of all the senses. You can only get out of it in depth what you have felt, appreciated, and applied. If I have learned anything from fifty-three years of ardent and enthusiastic sex it is this one thing. Sexual intercourse is so wonderful and so satisfying because God has made it the perfect way for a man and a woman to say to each other, 'I love you.' "

Is there anything else?

No. The last sentence says it all.

REFERENCES

This is a token list of the references which I used in writing this book. Actually there are more books on sexuality on one wall of my study than the total number of articles listed here —but anyone who wants to read them can find their titles in the card file of the nearest university library. The collection of books and medical journal articles that follows includes only those that introduced new concepts or are typical of the category. The actual bibliography that I worked from contains over seven thousand individual articles and books which at this moment are strewn over the tops of my three desks. To list them all in detail would require another entire volume.

Included between the lines are the names of over five thousand patients who contributed sexual experiences, sexual attitudes, and sexual discoveries. However, because of my commitment to guard forever their identities, they must appear only in spirit and never in substance.

Afrodex and impotence. *Med. Lett. Drugs Ther.* 10:97–98, 1968.
AHMED, S. H. Treatment of premature ejaculation. *Brit. J. Psychiat.* 114:1197–1198, 1968.
AMOORE, J. E., and VENSTROM, D. Correlations between stereochemical

assessments and organoleptic analysis of odorous compounds. In *Olfaction and Taste*. Edited by T. Hayashi. Vol. 2. Oxford: Pergamon Press, 1967.

ANASTASOPOULOS, G., and KOKKINI, D. Temporal lobe epilepsy and endocrinopathy, *Acta Neuroveg.* 26:1, 1964.

ANDERSEN, A. P. Androgenic treatment of frigidity. *Geburtsh. Frauenheilk.* 18:632, 1958.

AQUINO, J. A., CUNNINGHAM, R. M., and FILBEE, J. F. Peyronie's disease, *J. Urol.* 97:492, 1967.

BABBOTT, D., RUBIN, A., and GINSBURG, S. J. The reproductive characteristics of diabetic men. *Diabetes* 7:33–35, 1958.

BARNETT, M. C. Vaginal awareness in the infancy and childhood of girls. *J. Amer. Psychoanal. Ass.* 14: 129–141, 1966.

BARR, M. L., and HOBBS, G. E. Chromosomal sex in transvestites. *Lancet* 1:1109, 1954.

BARSAM, P. C. Specific prophylaxis of gonorrheal *ophthalmia neonatorum. New Eng. J. Med.* 274:731, 1966.

BARTHOLOMEW, A. A. A long-acting phenothiazine as a possible agent to control deviant sexual behavior. *Amer. J. Psychiat.* 124:77–83, 1968.

BARTLETT, R. G., Jr. Physiologic responses during coitus. *J. Appl. Physiol.* 9:469–472, 1956.

BELL, D. S. The precipitants of amphetamine addiction. *Brit. J. Psychiat.* 119:171, 1971.

BENSON, R. A., and WEINSTOCK, I. Gonorrheal vaginitis in children. *Amer. J. Dis. Child.* 59:1083, 1940.

BERGLER, E. *Neurotic Counterfeit-Sex.* New York: Grune & Stratton, 1951.

———. Premature ejaculation. *Int. J. Sexology* 4:14, 1950.

———. Some recurrent misconceptions regarding impotence. *Psychoanal. Rev.* 27:450–466, 1940.

———. Some special varieties of ejaculatory disturbance not hitherto described. *Int. J. Psychoanal.* 16:84–95, 1935.

BERGLER, E., and KROGER, W. S. *Kinsey's Myth of Female Sexuality.* New York: Grune & Stratton, 1954.

BIEBER, I. *Homosexuality: A psychoanalytic study.* New York: Basic Books, 1962.

———. Olfaction in sexual development and adult sexual organization. In *Science and Psychoanalysis: Psychoanalysis and Human Values.* Edited by J. H. Masserman. Vol. 3. New York: Grune & Stratton, 1960.

BLUMER, D., and WALKER, A. E. Sexual behavior in temporal lobe epilepsy: A study of the effects of temporal lobectomy on sexual behavior. *Arch. Neurol.* (Chicago) 16:37–43, 1967.

BORELLI, S. On the prescription of sex hormones in male sex disorders *(impotentia coeundi)*. *Landarzt* 43:476–477, 1967.

BOSSELMAN, B. C. Castration anxiety and phallus envy: A reformulation. *Psychiat. Quart.* 34:252–259, 1960.

BOWERS, L. M., CROSS, R. R., and LLOYD, F. A. Sexual function and urologic disease in the elderly male. *J. Amer. Geriat. Soc.* 11:647–652, 1963.

BRANCH, G., and PAXTON, R. A study of gonococcal infections among infants and children. *Public Health Rep.* 80:347, 1965.

BRECHER, R., and BRECHER, E., eds. *An Analysis of Human Sexual Response.* Boston: Little, Brown, 1966.

BROWNING, W. J. Male climacteric and impotence. *Int. Rec. Med.* 173:-690–694, 1960.

BUMPASS, L., and WESTOFF, C. The "perfect contraceptive" population. *Science* 169:1177–1182, 1970.

BURFORD, E. H., and BURFORD, C. E. Combined therapy for Peyronie's disease. *J. Urol.* 78:765, 1957.

CALDWELL, B. M., and WATSON, R. I. An evaluation of psychologic effects of sex hormone administration in aged women: #1. Results of therapy after six months. *J. Geront.* 7:228–244, 1952.

CAMERON, D. M., and DAYAN, A. D. Association of brain damage with therapeutic abortion induced by amniotic-fluid replacement: Report of two cases. *Brit. Med. J.* 1:1010–1023, 1966.

CHAPPELL, B. S. Relief of impotency by cartilage implants: Presentation of technique. *J. S. Carolina Med. Ass.* 48:31–34, 1952.

CHOKYU, K. Studies on *diabetes mellitus* and functions of the male sexual glands. *Acta Urol. Jap.* 11:850–876, 1965.

CHRISTENSEN, G. C. Angioarchitecture of the canine penis and the process of erection. *Amer. J. Anat.* 95:227, 1954.

COLE, W. G. *Sex and Love in the Bible.* New York: Association Press, 1959.

Committee on Public Health of the New York Academy of Medicine. Resurgence of venereal disease. *Clin. Pediat.* 4:255, 1965.

CONTI, G. L'érection du pénis humain et ses bases morphologicovasculaires. *Acta Anat.* 14:217–262, 1952.

COOPER, A. J. A clinical study of "coital anxiety" in male potency disorders. *J. Psychosom. Res.* 13:143–147, 1969.

————. A factual study of male potency disorders. *Brit. J. Psychiat.* 114:719–731, 1968.

CUSHNER, I. The aftermath of liberalizing abortion legislation in Maryland: Problems and projections. Paper presented at the American Association of Planned Parenthood Physicians Eighth Annual Meeting. Boston, Mass., April 9–10, 1970.

DANESINO, V., and MARTELLA, E. Modern concepts of functioning of cavernous bodies of vagina and clitoris. *Arch. Ostet. Gynec.* 60:150–167, 1955.

DANNREUTH, W. T. Vaginal dyspareunia. *Amer. J. Obstet. Gynec.* 74:-747–752, 1957.

DAVIDSON, P. W., III. Transsexualism in Klinefelter's syndrome. *Psychosomatics* 7:94, 1966.

DEACON, W. E., et al. Identification of *neisseria gonorrhoeae* by means of fluorescent antibodies. *Proc. Soc. Exper. Biol. Med.* 101:322–325, June 1959.

DENGROVE, E., MARCUS, D. M., and COOK, E. N. Premature ejaculation. *J.A.M.A.* 183:389–390, 1963.

DESANCTIS, P. N., and FUREY, C. A., Jr. Steroid injection therapy for Peyronie's disease: A 10-year summary and review of 38 cases. *J. Urol.* 97:114, 1967.

DEVEREUX, G. The significance of the external female genitalia and of female orgasm for the male. *J. Amer. Psychoanal. Ass.* 6:278–286, 1958.

DEYSACH, L. J. The comparative morphology of the erectile tissue of the penis with special emphasis on the mechanism of erection. *Amer. J. Anat.* 64:111, 1939.

DUFFY, J. Masturbation and clitoridectomy: A nineteenth-century view. *J.A.M.A.* 186:246–248, 1963.

EDISON, G. R. Amphetamines: A dangerous illusion. *Ann. Int. Med.* 74:605, 1971.

ELLINWOOD, E. H., and COHEN, S. Amphetamine abuse. *Science* 171:420, 1971.

EL SENOUSSI, A., COLEMAN, D. R., and TAUBER, A. S. Factors in male impotence. *J. Psychol.* 48:3–46, 1959.

EMMENS, C. W. Postcoital contraception. *Brit. Med. Bull.* 26:45–51, 1970.

Epidemiological treatment of syphilis. Editorial in *J.A.M.A.* 188:820, 1964.

ESSENHIGH, D. M., ARDRAN, G. M., HOVELL, G. J. R., and SMITH, J. C. The vesical sphincters and ejaculation in the ram. *Br. J. Urol.* 41:190, 1969.

ETTER, E. A. Hypogonadal impotence in middle-aged men. *Arizona Med.* 17:217–220, 1960.

FEAR, R. E. Laparoscopy: Valuable aid in gynecologic diagnosis. *Obstet. Gynec.* 31:297, 1968.

FERBER, A. S., TIETZE, C., and LEWITT, S. Men with vasectomies: A study of medical, sexual, and psychosocial changes. *Psychosom. Med.* 29:354–366, 1967.

FINKLE, A. L. Sexual potency after perineal prostatectomy. *Western J. Surg. Obstet. Gynec.* 70:55–57, 1962.

FINKLE, A. L., MOYERS, T. G., TOBENKIN, M. I., and KARG, S. J. Sexual potency in aging males:#1. Frequency of coitus among clinic patients. *J.A.M.A.* 170:1391–1393, 1951.

FISHER, S., and OSOFSKY, H. Sexual responsiveness in women: Psychological correlates. *Arch. Gen. Psychiat.* (Chicago) 17:214–226, 1967.

FITZHERBERT, J. Scent and the sexual object. *Brit. J. Med. Psychol.* 32:-206–209, 1959.

FIUMARA, N. J.: The treatment of syphilis. *New Eng. J. Med.* 270:1185–1188, May 28, 1964.

————. Venereal disease. *Pediatric Clinics of North America* Vol. 16, No. 2:333–345, May 1969.

FORD, R. Death by hanging of adolescent and young adult males. *Forensic Sci.* 2:171–176, 1957.

FOSS, G. L. The influence of androgens on sexuality in women. *Lancet* 260:667–669, 1951.

FREEMAN, J. T. Sexual capacities in the aging male. *Geriatrics* 16:37–43, 1961.

FRIEDMAN, P. Some observations on the sense of smell. *Psychoanal. Quart.* 28:307–329, 1959.

FRIGOLETTO, F. D., and POKOLY, T. B. Electrolyte dynamics in hypertonic saline-induced abortion. *Obstet. Gynec.* 38:647–652, 1971.

FUSSELL, E. N., ROUSSEL, J. D., and AUSTIN, C. R. Use of the rectal probe method for electrical ejaculation of apes, monkeys and a prosimian. *Lab. Animal Care* 17:528–530, 1967.

GARRISON, P. L., and GAMBLE, C. J. Sexual effects of vasectomy. *J.A.M.A.* 144:293–295, 1950.

GIRARD, P. F. Male impotence. *Acta Neurol. Belg.* 65:587–597, 1965.

GOULD, W. L. New therapeutic approach to aging. *Clin. Med.* 64:865–868, 1957.

GRAFENBERG, E. The role of the urethra in female orgasm. *Int. J. Sexology* 3:145–148, 1950.

GREEN, R. Physician emotionalism in the treatment of the transsexual. *Trans. N. Y. Acad. Sci.* 29:440, 1967.

HALL, R. E. A reappraisal of intrauterine contraceptive devices. *Amer. J. Obstet. Gynec.* 99:808–813, 1967.

HALL, S. P. Vaginismus as cause of dyspareunia: Report of cases and method of treatment. *Western J. Surg. Obstet. Gynec.* 60:117–120, 1952.

HAMBURGER, C. The desire for change of sex as shown by personal letters from 465 men and women. *Acta. Endocr.* 14:361, 1953.

HASLAM, M. T. The treatment of psychogenic dyspareunia by reciprocal inhibition. *Brit. J. Psychiat.* 111:280–282, 1965.

HECKEL, G. P., and ALLEN, W. M. Maintenance of corpus luteum and inhibition of parturition in rabbits by injection of estrogenic hormone. *Endocrinology* 24:137, 1939.

HELLER, C. G., and MYERS, G. B. Male climacteric: Its symptomatology, diagnosis and treatment; use of therapeutic test with testosterone propionate (androgen) and testicular biopsies in delineating male climacteric from psychoneurosis and psychogenic impotence. *J.A.M.A.* 126:472–477, 1944.

HERTZ, J., TILLINGER, K. G., and WESTMAN, A. Transvestism. *Acta Psychiat. Scand.* 37:283, 1961.

HIRT, N. B. Sexual difficulties after 50: Psychiatrist's view. *Canad. Med. Ass. J.* 94:213–214, 1966.

HOLLANDER, D. H., TURNER, T. B., and NELL, E. E. The effect of long continued subcurative doses of penicillin during the incubation period of experimental syphilis. *Bull. Johns Hopkins Hosp.* 90:105–120, 1952.

HOLLENDER, M. H. Women's fantasies during sexual intercourse. *Arch. Gen. Psychiat.* (Chicago) 8:86–90, 1963.

HOTCHKISS, R. S., and FERNANDEZ-LEAL, J. The nervous system as related to fertility and sterility. *J. Urol.*, 78:173–178, 1957.

HUGHES, J. M. Failure to ejaculate with chlordiazepoxide. *Amer. J. Psychiat.* 121:610–611, 1964.

INMAN, W. H. W., and VESSEY, M. P. Investigation of deaths from pulmonary, coronary, and cerebral thrombosis and embolism in women of child-bearing age. *Brit. Med. J.* 2:193–199, 1968.

IRISAWA, S., et al. Sexual disturbances in diabetes. *Tohoku J. Exp. Med.* 88:311–326, 1966.

ISKRANT, A. P., BOWMAN, R. W., and DONOHUE, J. F. Technique in evaluation of rapid anti-syphilitic therapy. *Public Health Rep.* 63:965–980, 1948.

ISMAIL, A. A. A., and HARKNESS, R. A. Urinary testosterone excretion in men, in normal and pathological conditions. *Acta Endocr.* (Kobenhavn) 56:469–480, 1967.

JACOB, D., and MORRIS, J. Estrogenic activity of postcoital antifertility compounds. *Fertil. Steril.* 20:211–222, 1969.

JOHNSON, J. Androgyny and disorders of sexual potency. *Brit. Med. J.* 2:572–573, 1965.

———. Prognosis of disorders of sexual potency in the male. *J. Psychosom, Res.* 9:195–200, 1965.

JONES, H. W., Jr., SCHIRMER, H. K., and HOOPES, J. E. Sex conversion operation in males with transsexualism. *Amer. J. Obstet. Gynec.* 100:101, 1968.

KALLMAN, F. J. Comparative twin study on genetic aspects of male homosexuality. *J. Nerv. Ment. Dis.* 115:283, 1952.

KALOGERAKIS, M. G. The role of olfaction in sexual development. *Psychosom. Med.* 25:420–432, 1963.

KARACAN, I., GOODENOUGH, D. R., SHAPIRO, A., and STARKER, S. Erection cycle during sleep in relation to dream anxiety. *Arch. Gen. Psychiat.* (Chicago) 15:183–189, 1966.

KEGEL, A. H. Sexual functions of the pubococcygeus muscle. *Western J. Surg. Obstet. Gynec.* 60:521, 1952.

KELLY, G. L. Problems of impotence in aging males. *J. Amer. Geriat. Soc.* 3:883–889, 1955.

KEYS, T. F., HALVERSON, C. W., and CLARKE, E. J. Single-dose treatment of gonorrhea with selected antibiotic agents. *J.A.M.A.* 210:857–861, 1969.

KINCH, R. A. Sexual difficulties after 50: The gynecologist's view. *Canad. Med. Ass. J.* 94:211–212, 1966.

KOLODNY, R. C., MASTERS, W. H., HENDRYX, J., and TOTO, G. Plasma testosterone and semen analysis in male homosexuals. *New Eng. J. Med.* 285:1170, 1971.

KORENMAN, S. G., WILSON H., and LIPSETT, M. B. Testosterone production rates in normal adults. *J. Clin. Invest.* 42:1753–1760, 1963.

KUPPERMAN, H. The endocrine status of the transsexual patient. *Trans. N. Y. Acad. Sci.* 29:434, 1967.

KURLAND, M. L., LAYMAN, W. A., and ROZAN, G. H. Impotence in the male. *GP* 32:113–116, 1965.

LAIRD, D. A. Some normal odor effects and associations of psychoanalytic significance. *Psychoanal. Rev.* 21:194–200, 1934.

Lang, C. M. A technique for the collection of semen from squirrel monkeys *(Saimiri sciureus)* by electroejaculation. *Lab. Animal Care* 17:218–221, 1967.

LASH, H. Silicone implant for impotence. *J. Urol.* 100:709–710, 1968.

LEAVY, Z., and CHARLES, A. California's new Therapeutic Abortion Act: An analysis and guide to medical and legal procedure. *UCLA Law Review* 15:1, 1967.

LECKIE, F. H. Hypnotherapy in gynecological disorders. *Int. J. Clin. Exp. Hypn.* 12:121–146, 1964.

LEDGER, W. J., and WILLSON, J. R. Intrauterine contraceptive devices and the recognition and management of uterine perforation. *Obstet. Gynec.* 28:806–811, 1966.

LINO, B. F., BRADEN, A. W. H., and TURNBULL, K. E. Fate of unejaculated spermatozoa. *Nature* (London) 213:594, 1967.

LITKEY, L. J., and FENICZY, P. An approach to the control of homosexual practices. *Int. J. Neuropsychiat.* 3:20–23, 1967.

LITMAN, R. E. Interpersonal reactions involving one homosexual male in a heterosexual group. *J. Group Psychother.* 4:440–449, 1961.

LOEFFLER, R. A., SAYEGH, E. S., and LASH, H. The artificial os penis. *Plast. Reconstr. Surg.* 34:71–74, 1964.

LORRAINE, J. A., ISMAIL, A. A. A., ADAMOPOULOS, D. A., and DOVE, G. A. Endocrine function in male and female homosexuals. *Brit. Med. J.* 2:406, 1970.

LUCAS, J. B., PRICE, E. L., THAYER, J. D., et al. Diagnosis and treatment of gonorrhea in the female. *New Eng. J. Med.* 276:1454–1459, 1967.

LUKIANOVICZ, N. Survey of various aspects of transvestism in the light of our present knowledge. *J. Nerv. Ment. Dis.* 128:36, 1959.

LYNN, E. J. Amphetamine abuse: A "speed" trap. *Psychiat. Quart.* 45:92, 1971.

MacCULLOCH, M. U., and Feldman, M. P. Aversion therapy in the management of 43 homsexuals. *Brit. Med. J.* 2:594, 1967.

MACLEAN, P. D. Cerebral representation of penile erection. *J. Neurophysiol.* 25:29, 1962.

————. New findings relevant to the evolution of psychosexual functions of the brain. *J. Nerv. Ment. Dis.* 135:289–301, 1962.

MAGNUSON, E. H., and EAGLE, H. The retardation and suppression of experimental early syphilis by small doses of penicillin comparable to those used in the treatment of gonorrhea. *Amer. J. Syph. Gonor. Vener. Dis.* 29:587–596, 1945.

McLEOD, P. A. Uterine perforation secondary to IUD: Comment. *J.A.M.A.* 210:728, 1969.

MANN, T. Effects of pharmacological agents on male sexual functions. *J. Reprod. Fertil.* 4(Suppl.):101–114, 1968.

MARGOLESE, M. S. Homosexuality: A new endocrine correlate. *Horm. and Behav.* 1:151, 1970.

MARSH, E. M., and VOLLMER, A. M. Possible psychogenic aspects of infertility. *Fertil. Steril.* 2:70–79, 1951.

MASTROIANNI, L., Jr., and MANSON, W. A. Collection of monkey semen by electroejaculation. *Proc. Soc. Exp. Biol. Med.* 112:1025–1027, 1963.

MAWDSLEY, C., and FERGUSON, F. R. Neurological disease in boxers. *Lancet* 2:795–801, 1963.

Medical Research Council Subcommittee. Risk of thromboembolic disease in women taking oral contraceptives. *Brit. Med. J.* 2:355–359, 1967.

MEYERS, R. Evidence of a locus of the neural mechanisms for libido and penile potency in the septo-fornico-hypothalamic region of the human brain. *Trans. Amer. Neurol. Ass.* 86:81–85, 1961.

MINNICK, R. S., WARDEN, C. J., and ARIETI, S. The effects of sex hormones on the copulatory behavior of senile white rats. *Science* 103:749–750, 1946.

MIROWITZ, J. M. The utilization of hypnosis in psychic impotence. *Brit. J. Med. Hypn.* 17:25–32, 1966.

MOORE, M. B., JR., PRICE, E. V., KNOX, J. M., et al. Epidemiologic treatment of contacts to infectious syphilis. *Public Health Rep.* 78:966–970, 1963.

National survey indicates lack of reporting masks VD climb. News item in *J.A.M.A.* 207:21, 1969.

NAZARIAN, L. F. The current prevalence of gonococcal infections in children. *Pediatrics* 39:372, 1967.

NICHOLS, G. DE LA M., and EDGAR, D. G. A transistorized rectal probe for ejaculating rams. *N.Z. Vet. J.* 12:145, 1964.

NUTTING, E. F., and SAUNDERS, F. J. Postcopulatory effect of two antifertility agents on ova transport and implantation. *Soc. Exp. Biol. Med.* 131:1326–1331, 1969.

O'HARE, H. Vaginal versus clitoral orgasm. *Int. J. Sexology* 4:243–246, 1951.

ORR, D. W. Anthropological and historical notes on the female sexual role. *J. Amer. Psychoanal. Ass.* 16:601–612, 1968.

OVESEY, L. *Homosexuality and Pseudohomosexuality.* New York: Science House, 1969.

PARKES, A. S., and BRUCE, H. M. Olfactory stimuli in mammalian reproduction. *Science* 134:1049–1054, 1961.

PATTERSON, R. M., and CRAIG, J. B. Misconceptions concerning the psychological effects of hysterectomy. *Amer. J. Obstet. Gynec.* 85:105–111, 1963.

PFEIFFER, E., VERWOERDT, A., and WANG, H. S. The natural history of sexual behavior in biologically advantaged groups of aged individuals. *J. Geront.* 24:193–198, 1969.

PLOTKE, F., EISENBERG, H., BAKER A. H., et al. Penicillin in the abortive treatment of syphilis. In *A Symposium on Current Progress in the Study of Venereal Disease.* 260–266. Division of Venereal Disease, Public Health Service, 1949.

POST, D. F. Perforation of the uterus and partial extrusion of a Lippes Loop. *Obstet. Gynec.* 34:859–860, 1969.

POWER, F. H., and BARNES, A. C. Sterilization by means of peritoneo-scopic tubal fulguration. Preliminary report. *Amer. J. Obstet. Gynec.* 41:-1038, 1941.

PRINZMETAL, M., ORNITZ, E. M., JR., SIMKIN, B., and BERGMAN, H. C. Arterio-venous anastomoses in liver, spleen and lungs. *Amer. J. Physiol.* 152:48, 1948.

RABOCH, J., BARTAK, V., and NEDOMA, K. Types of sexual reactivity in gynecological patients. *J. Sex Res.* 4:282–287, 1968.

RADO, S. Critical examination of the concept of bisexuality. *Psychosomat. Med.* 2:459, 1940.

RATNAM, S. S., and YIN, J. C. K. Translocation of Lippes Loop (the missing Loop). *Brit. Med. J.* 1:612–614, 1968.

REED, W. A., and LALLY, J. F., JR. A clinical trial with testosterone cyclopentylpropionate. *J. Louisiana Med. Soc.* 105:172–174, 1953.

RODGERS, D. A., and ZIEGLER, F. J. Changes in sexual behavior consequent to use of noncoital procedures of contraception. *Psychosom. Med.* 30:495–505, 1968.

ROSEN, I. The male response to frigidity. *J. Psychosom. Res.* 10:135–141, 1966.

282

ROWAN, R. L., HOWLEY, T. F., and NOVA, H. R. Electro-ejaculation. *J. Urol.* 87:726–729, 1962.

ROWAN, R. L., and HOWLEY, T. F. Premature ejaculation. *Fertil. Steril.* 14:437–440, 1963.

Royal College of General Practitioners. Oral contraception and thromboembolic disease. *J. Coll. Gen. Pract.* 13:267–279, 1967.

RUBIN, A. Studies in human reproduction: #2. The influence of *diabetes mellitus* in men upon reproduction. *Amer. J. Obstet. Gynec.* 76:25–29, 1958.

RUBIN, A., and BABBOTT, D. Impotence and *diabetes mellitus*. *J.A.M.A.* 168:498–500, 1958.

SARTWELL, P. E., MASI, A. T., ARTHES, F. G., GREENE, G. R., and SMITH, H. E. Thromboembolism and oral contraceptives: An epidemiological case-control study. *Am. J. Epidem.* 90:365–380, November 1969.

SCHAPIRO, B. Premature ejaculation: Review of 1130 cases. *J. Urol.* 50:374–379, 1943.

SCHROETER, A. L., and PAZIN, G. J. Gonorrhea. *Ann. Intern. Med.* 72:553–559, 1970.

SCUTCHFIELD, F. D., and LONG, W. N. Perforation of the uterus with Lippes Loop. *J.A.M.A.* 208:2335–2336, 1969.

SHADER, R. I., and DiMASCIO, A. Endocrine effects of psychotropic drugs:#6. Male sexual function. *Conn. Med.* 32:847–848, 1968.

SHANKEL, W., and CARR, A. Transvestism and hanging episodes in a male adolescent. *Psychiatric Quart.* 30:478–493, 1956.

SHOR, J. Female sexuality: Aspects and prospects. *Psychoanalysis* 2:47–76, 1954.

SIMPSON, G., BLAIR, M., and AMUSO, D. Effects of antidepressants on genito-urinary function. *Dis. Nerv. Syst.* 26:787–789, 1965.

SMITH, D. C. Removal of an ectopic IUD through the laparoscope.*Amer. J. Obstet. Gynec.* 105:285–286, 1969.

SPENCE, A. W. Sexual adjustment at the climacteric. *Practitioner* 172:427–430, 1954.

SPIEGEL, H. Is symptom removal dangerous? *Amer. J. Psychiat.* 123:1279–1283, 1967.

STAFFORD-CLARK, D. The aetiology and treatment of impotence. *Practitioner* 172:397–404, 1954.

STEARNS, H. C., and SNEEDEN, V. D. Observations on the clinical and pathological aspects of the pelvic congestion syndrome. *Amer. J. Obstet. Gynec.* 94:718–732, 1966.

STOKES, W. R. Sexual function in the aging male. *Geriatrics* 6:304–308, 1951.

STROLLER, R. Pornography and perversion. *Arch. Gen. Psychiat.* 22:-490–499, 1970.

TALBOT, H. S. The sexual function in paraplegia. *J. Urol.* 73:91–100, 1955.

TAUBEL, D. E. Mellaril: Ejaculation disorders. *Amer. J. Psychiat.* 119:87, 1962.

TIETZE, C. Problems of pregnancy resulting from a single unprotected coitus. *Fertil. Steril.* 11:485–488, 1960.

Transsexuality. Editorial in *Brit. Med. J.* 1:873, 1966.

TRUAX, R., and TOURNEY, G. Male homosexuals in group psychotherapy. *Dis. Nerv. Syst.* 32:707, 1971.

TUTTLE, W. B., COOK, W. L., JR., and FITCH, E. Sexual behavior in postmyocardial infarction patients. *Amer. J. Cardiol.* 13:140, 1964.

VALERIO, D. A., ELLIS, E. B., CLARK, M. L., and THOMPSON, G. E. Collection of semen from macaques by electroejaculation. *Lab. Animal Care* 19:250–252, 1969.

VAUGHAN, E., and FISHER, A. E. Male sexual behavior induced by intracranial electrical stimulation. *Science* 13:758–760, 1962.

VERWOERDT, A., PFEIFFER, E., and WANG, H. S. Sexual behavior in senescence: #2. Patterns of change in sexual activity and interest. *Geriatrics* 24:137–154, 1969.

VESSEY, M. P., and DOLL, R. Investigation of relation between use of oral contraceptives and thromboembolic disease: A further report. *Brit. Med. J.* 2:651–657, 1969.

WALDEN, P. Retrograde ejaculation. *Lancet* 1:308, 1969.

WALKER, K. The celibate male. *Practitioner* 172:411–414, 1954.

WAXENBERG, S. E., FINKBEINER, J. A., DRELLICH, M. G., and SUTHERLAND, A. M. The role of hormones in human behavior: #2. Changes in sexual behavior in relation to vaginal smears of breast-cancer patients after oophorectomy and adrenalectomy. *Psychosom. Med.* 22:435–442, 1960.

WEISBROTH, S., and YOUNG, F. A. The collection of primate semen by electroejaculation. *Fertil. Steril.* 16:229–235, 1965.

WHEELESS, C. R. A rapid, inexpensive and effective method of surgical sterilization by laparoscopy. *Reprod. Med.* 5:255, 1969.

WHITELAW, G. P., and SMITHWICK, R. H. Some secondary effects of sympathectomy with particular reference to disturbance of sexual function. *New Engl. J. Med.* 245:121, 1951.

WILLIAMS, J. L., and THOMAS, G. G. The natural history of Peyronie's disease. *J. Urol.* 103:75, 1970.

YAP, P. M. KORO. A "culture-bound" depersonalization syndrome. *Brit. J. Psychiat.* 111:43–50, 1965.

ZEITLIN, A. B., COTTRELL, T. L., and LLOYD, F. A. Sexology of the paraplegic male. *Fertil. Steril.* 8:337–344, 1957.

ZIEGLER, F. J., and RODGERS, D. A. Vasectomy, ovulation suppressors, and sexual behavior. *J. Sex Res.* 4:169–193, 1968.

INDEX

Abortion, 57–64, 233
  babies born alive, 60
  cost of, 57
  do-it-yourself, 61–64
    danger of infection, 63
    by hormone, 63–64
    menstrual extraction, 62–63
  killing and, 60–61
  late (after sixteenth week), 59–60
  safety factor, 57–58
  vacuum cleaner type of, 58–59
  See also Birth control
Absolute impotence, 128, 137, 150, 153, 158–161
  brain and, 127
  meaning of, 128
  penis–breast relationship, 153
  spontaneous erection and, 158–161

Adam's apple, surgical removal of, 123
Adolescent masturbation, 107, 108–109, 163
Adrenal gland, 63, 252
Alcohol, 146, 149, 256
American Family Physician (Magazine), 106, 107
American Medical Association, 65, 205
American Social Health Association, 205
Ampicillin, 215, 216, 217
Anatomy
  muco-cutaneous junction, 81
  orgasm and, 22–23
Anterior-posterior (A-P) repair, 16–18
Anxiety
  homosexuality and, 186
  impotence and, 131–137

Dykes, 191

Erections
    among lower animals, 8
    clitoral, 95
    getting, 163–168
        by PSR, 163–166
        by stuffing of, 167–168
    curving upward, 10–11
    longer-lasting,   circumcision
        and, 6–7
    of the nipples, 83
    plastic implant, 7–8
    prolonged, 8–9
    spontaneous, 158–161
        foolproof method for, 158–
        159
    teen-age, 227
    using cocaine on, 19
Eskimos, VD problems, 207
Estrogens, 252
    after hysterectomy, 270, 271
*Everything You Always Wanted to
    Know About Sex* (Reuben), 212

Fallopian tubes, sealing, 76–77
    without surgery, 77
Family planning, 57
Fear, impotence and, 131–137
Fellatio, 83, 85–92, 153
    Catholic marriage manual on,
        93
    as   exhilarating   experience,
        85–86
    homosexual, 92
    with ice cubes, 104
    laws against, 89
    in massage parlor, 87–88
    as pleasure for a woman, 86
    for Positive Sexual Reinforce-
        ment (PSR), 164–165
    pre-fellatio rinse, 103
    principle of, 85
    from prostitutes, 88–89
    semen etiquette, 91–92

taking the initiative, 87
in tea-rooms, 189–190
VD infections from, 221
what it means to men, 86, 87
why men like it, 89–90
why women enjoy it, 90–91
Fellatrices, 89
Feminine hygiene products, 13
Femmes, 191
Fetishes and perversions, 114–125
    cross-dressing, 120–122
    discipline and bondage, 118–120
    drag queens, 121–122
    foot, 116
    harmless variety, 116–117
    spanking, 115–116
    textbook definitions of, 115
    trans-sexuals, 122, 123–125
    transvestism, 121
Fiberoptics scope, 76
Fiberoptics sterilization, 76
Foam, safety factor statistics, 69
Food and Drug Administration, 65,
    66
Foot fetishists, 116
Foreskin, penis, 5–7
    grafting back onto circumcised
        penis, 7
    smegma accumulation, 5
French kissing, 81, 82
Frozen-sperm bank, 73

Gangrene, 19
Gauguin, Paul, 225
Gay bars, 190–191, 194
Gay Liberation, 209
Gay people, *see* Bisexuals; Homosex-
    uals and Homosexuality; Lesbians
Goering, Hermann, 118
Gonorrhea, 76, 77, 84
    diagnosis of, 206
    Eskimos, 206
    homosexuals, 206, 208–209, 216,
        221, 223
    immunity against, 212

Washington, D.C., VD rate of infection, 207, 226

Water sport masturbation, 113

Wilde, Oscar, 225

Wilhelm II, Kaiser, 225